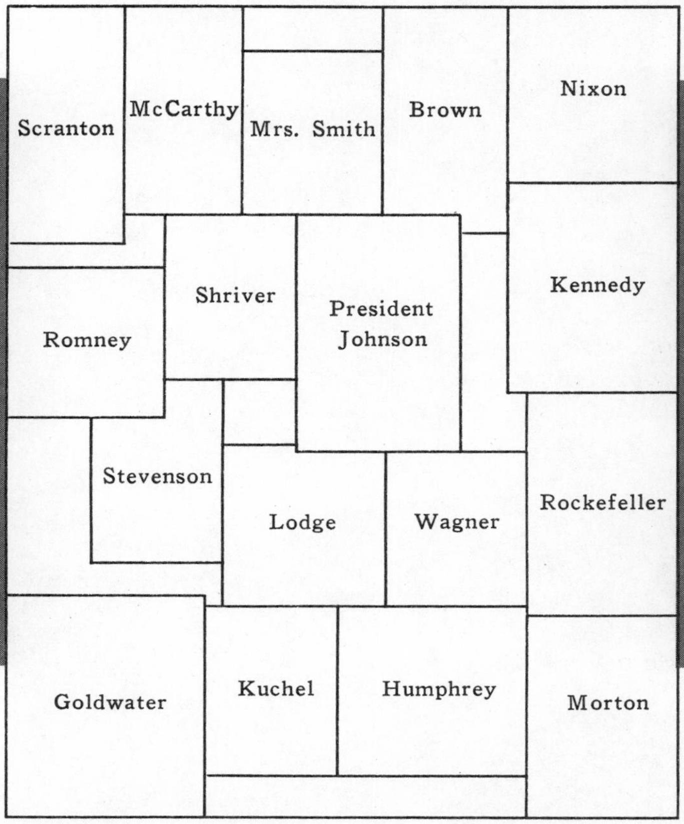

Scranton

McCarthy

Mrs. Smith

Brown

Nixon

Romney

Shriver

President Johnson

Kennedy

Stevenson

Lodge

Wagner

Rockefeller

Goldwater

Kuchel

Humphrey

Morton

ELECTIONS 1964

By Edwin A. Roberts, Jr.

NEWSBOOK

The National Observer
Silver Spring, Md.

Published by The National Observer
11501 Columbia Pike, Silver Spring, Md.

Library of Congress Catalog Card Number: 64-17811

Printed in the United States of America
By Danner Press of Canton, Inc. Canton, O.

Contents

Introduction

One evening in November four years ago, a family was gathered near a television set to watch history decide upon a course. Millions of Americans had voted for a President that day and now the returns were coming in.

Here was the climax to a long drama, and the family following the vote count was silent, save for an occasional murmur of elation or disappointment. Suddenly a small voice caused adult heads to turn toward the staircase. The question came simply and forthrightly, as children's questions do.

"What's happening?"

It was a fair question—worth more than the short answer it elicited. And the question is just as apt this very moment.

What's happening?

Who are the candidates? What are their backgrounds? Their records? Their strengths and weaknesses? Their strategies?

What are the issues? Why are they issues and what are their roots?

What are the mechanics of the electoral process? How did they originate? What are their defects?

What's the story on Presidential primaries, state conventions, national conventions, back-room politicking, campaign techniques, favorite sons, dark horses and special interest groups?

What have their most significant political battles taught the American people about the practical problems of representative government?

"What's happening?" covers a lot of territory, and so does *Elections 1964*. As the first Newsbook in a series dealing with vital topics of our times, this volume is designed to provide answers, quickly and interestingly, for busy readers. A generous sprinkling of the oddities that help make up the folklore of American politics lends color and humor to the story. Scores of photographs, maps, charts and tables augment the text.

Elections 1964 is a handy guide that you will want to refer to again and again as the current Presidential race progresses. It's a book to keep in your library or, better yet, next to your favorite chair.

☆　☆　☆

Elections 1964 was prepared in the news room of The National Observer. James L. Clunan assisted in the research, preliminary writing and general preparation of the book. The illustrations and page layouts are by Kathryn Henkel.

The cover design is by Edwin A. Roberts, Sr. The photographs of President Kennedy's office on Page **8** and of the White House on the inside back cover are by Larry Stevens. All other photos not otherwise credited are from the Associated Press and United Press International.

The staffs of the Library of Congress and the Smithsonian Institution were especially helpful in the preparation of historical material incorporated in this Newsbook.

Chapter I

Elections 1964

Part I: The Men

Every four years, since the Republic was founded, the American people have gone to the polls to elect a President. On November 3, 1964, they will make their decision for the 45th time. The electoral process has continued despite civil war, world war, epidemic, depression and assassination. Never has an election scheduled by the Federal or state constitutions, or by statute, been cancelled or postponed.

But while America's political machinery has been strong enough to withstand a variety of shocks, it has at the same time been acutely sensitive to them. Outwardly, the machinery remains undisturbed. Inwardly, the gears and rods thump and whack until a new series of motions is worked out. The thumping and whacking we hear today began with the last of three rifle shots in Dallas last November 22.

The assassination of President John F. Kennedy changed the prospects of all the Republicans who had been discussed by their colleagues and the press as possible GOP Presidential candidates in 1964. The old estimates of this or that fellow's strengths and weaknesses had to be revised. The Republican Problem would not be John F. Kennedy; it would be Lyndon Baines Johnson *and* John F. Kennedy.

Style and Capabilities

No Vice President has ever succeeded to the Presidency so late in his predecessor's term. Thus, Lyndon Johnson, the first Southern President since Andrew Johnson, will have had less than a year to convince the people of his capabilities and to sell them on his style. He must seek re-election on what is essentially the Kennedy record and what will be billed as a Johnson-Kennedy program. But if there is less time for the President to display his Presidential qualities, there is also less time for him to make mistakes, or to make the hard decisions that inevitably make enemies.

By one of the ironies that punctuate American politics, the man who was the Republican front-runner before Kennedy's death, Senator Barry Goldwater of Arizona, the leading spokesman for the American Right, lost much of his lead when the Republicans' expected opponent in 1964 was gunned down by a leftist madman. Goldwater's strength was in the South and much of the West, areas to which Texan Lyndon Johnson had long laid claim among the Democrats. Both men have been rated lowest in the industrial cities of the North.

And as Goldwater slipped back closer to the pack (at that time he controlled far more delegates than any other Republican), other GOP names were given renewed attention: Governor William Scranton of Pennsylvania; Richard M. Nixon, the 1960 Republican nominee; Henry Cabot Lodge, U.S. Ambassador to South Vietnam and Nixon's running mate four years ago; and Governor George Romney of Michigan.

Governor Nelson Rockefeller of New York, the first GOP candidate to announce his intentions, appeared to be affected least by the Goldwater slippage, but Rockefeller pledged himself to remain in the race "all the way."

One of these men will most likely face Lyndon Baines Johnson in the fall; the chance of a dark horse in the traditional sense getting the nomination is slim. For reasons which will be discussed later, the era of the successful dark horse is over.

Along with the problems peculiar to his own candidacy, each GOP hopeful is faced with the problem of Lyndon B. Johnson. The resemblances between President Johnson and President Kennedy are few.

The late John F. Kennedy was a member of a wealthy Eastern family that has comparatively short American roots. He was the son of a tenacious Boston businessman who turned a $5,000 stake into a $500 million fortune. He

was the grandson of two storybook Irish-American politicians. He was a product of an Eastern prep school and of Harvard. In his youth he was given the money and a family mandate to show the world of American politics what a Kennedy could do.

That he was born for such a mission there is no doubt. He was an intellectual without intellectual affectations, a practical, pragmatic politician who looked and sounded like the All-American boy. He was serious about his responsibilities but not bent by them. Armed with surpassing confidence in his gifts, he was yet less arrogant than many who worked for him. He never took men as seriously as he took their institutions. Nor did he take himself as seriously as others had to.

A Tree Full of Starlings

Life short-changed John F. Kennedy only in years. He had become the best known member of the best known family in the nation, and because his youthful presence and attractive manner were so familiar, his violent death left a real ache in the American heart. But as all families learn in time, life's business must proceed despite an empty chair. And so the country's business has proceeded.

The American voter, trying to assess the political picture following the Dallas tragedy, could liken the confused situation to a tree full of starlings suddenly rocked by an explosion. The birds scatter, wheel and hang in the air uncertainly until, finally, a few leaders return to the tree and the others take up new positions near them. Such is the continuing re-arrangement caused by Johnson's succession, and Johnson's new dominant position in the political tree is the clearest aspect amid the beating wings and bird chatter.

The difference between Johnson the Vice President and Johnson the President is no less than remarkable, and it is this difference that is influencing the prospects and the style of the Republican contenders. To most people LBJ was a legislative mastermind who got to run with Kennedy in 1960 because he happened to be born in a Southern state. His campaign personality was hammy and schizophrenic. His Southern audiences were regaled by an exaggerated drawl and dozens of Dixie colloquialisms. His Northern audiences heard Johnson the New Frontiersman talk liberally about getting the country moving again.

DARK HORSE

Originally a sporting term, this expression was in use around 1832, referring to a horse from which little was expected at the start of a race but which turned out to be the winner.

The first known political appropriation of the term was by Hamilton Fish, a U.S. Congressman and Senator, Governor of New York, and later a Secretary of State under President Grant.

Speaking on behalf of a little known Presidential aspirant, Fish declared: "We want a log-splitter, not a hair-splitter; a flat-boatman, not a flat-statesman; log cabin, coonskin, hard cider, old Abe, and dark horse—HURRAH!"

The expression came into general political use in 1876.

Shortly after the 1960 elections, President-elect Kennedy flew to the LBJ Ranch to confer with his running mate. Three years and one week later, Kennedy went to Texas for the last time.

Even as Vice President he retained his folksy ways, and when he went abroad he shocked some American critics and pleased many foreigners with his kindly, personal, homespun manner.

But when he assumed the Presidency, Johnson displayed dignity and determination. He left no doubt that he understood his job and had strong ideas about what he wanted to do with it. On November 27, five days after taking office, he addressed a joint session of Congress and pledged himself to continuing the Kennedy program while working for more economy in Government.

And it wasn't what he said so much as the way he said it. Johnson the bouyant glad-hander had vanished and in his place stood a man who seemed to realize that the historians were scribbling even as he spoke.

"A great leader is dead, a great nation must move on," he told the world in measured tones. "Yesterday is not ours to recover but tomorrow is ours to win or to lose."

The President's energy is famous, and the pace he set during one early week in office was not to let up. In his office he received more than 100 visitors, issued 10 statements, officiated at 10 large meetings, and spoke on the telephone more than 250 times. Some of the calls were made from his limousine as he roared to and from the White House at 65 miles an hour.

"The guy's a human tornado," said one veteran Washington reporter.

LBJ began immediately to claim as his own the large middle ground in American politics. He promised to push for equal Negro rights and thus pleased the civil rights forces. He promised Federal action to reduce unemployment and so made the AFL-CIO happy. And he ordered a realistic review of Government employment policies and defense spending to cut wasteful practices—thereby making friends among the many Americans who had been pleading for such a review for years.

President Johnson seemed to be thinking about everything except his heart. He had suffered a heart attack in 1955.

His doctors have ordered him to keep to a strict diet and to exercise regularly in the White House pool. He is partially successful in watching his diet but he usually doesn't do much in the pool except dog-paddle a little as he talks to aides and reporters.

Although he has refused to adopt any one format, he prefers small, informal press conferences with the reporters who are regularly assigned to the White House.

True to His Heritage

Some observers believe that it is essential for a modern Presidential candidate to have a warm sense of humor. This is not the same as a willingness to tell jokes. John F. Kennedy, for instance, would privately poke fun at himself and his listeners would be charmed off their chairs. Some other politicians, however, have no understanding of humor but try to be funny just the same. The results are often horrendous.

Johnson possesses a rather homespun humor. He tells stories that are true to his Southwestern heritage, and they often make a point. There is, of course, a great advantage in being President when telling a story; the listener is always more than eager to chuckle at a witty remark by the great man. Such is the nature of the human nervous system.

Some people who have watched the President at close range think he may not score too well before big Northern audiences.

Said one long-time friend: "Lyndon may strike certain people in the North like a riverboat gambler. He's tall and handsome and has an air of slickness about him. Inside, of course, he's dead on the level and his sincerity will probably come across. Still, he's got to be careful about his manner."

On August 27, in the midst of the 1964 Democratic National Convention, Johnson will mark his 56th birthday. He first came to wide public notice in the 1950s when, as Senate Majority Leader, he successfully pushed through the upper house a variety of controversial bills, including the first civil rights legislation of modern times. His reach for the Democratic Presidential nomination in 1960 was short, but running for Vice President he enabled his party to carry the South.

His family has been in Texas since 1846, when Grandfather Sam Ealy Johnson, then eight years old, moved west with his family from Alabama. Grandfather Johnson grew up to be a cattle driver, an Indian fighter, a Confederate soldier and a state legislator. He and a brother built a fort to keep the Indians away; the fort grew into the community now known as Johnson City. Lyndon's father, Sam Ealy Johnson, Jr., worked on his father's small ranch and during his school days picked up extra money clipping cowboys in the local barber shop. He gave up barbering for teaching and eventually entered the Texas legislature.

LBJ's maternal grandfather was Texas secretary of state and editor of a newspaper in the town of McKinney. His daughter, Lyndon's mother, was a reporter who met Lyndon's father when she called on him for an interview.

Their first born was named Lyndon, but he wasn't named Lyndon right away. Papa Sam wanted to name the baby after two cronies— lawyers named Clarence and Dayton. But Lyndon's mother, Rebekah, thought Clarence and Dayton drank too much and refused to accept either name. The baby remained nameless for three months while its parents and relatives held caucus after caucus.

Finally, when it appeared family legislation on the matter might be permanently stalled, Rebekah agreed to name her son after Judge W. C. Linden of San Antonio. But she attached a rider. She would spell the name L-y-n-d-o-n. In time that first name was to become more instantly identifiable than "Johnson."

A Variety of Jobs

Lyndon was born on the ranch Grandfather Johnson had built near Stonewall, Texas, about 50 miles west of Austin. When Lyndon was five, the family moved to nearby Johnson City where he attended public schools and was graduated from high school when he was not quite 16.

Money was tight in the Johnson family and the future President took many part-time jobs— on a highway construction gang, as a handyman, car washer and goatherd. There's no telling which of these experiences was to help him most when he was Senate Majority Leader, but some people think they know.

The young LBJ was graduated in 1930 with a bachelor of science degree from Southwest Texas State Teachers College in San Marcos, which is about 40 miles from Johnson City. He taught debating and public speaking at a Houston high school from 1930 to 1932.

There was little in Lyndon B. Johnson's formative years to suggest he would rise to power in national politics. But in 1932 he was given the job of secretary to Congressman Richard

THE LITTLE BOX THAT COULD

The most important ballot box in the long career of Lyndon B. Johnson was Box 13 from Jim Wells County, Texas. And a wonderful box it was.

Back in August, 1948, Texas Democrats held a run-off primary election to see whether the then Congressman Johnson or Governor Coke R. Stevenson would be the party's Senatorial nominee in the general elections. The final tally was 494,191 votes for LBJ and 494,104 for Stevenson—an 87-vote margin for Johnson who went on to defeat the Republican candidate in November. But those 87 votes are still the subject of some discussion in the Lone Star State.

It seems that right after the run-off primary in 1948, a dispute arose about all the votes cast in Box 13, Jim Wells County, a South Texas area. Most of the voters in this area are Latin-Americans, and there have been long-standing complaints (from those failing to benefit) that the citizens of Jim Wells County vote in a bloc for whomever local leaders direct them to.

One report at the time said that three South Texas counties gave Johnson 10,547 to 368 for Stevenson in the run-off primary—before a late "correction" from Box 13 increased Johnson's margin by 201 votes.

On the basis of unofficial—but usually very reliable—Texas Election Bureau (a firm financed by Texas newspapers) calculations, returns from all counties in the state five days after the election showed Stevenson leading by 113 votes.

Nevertheless, Johnson claimed victory. And six days after the election a recount of Box 13, adding 202 votes to Johnson's total, was reported. This raised the box's total to 967 for Johnson and 61 for Stevenson. The recount added one vote for Stevenson. These figures changed the state-wide tallies, giving Johnson an 87-vote edge.

The state Democratic executive committee decided by a one-vote margin, 29 to 28, to accept the revised Box 13 returns. This decision, in turn, was accepted by the state Democratic convention and Johnson was declared the nominee.

An unofficial investigation conducted by Stevenson's friends, including a Texas Ranger and two former FBI agents, revealed that the 203 belatedly reported names on the Box 13 poll list were written in green ink, alphabetically, although all other voters' names had been written in black ink. The investigators were denied access to the poll list, but they did uncover 15 of the "green-ink" names. They had trouble finding the addresses of the 15 people.

Johnson and Stevenson went up through the courts getting injunctions against each other until, finally, U.S. Supreme Court Justice Hugo L. Black signed an order staying a lower court order that would have prevented Johnson's name from appearing on the November ballot until an official investigation had been conducted. The Supreme Court delegates certain territory to individual justices, for the issuance of emergency orders, pending full hearing by the Court.

But Johnson was elected Senator before any Court hearing was held on the merits of the dispute, and he was seated by the Senate. In fact, no court inquiry has ever been held in the case.

Nor, considering everything, is one likely any time soon.

M. Kleberg, a lawyer, banker, and cattleman. This Washington job brought Johnson into contact with the administration of Franklin D. Roosevelt and, in 1935, the President appointed him Texas State Director of the National Youth Administration.

In 1937, at the age of 29, LBJ was elected to the House. With seven months out for duty with the Navy, he remained in Congress until he resigned from the Senate January 3, 1961, to assume the Vice Presidency.

Lyndon Johnson likes to say that he is basically a Roosevelt New Dealer. He got to know FDR personally in the 1930s and, in his 1937 campaign for the House, he backed Roosevelt's social legislation and his controversial plan for increasing the size of the Supreme Court.

But the ambitious young Texan was to know the taste of defeat, too. In a special primary election for a Senate seat in 1941, Johnson ran second to W. Lee (Pappy) O'Daniel in a 29-man race. Trying again when O'Daniel retired in

1948, Johnson beat ex-Governor Coke Stevenson by 87 votes (out of one million cast) in the Democratic primary, and then went on to swamp his Republican opponent in the November election.

When war broke out with Japan, Johnson was among the first Congressmen to go on active duty; he was a lieutenant commander in the Naval Reserve and his assignment was a special intelligence mission in the South Pacific.

In 1942, LBJ volunteered for an aerial observation mission that another officer at the time described as "certain suicide." Near Port Moresby, New Guinea, Johnson's patrol bomber was attacked by eight Japanese fighters. Somehow, the eight Japanese fighters were unable to shoot down the lone U.S. bomber, but they did damage it. The bomber got back on a wing and and a prayer and the future President of the United States was awarded the Navy's Silver Star for gallantry. LBJ remained on duty for seven months—until Roosevelt ordered all members of Congress back to their jobs in Washington.

A Tough Arm-Twister

Johnson was elected Democratic whip in the Senate in 1951; his star was to take on particular brilliance during the Eisenhower Administration when he was Senate Majority Leader. Although he was one of the first Democrats to speak out in criticism of the popular Republican President (May 25, 1953), he was decidedly not a legislative obstructionist. During Ike's eight years in office, Johnson earned a reputation for possessing an almost unearthly power over his fellow Senators. He was a master salesman, a friendly persuader, a tough arm-twister and an expert parliamentarian.

He made known his philosophy for running the Senate at the outset. On July 27, 1953, he announced that Democrats would supply President Eisenhower with "constructive support" and would oppose him only when they felt longstanding principles were at stake. His appraisal of the first session of the 83rd Congress is revealing.

On September 14, 1959, he declared:

"When government is divided, public officials are faced with a choice of doing something or doing nothing—of creating laws or creating issues. In divided government no one group can have everything exactly as desired. Congress acted in many fields. It sought to act in others. We went as far as we reasonably could to meet

Congressman Johnson and tutor.

the executive. And by sheer persistence, we succeeded in achieving laws—not just issues."

Johnson's legislative skill is considered the key factor in winning Congressional approval of the 1957 and 1960 civil rights bills, the first such laws since the Grant administration. But his leadership in the Senate was not unchallenged.

Opposition was most widely heard from the Democratic Advisory Council and liberal Democratic Senators. LBJ was accused of abandoning programs that Democrats believed in, of aping the Republican Party, and of hurting the Democrats' chances in 1960 by accommodating the opposition. The critical chorus was led by Democratic Senators William Proxmire, Paul H. Douglas, Joseph S. Clark, Wayne Morse, Pat McNamara and Albert Gore. The liberal attack was also aimed at the late Speaker of the House, Sam Rayburn, who for years was Johnson's close friend and mentor.

When the liberals brought their dispute with Johnson to a showdown in 1960 with an attempt to increase the number of party caucuses (usually only one was held each year) and to diversify party leadership, they won concessions which they claimed amounted to a victory. In two test votes, however, Johnson's leadership

Early in 1942, Congressman Johnson put on his Naval officer's hat and reported for special duty in the South Pacific.

In the summer of 1961, with the Wall going up, the U.S. Vice President went to West Berlin to assure its people of American support.

was reaffirmed, 51 to 12 and 51 to 11.

His record during his last years in Congress and his three years in the Vice Presidency rate him the elastic adjective, "moderate." On selected issues, for instance, the very liberal Americans for Democratic Action calculated that Senator Johnson had voted the "liberal position" 54% of the time in 1957, 67% of the time in 1958, and 58% in 1959.

Specifically, Senator Johnson favored an expanded social security program, a $1.25 minimum wage, and an attempt to reduce unemployment through Federal action. At the same time he voted for legislation to curb the abuses of organized labor (the AFL-CIO scorekeeper rates 46% of his Senate votes from 1948 through 1960 as "pro-labor").

As for defense, LBJ was no different than most other Congressmen: More money for more might. He was not then one to quibble with the Pentagon over another billion or three.

He steered a middle course on civil rights, pushing new Negro-aiding legislation through while opposing attempts to curtail the filibuster. He was mildly critical of the use of Federal troops in Little Rock in 1957, but supported passage of the 24th Amendment which has outlawed the poll tax (Texas had a poll tax).

Like his predecessor Richard Nixon, Lyndon Johnson was an active Vice President.

At the outset of the Kennedy administration, Senate Majority Leader Mike Mansfield sought to have Johnson preside over the Senate's Democratic caucus. But Johnson's old liberal foes were against the idea and, although the liberals were outvoted 45 to 18, the Vice President was prevented from playing a major role in the Senate for fear of splitting the party there. LBJ was, however, very influential in securing passage of the Kennedy-backed resolution to expand the House Rules Committee early in 1961 — thus loosening the conservative grip on that panel.

As President of the Senate (another hat the U.S. Vice President wears), a Johnson ruling sent an administration measure outlawing arbitrary literacy tests in voting requirements to the Judiciary Committee, which is equivalent to burying it under six feet of sod. In the same capacity he refused to rule to cut off debate on a liberal attempt to modify the Senate's cloture rule. Under this rule a filibuster can be stopped if two thirds of the Senators vote to end it. As a result, the liberal effort was talked to death.

Johnson's foes will have trouble pinning an anti-civil rights label on him. As Vice President he was active in promoting equal job opportunities in companies holding Government contracts. In 1961 he campaigned on behalf of a Democratic Texan of Mexican ancestry who was running for a House seat. His man won.

In a series of speeches on civil rights last year, Johnson showed himself to be a pragmatist with convictions. In sum he declared that unless the problem of racial discrimination is solved by justice and fair play, force and violence are inevitable. He pointed out that while law can restrain unreasonable men from imposing their will on the community, it cannot implant reasonable attitudes among human beings. The ultimate solution will spring from the decisions of the people themselves. Still, he went on, the Government cannot sit by while unreasonable men prevent the people from making their own decisions.

A Creature of Congress

President Johnson is a creature of Congress. He has spent more than 30 years in Washington. The weak spot in his preparation for the Presidency has been foreign affairs.

To get at least some rudimentary foreign experience under his belt, Vice President Johnson visited all the Common Market countries, all the Scandanavian countries, Turkey, Greece, Iran, India, Pakistan, the Philippines and South Vietnam. He went to only one African country, Senegal, and did not go to South America at all.

He is a firm supporter of the Atlantic Alliance and as Vice President he visited all member nations except Canada and Britain, which are considered "safe" allies, and Portugal, which has a messy colonial situation the U.S. is not happy about.

LBJ's most important trip abroad was to Berlin in the crisis over the Wall in mid-August of 1961. His assignment was to emphasize America's commitment to the West Berliners.

At his side throughout the last 30 years has been Claudia Taylor Johnson, the vivacious Texas girl he married after a whirlwind courtship in 1934. So anxious was young Lyndon to get married and return to Washington that he forgot the wedding ring. Mrs. Johnson is known to

millions by her nickname "Lady Bird," given her in childhood. She is called "Bird" by relatives and close friends. The Johnsons have two teen-age daughters, Lynda Bird and Lucy Baines.

Billie Sol and Bobby

President Johnson is a member of the Christian Church; his wife and children are Episcopalians and the President often attends Episcopalian services.

A couple of years ago, Republicans attempted to link Johnson with Billie Sol Estes, a man who had swindled a variety of individuals and companies with a complicated scheme involving non-existent fertilizer tanks. There has never been any evidence, however, that Johnson had anything to do with Estes.

On October 7, 1963, Robert G. (Bobby) Baker resigned amid conflict-of-interest charges as the Senate's Secretary to the Majority, a job he had gotten through Johnson. Baker had diverse outside interests that made him a fortune and caused deep stirrings on Capitol Hill.

In an entirely different case, Fred Korth, a political associate of Johnson who became Secretary of the Navy in 1962, resigned under a cloud November 1, 1963.

Accusations of conflict of interest against Korth in the award of the TFX airplane contract to former business associates were not upheld, but an investigation showed Korth had violated the Administration's code of ethics.

Such incidents are ordinarily just a temporary embarrassment to a politician who is called upon to do numerous favors. But the Bobby Baker case is an unusually shadowy business. The President's connection with it— if that connection appears suspicious to the public—could be extremely damaging to him. Johnson cannot afford any question about his integrity to remain in the minds of the voters. A President must be up to the standards set for Caesar's wife: Above suspicion—and well above.

The Democratic story in 1964 is all, or nearly all, about Lyndon Baines Johnson, the man who declared on December 13, 1958: "I don't think anybody from the South will be nominated (for the Presidency) in my lifetime. If so, I don't think he will be elected."

There is also the matter of a running mate for LBJ, of course, and many possibilities have

The President's ladies are his wife, Lady Bird, and his daughters, Lynda Bird (left) and Lucy Baines. LBJ enjoys entertaining guests at his Texas ranch, which is equipped with an old-time outdoor dinner bell. The name of the horse is Lady B.

been mentioned. But meanwhile the Republicans are stirring, and their situation is far more complicated. The GOP has one man—Barry Goldwater—who, like the President, has strong ties to the South and West. Like the President, he must be concerned with his strength in the industrial North. The other Republican contenders have just the reverse of this problem, along with many other problems peculiar to each.

William Warren Scranton, the 46-year-old Governor of politically important Pennsylvania, brings a variety of assets into the fray for the GOP Presidential nomination. He comes from the "right" section of the country—the populous Northeast—and he is an Ivy League intellectual and the closest facsimile of John F. Kennedy the Republicans have. Like the late President, Scranton is handsome, hard-working, shrewd, sophisticated and rich. He also possesses a young, first-rate staff. He has heavy backing from some of the same Eastern industrialist groups that favored Eisenhower over Taft in 1952.

Value of a New Face

Governor ("Call-me-Bill") Scranton is an internationalist, a liberal on civil rights matters and a strong believer in bolstering the states' position in the Federal system. His economic views are close to Governor Rockefeller's; Scranton thinks the states should accept more responsibility for their own affairs and should modernize their governments to meet modern problems. Not his least asset is his "new face," something the Republicans have sorely lacked in recent times.

Nor is his newness to national politics a serious liability. If it's true that the first job of a candidate is to become known, then Scranton is handling that job in good fashion. Newspapers, magazines and television are already giving him plenty of exposure and the coverage will be stepped up as the race progresses.

The Pennsylvania Governor, however, does have some liabilities. For one thing, he's not a particularly dynamic campaigner. Although he traveled extensively around the state in the gubernatorial campaign, many neutral observers doubt he did much of a selling job.

Polls taken immediately after he was elected governor showed that great numbers of Pennsylvanians voted *against* the Democrats rather than *for* Scranton. The administration of Dem-

ocrat David Lawrence was hugely unpopular and most people wanted a change of party in Harrisburg, almost no matter who the GOP candidate was.

Another charge leveled at Scranton is that he is "too cute." Translated from the political vernacular, this means the Governor has in the past been extremely reluctant to go into a fight unless he was sure the odds were heavily in his favor.

Another example of Scranton's reluctance to take risks was his attitude toward the 1963 mayoralty election in Philadelphia. Public opinion polls showed the Republicans had an excellent chance to dislodge the Democratic machine in that city, chiefly because of a white "backlash" following Democrat-supported Negro demonstrations there. State Republicans wanted Scranton to pick a strong GOP candidate for mayor and campaign hard for him in the city.

Scranton, however, refused. He didn't want to risk his prestige in a battle where the odds were so close. As a result the Republicans didn't offer a first-rate candidate and they lost by a comparatively narrow margin. Many GOP pros believe that had Scranton entered the Philadelphia fight, the Republicans would have won.

GOP

However grand it may have been at the time, the Republican Party certainly wasn't very old in the 1880s when it began calling itself the GOP, for Grand Old Party. The term apparently was taken from Grand Old Man, the nickname given to England's William Gladstone, then at the peak of his fame. Democrats at first used the name GOP derisively, but the familiar letters have come to be a useful abbreviation—especially for newspaper headline writers and others who, unlike Democrats, can't think of anything else to call Republicans.

William Scranton has the fewest built-in liabilities of all the more liberal Republican contenders, and his strength in the North tends to make him automatically a good possibility to hit President Johnson where he is weakest. Even more importantly, Scranton hates intra-party rows. Before he decided to run for Congress in 1960, he demanded that all county leaders agree to his candidacy so his cause wouldn't be hurt by factional fighting. He did the same thing when he was asked to run for governor; his terms were simple. He would run if every Republican leader in the state would support him.

One Pennsylvania newspaper described this demand as "an impossible condition." Impossible or not, Scranton made it stick. He got the united backing he wanted.

Scranton knows, of course, that nobody can dictate such terms to a national convention. He is a new personality on the national Republican scene and only the coming months can tell how much else he knows about national politics.

Again in the field this year is Richard Milhouse Nixon, 51, Vice President under Dwight D. Eisenhower, defeated 1960 Republican Presidential candidate, defeated 1962 GOP California gubernatorial candidate, and New York lawyer.

Nixon's assets are his experience in domestic and foreign affairs, his long-time high rank in the Republican Party, and his near-miss in 1960. But since his unsuccessful campaign against John F. Kennedy, Nixon's list of liabilities has steadily grown.

The Republican defeat four years ago is, fairly or not, attributed by many party leaders to Nixon's campaign strategy. Had he not decided to debate Kennedy, had he not promised to visit all 50 states and thereby spread himself so thin, had he not "sold out" to Nelson Rockefeller on the platform, had he not ignored the advice of party chieftains on numerous matters—had he not done all these things, so the Monday morning quarterbacking goes, he would have won the election.

Moreover, Nixon lost the gubernatorial race in California in 1962, and in politics the source of power is victory at the polls. Nor did Nixon add to his stature by publicly bawling out the press after his California defeat. And, to round out his liabilities, the former Vice President, in moving to New York, became a politician without a political base.

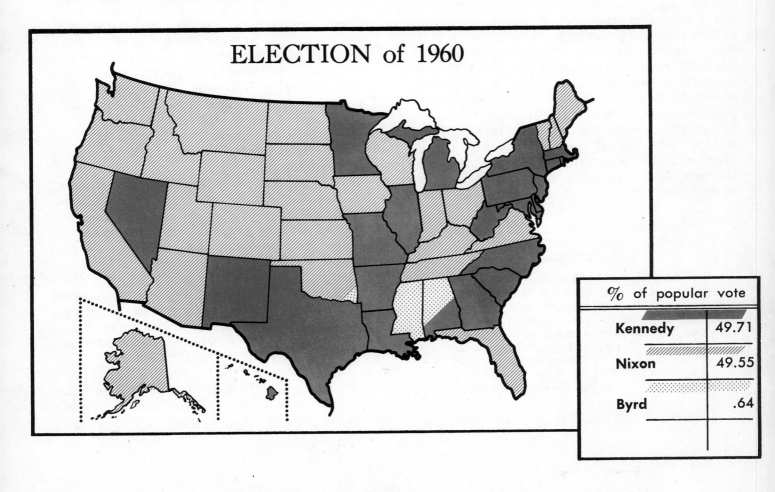

ELECTION of 1960

% of popular vote	
Kennedy	49.71
Nixon	49.55
Byrd	.64

As far as his philosophy goes, Nixon fits under the same "moderate" umbrella as all his major rivals for the nomination—except Goldwater. He is a liberal on civil rights but tends to take a more conservative attitude toward economic problems.

Nelson Aldrich Rockefeller, 55, despite the outrage he provoked among party pros four years ago when he forced the GOP national convention to modify its civil rights and defense planks, was considered the strongest candidate for the Presidential nomination until his remarriage in 1963.

Marriage on the Rocks

As Governor of New York State, he was automatically a leading contender for the White House. On top of this he had proven himself a solid vote-getter and an able administrator. His reputation as a liberal made him a good bet to score heavily in the Northern states with the big cities and the big electoral votes. But the odds on him were reversed when his private life took some quick turns.

After he was divorced by his wife of 31 years, Governor Rockefeller married a woman 18 years his junior, who herself had recently been divorced. Moreover, the second Mrs. Rockefeller did not obtain custody of her four young children and the family's explanation of this was considered vague. Whatever the popular reaction to the circumstances of the Governor's remarriage, Republican politicians immediately feared that reaction would be adverse. Down plunged Rockefeller's political stock.

After his election as governor in 1958, Nelson Rockefeller had been depicted by many journalists as "a grown-up Boy Scout." The changes in his personal life were viewed as costing him his merit badges. But the Gov-

HUSTINGS

Originally, in England, the word was used to describe a lord's household assembly ("house-thing"); but it gradually became the term applied to various English courts, and then to the temporary platform where politicians seeking a seat in Parliament formally stood for nomination. Now it means any place where political speeches are made.

ernor refused to give up. He is an unusually optimistic man, and he is as daring as William Scranton is cautious. He has strong ideas about national issues and is deeply convinced the nomination of a conservative like Barry Goldwater would wreck the Republican Party.

Down the Primary Path

His only chance was to convince the party powers that his remarriage is not an insurmountable obstacle on his path to the Presidency. And he knew he had to follow the primary route to do that.

Rockefeller's insistence on staying in the race has struck many people as odd. There is little love for him among party regulars outside the East, and even in the East the GOP pros doubt the remarriage issue will blow away.

But Rockefeller is almost as anxious to keep the nomination from Barry Goldwater as he is to win it himself. He feels his remarriage gave Goldwater his biggest boost and he thinks it's up to him to help block the conservatives from gaining control of the party.

And again, Rockefeller is an incurable optimist. He has often amazed his advisers with the way he interprets public opinion polls.

"Nelson may be near the bottom of some popularity poll," says one Rockefeller strategist, "but if he's a point or two higher than he was a week before he's tickled to death. Maybe he's just trying to boost everybody's morale, but it doesn't seem that way. There's very little that Nelson will admit is impossible. He's really got an invigorating attitude."

Hard-headed Republican chieftains, however, need more tangible evidence before a state of invigoration sets in.

George Wilcken Romney, 56, Governor of Michigan and former auto executive, is a handsome, dynamic personality whose name has been listed among the Presidential contenders because he is top man in a populous state and because he has gained a reputation for being ardently interested in the problems of the average American. It was Romney who popularized the "compact" car (he invented the term) which, so his advertising people said, was to save the consumer from the supposedly less economical models of his competitors.

His problems as a Presidential hopeful are several. He has had trouble getting his program through in Lansing, he has never really caught on with the Republican pros (largely

BANDWAGON

A bandwagon, for those too young to remember old-time parades, is a high, gaily decorated vehicle designed for brass bands to ride in. It is a happy affair that has come to symbolize the happy (winning) side in political contests. Politicians try to climb aboard a candidate's bandwagon when they're sure that is indeed the one that will win the race. Jumping on too soon is extremely risky beacuse it may not be going any place, and waiting too long may mean only a slippery seat on the rear fender.

because they think he is more an "independent" than a true-blue Republican), and he is a Mormon.

Romney's religion may pose a problem, especially among Negro voters. Some Negro leaders have charged that the Mormon Church officially regards Negroes as inferior persons.

Governor Romney has replied to these charges by saying he would not discuss "religious matters." Meanwhile he has re-emphasized his personal belief in human equality.

Barry Morris Goldwater, 55, entered the campaign as the best known spokesman for economic conservatism. He was strong politically where his ideas are strong—in the South and West. He began with many assets.

Behold, It's Barry

He is handsome (silver hair receding from a forehead almost always bronze from the Arizona sun), charming (a witty, ingratiating manner that delights Republican men and all but unhinges Republican women), articulate (an expert salesman of conservatism), and enormously popular within the GOP (the party's most-invited-to-dinner speaker).

His biggest liability was always the questionable appeal his attacks on the welfare state have in the big cities of the Northeast. In recent decades, Federal largess has replaced the handouts of the city political machine as a vote-getting agent. No candidate can hope to win the Presidency without carrying some of the industrial states with the big electoral votes (Goldwater, for instance, could win every state in the South and West, except California, and still lose the election).

Another potential liability shapes up among his supporters. Most of them are conservatives who are distressed at the growth of Federal power and spending. But there are also a number of others who think of themselves as conservatives but who are widely regarded as right-wing fanatics. The influence of such people has been greatly exaggerated, but they have made enough noise to confuse many people about the real nature of the conservative philosophy.

The status of Goldwater's candidacy has taken some odd turns. He emerged as the Republican front runner last year not because he

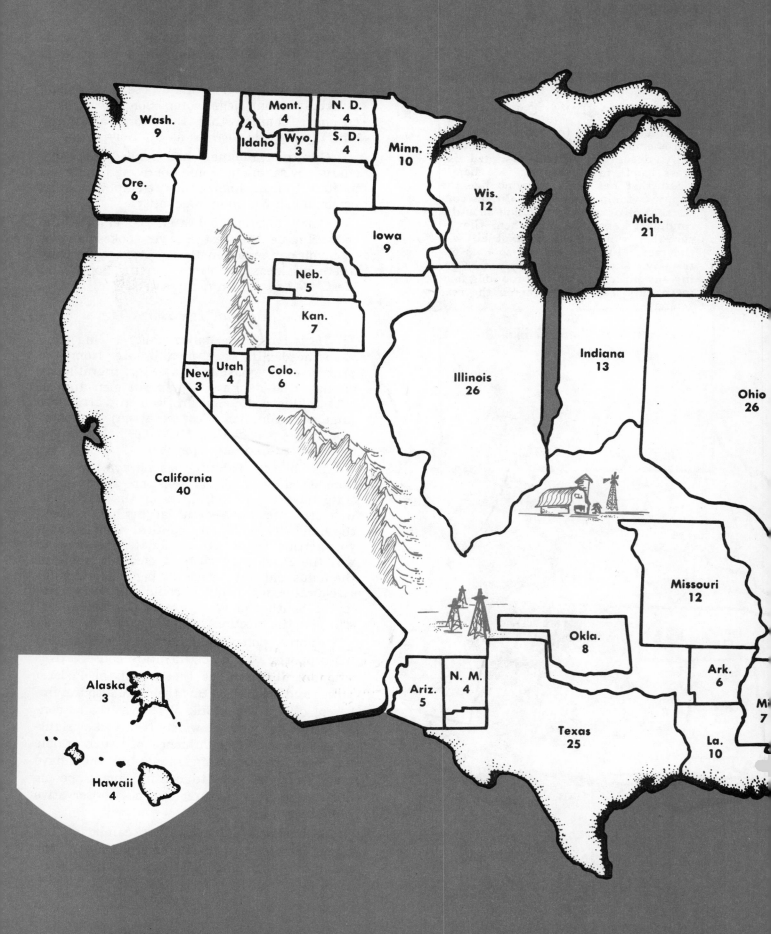

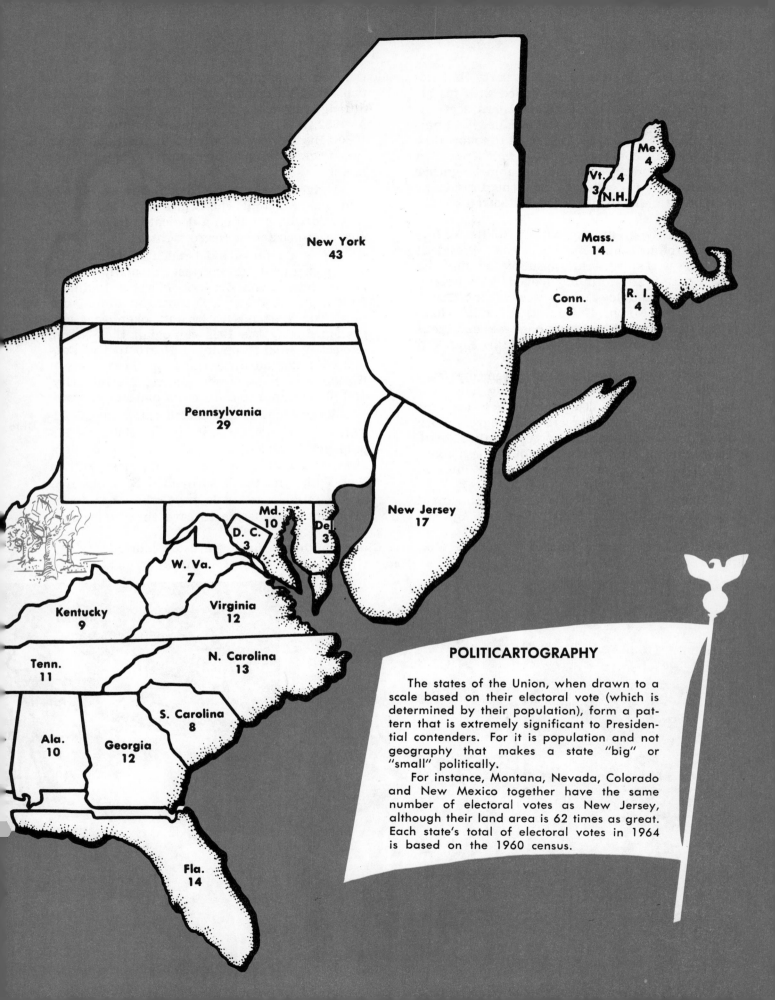

New York
43

Me.
4

Vt.
3

N.H.
4

Mass.
14

Pennsylvania
29

Conn.
8

R. I.
4

Md.
10

D. C.
3

Del.
3

W. Va.
7

New Jersey
17

Kentucky
9

Virginia
12

Tenn.
11

N. Carolina
13

S. Carolina
8

Ala.
10

Georgia
12

Fla.
14

POLITICARTOGRAPHY

The states of the Union, when drawn to a scale based on their electoral vote (which is determined by their population), form a pattern that is extremely significant to Presidential contenders. For it is population and not geography that makes a state "big" or "small" politically.

For instance, Montana, Nevada, Colorado and New Mexico together have the same number of electoral votes as New Jersey, although their land area is 62 times as great. Each state's total of electoral votes in 1964 is based on the 1960 census.

was suddenly discovered by the party, but because Rockefeller's prospects faded with his remarriage at the same time Southern segregationists' hostility toward the Kennedy Administration was mounting. It seemed to follow that a Republican conservative with wide appeal in the South and West might be able to gather enough electoral votes to win the Presidency even if he didn't capture the industrial Northeast.

Similarly, events over which Goldwater had no control lost him his long lead. President Kennedy was killed, Johnson succeeded him, and the South-West formula looked less potent. Johnson, like Goldwater, is weakest in the big cities of the North. But Johnson, unlike Goldwater, is President and thus possesses enormous leverage for making an appeal to Northern liberals.

Beyond that, Johnson is a Democrat and the Democrats nationally have long had their brand on the welfare state. They are the party of most union leaders and Negroes, both of whom are influential forces in the North. They will not stray from the fold unless Johnson gives them good reason to. And Johnson won't—if he can help it.

Henry Cabot Lodge, 61, who was appointed U.S. Ambassador to South Vietnam by the Democratic administration, has lost the last two times he ran for public office. Lodge was dislodged from the Senate by John F. Kennedy in 1952, and he was Nixon's running mate in 1960. His name was entered in the Republican sweepstakes this year by former President Eisenhower.

Lodge is a veteran Republican war horse, a long-time liberal who comes from the Northeast and who has been a dedicated internationalist and booster of Negro rights.

He is a man of independent mind, a little too independent for the taste of many Republican leaders who did not like his taking a diplomatic job under a Democratic administration. Too, he tends to be outspoken (his suggestion during the 1960 campaign that Nixon, if elected, would appoint a Negro to the Cabinet, did not advance the Republican cause). His dedication to public service, his integrity, and his personal courage are a matter of record.

Scranton, Nixon, Rockefeller, Romney, Goldwater and Lodge. At least five of these six Republican Presidential contenders are millionaires, and Lawyer Nixon is doing very well in New York. Inasmuch as Lyndon B. Johnson is also a millionaire, little boys who want to be President may decide to save their allowance.

Senator Thomas Kuchel of California.   Senator Margaret Chase Smith of Maine.   Senator Thruston Morton of Kentucky.

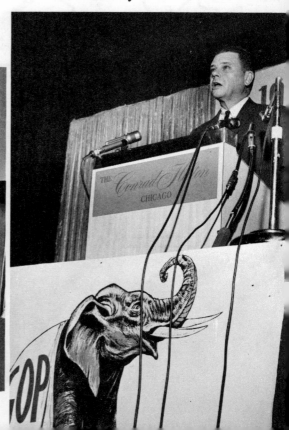

Senator Thruston Morton of Kentucky has been discussed as a long, long shot for the Republican nomination, and some people have mentioned Senator Thomas Kuchel of California. Harold Stassen has been mentioned by Harold Stassen.

Only Ike Since 1928

It is one of the interesting features of American politics that to become a Presidential possibility it is necessary only to have a friend or two to mention your name in that connection. And, if that mention is made on a dull news day, who can tell what will start rolling?

What could start rolling for the GOP this year is a battering-ram that might very well split the party apart. The conservative wing of the party has been frustrated for decades, because the national convention has repeatedly passed over conservative candidates and picked a liberal. When Eisenhower was chosen he was thought to be more liberal than he was and no Republican, except Ike, has beat a Democrat for the Presidency since Herbert Hoover beat Al Smith. And that was some time ago.

This year there is a real danger of a conservative revolt if Barry Goldwater doesn't get the nomination. Goldwater is a loyal party man who has campaigned for many party candidates. He has been a diligent fund raiser and after-dinner speaker. A lot of Republicans are in his debt and to many Republican stalwarts he is a shining knight who deserves a crack at the White House. Not a few of his supporters want to see him lead the Republicans this year to show the nation what they believe is the enormous conservative sentiment in grassroots America.

In any case, it's difficult to see how the GOP can escape a divisive brawl over the platform. Nixon was able to keep the seams from splitting in 1960, and this role of compromiser may be Nixon's trump card come July. Otherwise, the prospect of Goldwater supporting a liberal platform or Rockefeller supporting a conservative platform seems unlikely. Principles can stretch just so far, and then they are no longer principles.

The Vice Presidential nomination could go —and often has gone—to anybody. Considerations of geographical and philosophical balance usually prevail. Thus, if Scranton is nominated, for instance, a Westerner like California Senator Thomas Henry Kuchel, 53, might be chosen.

Scranton is generally considered a hair more conservative than, say, Rockefeller, and Kuchel is a liberal.

Another possibility is Senator Thruston Ballard Morton, 56, of Kentucky, a moderate who comes from a border state. The State of Maine's champion vote-getter, Senator Margaret Chase Smith, 66, a Presidential hopeful, would be happy with the second spot.

Kuchel has been in the Senate since Governor Earl Warren appointed him to fill the vacancy left by Richard Nixon's election as Vice President in 1952. He is probably best known for his Senate declamation against rumor-spreading crackpot groups. He comes from an old newspaper family (Anaheim Gazette) that has been in California since 1859.

Thruston Morton was elected to Congress in 1946 and served in the House until early 1953 when he was appointed Assistant Secretary of State for Congressional Relations by President Eisenhower. He was elected to the Senate in 1956 and was chairman of the Republican National Committee from 1959 to 1961.

A Woman's Place . . .

Senator Smith of Maine first went to Washington as secretary to her late husband, Representative Clyde Harold Smith, who served in Congress from 1937 to 1940. Upon her husband's death, Mrs. Smith was elected to his seat in the House where she served until 1948 when she ran successfully for the Senate. Senator Smith is one of the hardest working lawmakers in Washington; her attendance record is the best in the Senate.

There were scoffers when Mrs. Smith, in a memorable little speech, declared her candidacy for the Republican Presidential nomination. Some politicians, reflecting the feminine mystique, apparently believe that a woman's place is in the Senate.

There is hardly a limit to the names that might be mentioned as Vice Presidential contenders. The man who gets the top spot on the ticket will make his choice unless, as is extremely unlikely, he follows Adlai Stevenson's tactics in 1956 and throws the decision to the convention.

Similarly, President Johnson will pick the man to run with him in 1964. He will almost certainly choose a Northern liberal. Some prospects: Senator Hubert H. Humphrey of

(Continued on Page 40)

Barry Morris Goldwater

One day long ago, when he was minding the family department stores, Barry Goldwater decided to try his hand at fashion designing. He invented something called "antsy-pants," which were men's shorts with big red ants printed on them. The shorts were advertised in a sophisticated New York magazine and, for reasons best known to the magazine's readers, thousands of pairs were sold.

Such a novel creation must have come naturally to a man who hates to sit still. It is symbolic of the impatience that pervades the Goldwater character.

The 55-year-old junior Senator from Arizona is impatient with the Federal Government, which he believes is muscling in on the lives of private citizens while it postures almost sheepishly when challenged from abroad. He is impatient with state and local governments which in his view have contributed to the growth of Federal power by not solving their problems themselves. He is impatient with individuals who look to Washington for their personal security. And he is impatient with any routine that prevents him from being on the move.

East to Arizona

Goldwater has fitted this in-born impatience neatly into an in-born conservative outlook, and he has combined these characteristics with one of the most winning personalities in politics. Small wonder, then, that during a period of renascent conservatism, the Senator has been thrust forward as a major Presidential contender.

Barry Morris Goldwater's forebears headed east to Arizona in 1860. They headed east because they came from California, and they came neither as ranchers, farmers nor miners. They were peddlers seeking to sell their wares to prospectors drawn to the Southwest by the discovery of gold and silver. They were rugged folk who endured the hardships and dangers of the frontier, and eventually their peddler's wagon was replaced by a chain of department stores.

Young Barry grew up loving the outdoors and disliking the indoors, especially if being indoors meant being in school. Sitting on a hard bench for hours in a classroom was even less pleasant to him than it is to most boys. He spent four years at Staunton Military Academy in Virginia where he didn't set any academic records. Still disliking schoolwork as a freshman at the Unversity of Arizona in 1928, he decided to quit when his father died and enter the family business.

On September 22, 1934, Goldwater married Margaret (Peggy) Johnson of Muncie, Indiana, a girl he had first met when she was shopping in one of the family stores. They now have three grown children. The Senator's paternal forebears were Jewish; his mother, his wife and children and he himself are Episcopalians.

Before she met Barry, Peggy had plenty of suitors, including a Princeton man named G. Mennen (Soapy) Williams. The Princeton man went on to become governor of Michigan, and as liberal a politician as Goldwater is conservative. In the history of politics

A convinced conservative.

and/or love, the record does not show many more incongruous facts than that Soapy Williams wrote love poems to the girl who wound up marrying Barry Goldwater.

Senator and Mrs. Goldwater like many of the same activities, but they part company when it comes to flying. The Senator has been an avid aviator since long before World War II; Peggy Goldwater would rather stay on solid ground.

When the Japanese attacked Pearl Harbor, Barry decided he would become a fighter pilot. The Army Air Corps decided he would not—Goldwater had a disqualifying astigmatism. But he didn't want a desk job so he pressed for an assignment ferrying air transports between the United States and Asia. Yet even this occasionally hazardous job failed to provide enough excitement for the Arizonan.

One night in Calcutta, Barry and a friend were sitting in a bar waiting impatiently for their next assignment. They decided to give the natives a treat by holding a ricksha race down Calcutta's main street. They each got into a ricksha and ordered the ricksha boys to start stepping. The outcome of the race is lost to history, but it was the fact of the race that interested Goldwater. He was on the move.

After the war he returned home to organize Arizona's Air National Guard (today he is a major general in the Air Force Reserve), and resumed the life of department store executive. In 1949 he was named

Running, too, Suggests Impatience

Campaigning with Mrs. Goldwater.

Phoenix' "Man of the Year" and shortly thereafter he was elected to the Phoenix city council. In 1952, he won the Republican senatorial nomination in traditionally Democratic Arizona. His opponent was Senate Majority Leader Ernest W. McFarland, who was seeking a third term in the Senate.

The year 1952 saw many Americans worrying about Communist influence in the Federal Government and the growth of the welfare state. Goldwater campaigned hard against "coddling Commies," foreign aid and "creeping socialism."

Despite his rank in the Senate, McFarland was a match neither for the Goldwater personality nor the coattails of Dwight D. Eisenhower. It was especially the latter that pulled Goldwater across the finish line 6,725 votes ahead of his rival.

The freshman Senator quickly established himself, after the death of Senator Robert A. Taft of Ohio, as the foremost spokesman for conservatism in the Upper House. And, oddly, while many of his views were to the right of Taft's, Goldwater attained a personal popularity that had always eluded the astute, reserved Ohioan.

Barry served six years as chairman of the Republican Senatorial Campaign Committee, raising money and speaking in behalf of Republican Senators throughout the country. But it was in 1960 that two events occurred that brought Goldwater to national attention.

In that year he published a book, which was essentially a collection of his speeches, called "The Conscience of a Conservative." In it he pressed for a greater role for the states in the Federal system, and a tougher policy toward the Communist bloc. The book was an immediate best-seller.

Also in 1960, Goldwater backers pushed their man for the GOP Vice Presidential nomination (many non-Goldwater people are pushing him for that job this year to help pacify the party's conservative wing should a liberal get the top spot) and even then he was a favorite for the Presidential nomination among some convention delegates.

A Variety of Views

In recent years the Arizona Senator has been making more than 200 speeches annually. In them, and on the Senate floor, he has offered a variety of views.

While "utterly opposed to discrimination in any form," he would prefer a "states' rights" formula for solving racial problems. He's added, however, that if he were President he would see that Federal court orders were enforced. He has termed the public accommodations feature of the current civil rights measure "unworkable, unconstitutional and a violation of property rights."

He supports state "right-to-work" laws to bar compulsory unionism, and he wants a Federal law prohibiting unions from spending their funds for political purposes.

He has urged sale of the Tennessee Valley Authority to the states that benefit from it, with some of TVA's diverse facilities being sold to private industry. He would like to see the Social Security program made voluntary, but he has never urged its repeal as some of his critics contend. He is opposed to paying for the hospital care of elderly people through Social Security.

He voted against the 1963 nuclear test ban treaty, opposed the sale of wheat to Moscow, and he thinks the U.S. should pull out of the United Nations if Communist China is admitted.

And he has suggested that many poverty-stricken Americans are poor because they are stupid or lazy or both.

This last opinion illustrates the Senator's penchant for giving the hornets' nest a whack now and again. He likes to shock people and he likes to meet them. People, in turn, like to meet him. His charm is famous and his power in the Republican Party is real.

But not a few Washington observers think he may be running for President chiefly because he doesn't want to let down his legions of enthusiastic supporters. The Arizonan has always been impatient with routine and he may prefer the excitement of a campaign to the grim responsibilities that might await him at campaign's end. (He has said the prospect of being President "scares me to death"). Barry Goldwater is a man of action, it's true. But for some men of action, in rickshas or politics, the race is the thing.

Henry Cabot Lodge

That editorial writer is doubly blessed who can combine a commitment to principles with a mild case of colic. Such a man pushed his typewriter aside in 1933 and entered politics, where those qualities do not always guarantee victory. Nor have they always for Henry Cabot Lodge.

But at 61, this veteran politician-diplomat-soldier-journalist can reach for the Republican Presidential nomination on the basis of a record of public service that is at once lengthy and extraordinarily diverse. Before taking on the rugged ambassadorial job in Saigon, Lodge ran unsuccessfully for Vice President, represented the United States in the United Nations for eight years, spent 13 years in the U.S. Senate, and, during World War II, fought at Tobruk, El Alamein and in Italy and France.

"It's just as well Cabot didn't win the Vice Presidency in 1960," says a friend. "He wouldn't be much good in an easy job."

In His Element

If that's the case, Henry Cabot Lodge should be in his element today. Winning his party's Presidential nomination will be anything but easy, and many observers think the Lodge candidacy is all but hopeless. He increased his foes in the GOP by accepting President Kennedy's offer of the Saigon post—thus decreasing the value of Vietnam to the Republicans as a partisan issue—and his impatient, often abrupt personality has not endeared him to the party bosses to whom he must now pay court.

Henry Cabot Lodge comes from a family that has been in Massachusetts longer than Boston has, and whose sons have been going to Harvard College since soon after its founding (1636). His great-great-great grandfather served in the Second, Third and Fourth Congresses (1791-1796) as a Senator from Massachusetts, and his grandfather, also named Henry Cabot Lodge, spent three terms in the House and six terms in the Senate, from 1887 to 1924.

After Harvard ('24), young Cabot went to work on the Boston Evening Transcript as a cub reporter and later joined the staff of the New York Herald Tribune, where he wound up writing editorials.

In 1926, he married the former Emily Sears. They have two sons, George Cabot and Henry Sears Lodge. The former was defeated in his 1962 bid for the U.S. Senate by Edward (Ted) Kennedy, brother of the late President. It's easier to get nominated for something in Massachusetts if you've picked your family wisely.

Lodge wrote a book in 1932, *The Cult of Weakness,* in which he warned America of the dangers of military weakness in a disintegrating world.

Quitting his job as editorial writer on the Herald Tribune, he ran successfully for the state legislature in Massachusetts where he served for four years. His political liberalism (he is no late-comer to the liberal wing of the GOP) dates from these years as a state lawmaker, when he was chairman of the Massachusetts house legislative committee on labor and industries.

Vietnam: The latest tough job.

In 1936, at the age of 34, Henry Cabot Lodge took on, and whipped, Governor James Michael Curley in the contest for the U.S. Senate. It was this fight that built Lodge's pre-1952 reputation as a man who won tough political battles. The young Republican beat Curley by 142,000 votes while the Democrats were carrying all other statewide offices; he was the only Republican in the 1936 Roosevelt landslide to take a Senate seat away from the Democrats.

When Japan attacked Pearl Harbor, Lodge joined other Congressmen in volunteering for active duty. His tank outfit was assigned to the thin British line in Libya—the plan was to give the Americans combat experience and then return them to the United States where they would form the nucleus of units still to be trained.

Not a Little Bit Independent

Combat experience Lodge got quickly. The handsome Bostonian was under fire in the desert operations against Rommel's Afrika Corps, including the retreat from Tobruk and the famous defense of El Alamein that followed. Then he returned to the United States to report on the lessons learned in the blazing African dessert. In July, 1942, FDR ordered all Congressmen in the service back to their Washington posts.

After winning re-election to the Senate that year, Lodge tried to settle down to life on the home front. By February 3, 1944, his impatient disposition would let him sit still no longer. He resigned from the Senate and went back to war, the first member of Congress to take such a step since 1861. The late Senator Arthur H. Vandenberg was later to write of the event:

"In all my 20 years in the Senate, no single episode ever thrilled me so deeply as the quiet drama which saw young Lodge in his usual Senate seat on a late afternoon in February and the next morning heard his resignation read at the desk after his overnight departure to the fighting front. No one, including myself, had any idea Cabot planned to quit the Senate and go to war. It was typical of him. He made no valedictory speech to his colleagues and there was no band to escort him to the station. He just quit the Senate and went."

Lodge, who fought in the Italian compaign and later was American liaison officer with the First French Army, was awarded the American Bronze Star, the French Croix de Guerre and other decorations.

A Smashing Victory

At war's end, Lodge came home and unseated Massachusetts' aging Senator David I. Walsh, the lawmaker a young fellow named George Romney had worked for in 1929-30. Walsh had been in the Senate 26 years and was noted for his ability to attract Republican as well as Democratic votes. Lodge beat him by 329,000 votes.

Senator Lodge continued to support liberal policies, but he was a discriminating legislator. He favored a variety of bread-and-butter measures but voted for the Taft-Hartley Act, which was designed to curb the abuses of organized labor. He sought to make lynching a Federal offense, to eliminate the poll tax, to end racial segregation in the armed forces and housing (before such a stand was fashionable), and he pressed for a revision of the tax system to give the economy a lift.

During his postwar term in the Senate, Lodge became a leading figure in the international field. A member of the Senate Foreign Relations Committee, he carried on the Vandenburg policy of nonpartisanship in foreign policy. His role in this field expanded in 1950 when President Truman named him an alternate delegate to the United Nations.

After Lodge lost his Senate seat to fast-rising John F. Kennedy in 1952, he was named Ambassador to the U.N. by President Eisenhower. There, for eight years,

Lodge defended American policy to the world, often doing it on an eyeball-to-eyeball level with Russia's Vishinski and Gromyko. When Khrushchev visited the U.S. in 1959, Lodge was his official escort. In 1960, he was Richard Nixon's running mate.

Last summer, when the South Vietnam situation was rapidly deteriorating, President Kennedy asked Lodge to go there as the new U.S. ambassador. His experience in international affairs, his impeccable French, his military background and his "tough guy" reputation were all listed as assets in getting the regime of Ngo Dinh Diem to prosecute a more vigorous war against the Communist guerrillas.

Ambassador Lodge quickly made it clear the U.S. was changing its policy. He voiced official disapproval of the repressive measures of the Diem government, and he helped create the climate for the coup that brought down Diem on November 1, 1963.

Meanwhile, election-year stirrings were heard at home. The changed political situation after President Kennedy's assassination prompted former President Eisenhower, as titular leader of the GOP, to urge all prominent Republicans to consider running for the party's Presidential nomination. Lodge was one of them.

Eisenhower's gesture is a curious reversal of the 1952 situation when Lodge was instrumental in persuading Ike to run for the GOP nomination. (In Lodge's office in Saigon is a picture of the former President, inscribed: "To Senator Henry Cabot Lodge —my first 'campaign manager'—from his devoted friend—Ike Eisenhower").

That Lodge effort for Eisenhower in 1952 made him many enemies in the GOP conservative wing, which favored Senator Robert Taft. This, as well as his place on the losing 1960 ticket and his acceptance of a crucial diplomatic post under a Democratic administration, does not enhance his prospects for the GOP Presidential nomination in 1964.

But Lodge has long been a famous figure in American life, and his solid record of service and his independent personality are not without appeal. That he can be testy, his friends will agree. That he is tested, his enemies cannot deny.

Richard Milhous Nixon

Although he has been a Congressman, a Senator, and Vice President, and is a youthful 51, Richard Milhous Nixon is tabbed by some as a political has-been. His unsuccessful attempt to win the 1962 gubernatorial election in California was viewed by most observers as his last political battle.

Less than two weeks after this 1962 struggle, Nixon summed up his political career: "It is not whether we win or lose that counts but whether we fight to the best of our abilities for the cause in which we believe."

Despite this advocacy of fighting the good fight for its own sake, it has been Richard Nixon's bad luck that many people are convinced he simply wants to win the fight, good or bad.

None of Richard Nixon's political battles drew more attention than his 30 minutes on national television, September 23, 1952. Five days earlier a New York newspaper had charged that 76 wealthy Californians had raised a $18,235 "slush fund" for the "financial comfort" of the Vice Presidential nominee.

The charges were so serious that GOP Presidential candidate Eisenhower declined to say anything more than that he had an open mind on the affair. Most Republican newspapers criticized Nixon's judgment in accepting the fund. One such paper suggested that Nixon might have to quit the race. Democratic National Chairman Stephen Mitchell flatly demanded it. Nixon was near despondency; he felt that the party was deserting him without cause.

It wasn't, but the GOP was worried. The party underwrote the heavy expense of a half-hour, nationwide radio-television broadcast for Nixon's use to answer the charges made against him.

In defending himself Nixon did not dwell on his claim that the donations had been used solely for political, rather than personal purposes; nor did he make a careful audit of the precise use of his fund.

"Respectable Cloth Coat"

His defense was very different—and very successful. It was his family. Nixon told how he and his wife, Pat, had worked hard and accumulated their possessions like most young Americans—by going in debt ($30,000 in mortgages, $8,500 in other loans). Pat didn't wear a mink coat (a favorite symbol of political favor in 1952), she wore a "respectable Republican cloth coat."

The only gift the Nixons said they ever accepted from a political supporter was a cocker spaniel named Checkers that had been sent to their two daughters. They kept it, Nixon explained, because "the kids, like all kids, love the dog."

"Incredible corn," howled one Democratic newspaper. Republicans retorted that the talk was a masterpiece.

Masterpiece or corn, it was effective. Nixon had succeeded, deliberately or by accident, in identifying himself with the average American of the 1950s.

Richard Nixon's speech had been a personal fight for his own political survival. It also turned out to be a great boon for the Republican Party. "The common man was a Republican, for a change," said one commentator.

This Republican common man was born on January 9, 1913 near Los Angeles. His Quaker parents had a successful general store and filling station in nearby Whittier. Money was never plentiful, however, so Nixon worked his way through Whittier College (A. B. '34), graduating second in his class, and through Duke University Law School ('37), where he was an honors student.

Nixon returned to his hometown to practice law. When he joined a local theater group, he met a pretty, red-headed schoolteacher, Pat Ryan. They were married in 1940. During the war he put in four years in the Navy, including a 15-month tour as an air transport officer in the South Pacific.

A Hard Campaign

Late in 1945, Republicans in the 12th California Congressional District were looking for someone to unseat the five-term incumbent, New Dealer Jerry Voorhis. They found Richard Nixon.

Nixon fought a hard campaign, highlighted by a series of debates in which his legal training gave him an advantage over his less aggressive opponent. In the great Republican sweep of 1946, Nixon won his House seat with 57% of the votes cast.

As a member of the House Un-American Activities Committee, Nixon played an important role in the exposure of the connections between Alger Hiss, a former Federal employe, and a Communist espionage apparatus in the 1930s. With the Hiss case, the issue of Communist infiltration of the Federal Government became a major one, and Nixon earned a national reputation as a leading fighter against Communists.

In his Senate campaign of 1950 against the Democrats' actress-politician Helen Gahagan Douglas, Nixon made extensive use of the issue of domestic Communism. Opponents called this tactic a smear. Nixon won by 680,000 votes.

After Richard Nixon completed eight years as the 36th Vice President, the entire concept of the office had been redefined. Harry Truman began the upgrading after he got a Vice President in 1948. (As Vice President, Truman had never heard of the atomic bomb, then under development, until he became President.)

With Eisenhower and Nixon the office assumed its present importance. Eight years of high responsibility gave Nixon a strong claim to the GOP Presidential nomination in 1960. And eight years as the party's number two man gave him the political leverage to control a majority of the delegates far ahead of the convention.

No one in his generation had soared so high, so suddenly, except John Kennedy. After he lost out to Kennedy in the closest Presidential election since 1880, Nixon quickly fell from political prominence.

Counselor Seeks Another Hearing

He returned to the private life he had put aside in 1946. His law practice, his autobiography, and a newspaper column enabled him to make more money in the first 10 months after he left office than in all his 14 years in Washington. Yet Richard Nixon, like many other men, was irresistibly drawn to politics. He toyed with the idea of running for the House again, but decided to try for the California governorship.

It was risky business. Four years earlier, William Knowland, former Republican Senate Majority Leader with 14 years on Capitol Hill had been dumped into oblivion after he had failed in a try for the same office. Nixon faced the same man who defeated Knowland, Governor Edmund G. (Pat) Brown, and he was hard pressed to find a major issue in the record of Brown's administration.

Nixon had compounded his troubles by alienating the working press (after losing to Brown, he called a news conference to bawl out the press for giving him what he felt was unfair treatment during the campaign). Many reporters got the impression that Nixon was persisting in the aloof manner of a Vice President running for the Presidency, rather than a lawyer running for governor.

With few issues on which he could successfully attack the Brown administration, Nixon concentrated on blitz strategy; he would overwhelm his opponent with sheer energy; he would win on personality. As often occurs in campaigns of this type the rivals spent most of their time denying charges made against them.

Eastward, Ho!

Brown won by more than 200,000 votes. Seven months later Nixon moved his residence to New York City, where he became a senior partner in an established firm specializing in international and corporate law, and he quickly earned a reputation for being a very good lawyer. The essay Nixon submitted for admission to the New York bar was praised by the chairman of the reviewing committee as the "finest" he had seen in 28 years.

Well settled in his $135,000, 12-room apartment, Richard Nixon has repeatedly stated that he is not a candidate for the GOP nomination. Republican politicians agree that Nixon could find no friendly delegates in Nelson Rockefeller's own political preserve. Yet the possibility of a convention deadlock is a real one. And few GOP pros have forgotten Nixon's near miss in 1960.

A good lawyer doesn't reveal his strategy until all the facts and forces that will be potent at the decisive moment are apparent. As the campaign got underway, lawyer Nixon announced his availability for a draft. Otherwise, he wasn't talking.

Ready and waiting.

Some thoughts on American journalism.

Nelson Aldrich Rockefeller

Nominated again for governor—1962.

Showing Berlin to the new Mrs. Rockefeller.

The Rockefellers of Pocantico Hills, New York, are the richest upper-class family in the country. At the same time, they are the richest middle-class family, for it has been their adherence to middle-class notions of family life that has helped to mollify the public's old hostility toward the founding father, John D. Rockefeller, Sr.

Thus, it's not hard to account for the seismographic shock caused by the divorce and remarriage of Nelson Aldrich Rockefeller. But it was the circumstances of the events, rather than the events themselves, that were responsible for the impact on the nation.

As Governor of New York, Nelson Rockefeller had proven his administrative ability and his popularity with the voters, and his chances of winning the 1964 Republican Presidential nomination were, before his divorce, rated excellent. But on March 16, 1962, this man—whose strict religious upbringing had been amply publicized—was divorced by his wife after nearly 32 years of marriage. A year later, Governor Rockefeller married a New York neighbor, herself divorced only four weeks before. The Governor was 54; his second wife was 36. The new Mrs. Rockefeller had four young children by her previous marriage, and her former husband obtained custody of them.

Professional politicians, as a breed, are not dogmatists about such things as divorce and remarriage, but they are acutely sensitive to what they think the popular reaction to such events might be. Divorce is hardly regarded as shameful in American society, but it is generally felt to be a liability for a Presidential contender.

A Certain Amount of Leverage

Governor Rockefeller's political problems, then, are largely of his own making. To be a Rockefeller and have problems, it's almost necessary to make them yourself. A family fortune estimated at more than $3 billion, a fortune that permits the family to control investments worth more than $10 billion, gives a Rockefeller a certain amount of leverage in his dealings with his fellow man. But only personal achievement can provide real satisfaction, so the New York Governor has pursued a political career in the hope that he can get something from it that his $5 million-a-year income can't buy.

Nelson Rockefeller was born July 8, 1908, the second of five sons of John D., Jr., and Abby Greene Aldrich Rockefeller. Grandfather Rockefeller had made so much money in the oil business that his son made giving away millions a full-time job.

Fearful that incredible wealth might have a damaging effect on the character of their children, the parents raised them carefully. They were taught that wealth gave them a responsibility to the community, that prudence was essential to the care and feeding of money, and that a strong religious faith was an essential ingredient of a worthwhile life.

After private school in New York, Nelson went off to Dartmouth. Family legend has it that he

The Major Issue Is Domestic

muddled along without distinction for three years but, when he found his roommate would earn the Phi Beta Kappa award, bore down on the books and won this honor for himself.

At the Rockefeller summer home on the Maine Coast, Nelson had grown up near Philadelphia heiress Mary Todhunter Clark. Six days after he was graduated from Dartmouth, they were married. Together they took a trip around the world.

After clerking at a New York bank and working for a time at Rockefeller Center, the family's office-building complex in Manhattan, Nelson was assigned to a supervisory post in Venezuela where the family had oil interests. This hitch in South America profoundly affected the friendly, energetic young man who was astonished by the extreme poverty of most people in that mineral-rich land. His Venezuela experience led him to put up the capital for industrial and housing developments there and in Puerto Rico.

"Open Skies" Inspection Plan

When World War II broke out, President Roosevelt appointed Nelson assistant secretary of state for Latin America. His performance in that job led to other important posts under FDR and Truman. President Eisenhower made him Undersecretary of the newly-created Health, Education and Welfare Department. Later it was Nelson who suggested the "open skies" aerial inspection plan put forth by Ike.

Although this record of national service would have satisfied many men, it did not satisfy Rockefeller. He sought the special rewards that only elective office can bring, and from the beginning he never doubted what elective office he wanted. Even before he entered the gubernatorial race in New York in 1958, Nelson Rockefeller's eye was on the White House. But all in good time.

His first task was to win the GOP nomination for governor. This was not hard. He had a long record of public service and his family had been a generous contributor to the state Republican Party for generations.

Rockefeller began his campaign against incumbent W. Averell Harriman as the underdog. But he waged a vigorous campaign that took advantage of his two main assets, personality and ample funds. And he attracted many Democratic voters by playing down his party affiliation while stressing his liberal philosophy.

His victory in 1958 bucked the biggest Democratic tide in years. Democrats gained 13 seats in the Senate, 46 seats in the House, and increased their control of governorships from 29 to 34. In the face of this rampaging donkey, Rockefeller scored a landslide victory with a plurality of 500,000 votes.

He came out strong for civil rights, for more public housing, for no fare increase on New York's debt-ridden subway system, against cuts in the state's vast relief program, and against right-to-work legislation. Many state Republicans felt that Rockefeller was really a Democrat in disguise.

In 1960, the New York Governor made a try for the GOP Presidential nomination, was discouraged early by party leaders, but made his influence felt on the Republican platform (See Chapter III).

In 1962, he was re-elected governor; this time his victory was less impressive as he ran last among Republican winners on the statewide ticket. In the years since 1958 his personal life had changed radically, and the changes had not served his political ambitions.

A quiet, but effective, campaigner in 1958 had been Mrs. Rockefeller. Slender, aristocratic in feature, elegantly but conservatively turned out, she had a special appeal for the Republican ladies she met at teas, receptions and suppers. Her unaffected little speeches were gracious and only covertly political. She may not have enjoyed politics, as some reports have maintained, but she handled her role of candidate's wife with poise and warmth.

Less conspicuous on the Rockefeller campaign scene was Mrs. James Slater Murphy (formerly, Margaretta "Happy" Fitler), wife of a microbiologist at the Rockefeller Institute. She had grown up on the Philadelphia Main Line, and at the summer colony where Rockefeller had. She and her husband moved in the select social group that revolves around the Rockefeller family, and she was a key member of Nelson's political team until she quit in May, 1961.

On November 17, 1961, the Rockefellers revealed they would dissolve their marriage after nearly 32 years. A brief announcement to the press was their first and last public comment on their personal difficulties.

The tragic disappearance of their youngest son, Michael, off the coast of New Guinea temporarily quieted the talk about the Governor's marital troubles. Then the rumors started. Mrs. Rockefeller was granted a Nevada divorce on grounds of mental cruelty after an eight-minute hearing behind closed doors.

One year later, Mrs. Murphy obtained an Idaho divorce and, one month after that, she married Nelson.

A Lot of Head Shaking

Rockefeller's supporters looked at the ground and shook their heads. The Press and the politicians looked at the public opinion polls and shook their heads. The clergy looked at the sky and shook their heads. Nobody seemed to think the Governor's remarriage was a good idea except Nelson and Happy.

But Nelson Rockefeller is not a man to shrink before personal criticism or long odds. He decided to pursue the White House despite his divorce and remarriage because he is ambitious, because he believes it's up to him to battle Goldwater conservatism for the sake of the GOP, and because he thrives on the tempo of big-time politics.

Politics, to the Governor of New York, is a high calling, an exercise in practical patriotism, and the climb toward the Presidency is the greatest challenge of all. For a Rockefeller, where else is there such a mountain?

George Wilcken Romney

If America attached as much romance to the nail-spitter as it does to the rail-splitter, George Wilcken Romney might have a better chance of moving into the White House.

As a boy, George helped his father in his work as a carpenter and builder. George's specialty was lathing—putting up strips of wood on walls as a groundwork for plastering. Young Romney would fill his mouth with nails and spit them out point first so fast that he could place 3,000 laths a day when the standard was only 1,600.

This earnestness on the job is characteristic of the man, who, as Republican Governor of Michigan, is a long-shot contender for the GOP Presidential nomination in 1964. At 56, Romney is as energetic a politician as he was a businessman, but he has learned that demonstrative leadership is not enough in the give-and-take, rough-and-grumble world of politics. Although his native idealism (his detractors call it naivete) remains, he has lost many of his illusions about what one good citizen can do upon entering public service.

Fight for Better Schools

He got his first taste of civic combat in 1956 when, as president of then-struggling American Motors, he became leader of a citizens group fighting for better schools in Detroit. The group's efforts were climaxed with a dramatic campaign for bond issues and a tax boost to pay for the new schools the Romney committee was convinced the city needed. Thanks largely to Romney's spirited leadership, the school referendum passed after a hard uphill battle.

Meanwhile, the State of Michigan had been having acute economic troubles for years. In 1959, the level of private income was high but unemployment—more than twice the national rate—was a major problem. Moreover, the Democratic governor and the Republican legislature were, as usual, deadlocked over revenue measures. The state's troubles were not helped by a state constitution that, though it was somewhat revised in 1909, was substantially the one that had been written in 1850. And unlike the U.S. Constitution, state constitutions were not written for the ages.

A crisis came in April, 1959, when the state couldn't meet its payroll and 26,000 state employes, including its 144 legislators, went unpaid.

George Romney believed that another citizens' committee, like the one that helped solve Detroit's school crisis, could work its own kind of democratic magic on the state's problems. He blamed the mess in Michigan on both parties, contending that it was the result of a deterioration of public responsibility over more than 30 years as the state was transformed to an urban-industrial complex.

The "Citizens for Michigan" (CFM) group that he helped form was a voluntary, nonpartisan organization. It was Romney's concern about excessive concentrations of power in Michigan politics that led to the requirement that contributions to the group be limited to individual gifts and be no more than $100.

Off to restyle Michigan.

He was convinced the state GOP organization was dominated by Ford and General Motors, and that the Democrats were under the thumb of Walter Reuther's United Auto Workers.

The CFM agitated for a state constitutional convention and, when one was finally called, Romney was named a convention vice president. In 1962, he quit as president of American Motors to run for governor on the Republican ticket. Elected by 80,000 votes (he captured 51.4% of the votes cast), Romney became Michigan's first GOP governor in 14 years.

The Republican-controlled legislature passed a large portion of his initial recommendations, but turned down a $1.15 minimum wage bill. And over bitter Democratic and organized-labor opposition, Romney won voter approval of a new state constitution last spring.

Lansing Is Not Detroit

The Romney-for-President talk grew more audible. With the boom in automobile sales, the state's unemployment total fell to an eight-year low, and state finances finally moved out of the red. But George Romney's extraordinary good fortune was not to last.

Last November the Romney tax-reform proposal foundered in the legislature. The Governor had gone ahead with his full tax program despite the encouraging fiscal picture and despite the opposition of Democrats and conservative Republicans. Why, the analysts asked, did Romney push his whole tax plan when he could so easily have used the state's unexpectedly happy financial situation as an excuse to put off or modify the tax reform he had pledged in the 1962 campaign.

Part of the answer, even his foes concede, does him credit: Convinced that tax reform is needed, he is the kind of man who fights for what he believes. Secondly, he was supremely confident in his ability to rally public sentiment and sway hostile legislators. Also, Romney was aware that failure to follow through on the most widely publicized pledge of his campaign would be a big liability in the next election.

But the Governor had underestimated his political opposition. And his dashing, independent, unorthodox behavior had irritated many of the Republicans whose support he needed.

"George just isn't a real politician, says one friend. "He's just plain Romney."

Just plain Romney was born July 8, 1907, in northern Mexico in a settlement of members of the Church of Jesus Christ of Latter-Day Saints. His father, Gaskell Romney, was a furniture maker. His family were devout Mormons, as Governor Romney is today.

The Mormon colonists, including the Romneys, were driven out of Mexico during the 1912 revolution in that country. By the time he was 14, young George had lived in Mexico, Texas, California, Utah and Idaho. He attended public schools in Salt Lake City and completed a year of junior college there. For two years thereafter he served as a Mormon missionary in England and Scotland.

George returned to the United States when he was 21; he got a part-time job and entered the University of Utah. But his high-school sweetheart, a lovely girl with the lovely name of Lenore LaFount, was living in Washington (her father was a Coolidge appointee to the Federal Radio Commission, forerunner of the Federal Communications Commission). With one of his brothers, Romney drove east to the capital.

Through a newspaper ad, George found a job as stenographer for Senator David I. Walsh of Massachusetts. Bright and aggressive, Romney soon assumed duties as a staff assistant in legislative matters. He worked hard on pending legislation and spent long hours in the company of Walsh and other Senators. Through the daily tasks of the lawmaker's office, the young man got a valuable grounding in how to deal with Congressmen—training he would use later.

In 1930, Romney became a legislative representative (that's code for lobbyist) for the Aluminum Company of America, and in 1931 he married Lenore after a courtship of nearly eight years. Brigham Young had once declared: "An unmarried man 25 years of age is a dangerous element in a community." Strict Mormon Romney made it just under the wire; had he waited another year to wed, he would have become a "dangerous element."

During his years in Washington, Romney frequently entertained politicians and reporters in his home. Because the Romneys neither drink nor smoke, they at first didn't stock in a supply of liquor.

But this was changed when George found out that his guests, before arriving at his house, usually made it a point to have several snorts on the way over.

Super-Salesman

Romney became Detroit manager of the Automobile Manufacturers Association in 1939. Two years later, Romney was named director of the Automotive Council of War Production, which coordinated the efforts of all the companies connected with the auto industry in turning out more than $30 billion of war material. After the war he joined Nash-Kelvinator and rose steadily in its ranks. After consolidating with other firms, the company was renamed American Motors. It was as president of American Motors that Romney came to national attention as the super-salesman of the "compact" car.

Romney infuriated the auto industry and delighted the public with remarks such as: "Cars 19 feet long, weighing two tons, are used to run a 118-pound housewife three blocks to the drugstore for a package of bobby pins and lipstick."

During his reign at American Motors, the company prospered—against the stiffest kind of competition. And as George Romney took care of his company's health, he also took care of his own. He was on the golf course every morning at dawn, playing several balls at once and running after them down the fairway.

As a politician, he is still running hard. But he is coming upon traps and bunkers he's never known before.

An evening out with Mrs. Romney.

William Warren Scranton

Barry Goldwater claims that only he, among all the Republican Presidential contenders, is in a distinguishable position in an era of conspicuous conformity. But that's not necessarily so.

There's another GOP prospect who possesses at least two claims to special status. William Warren Scranton entered the Presidential race less well known to party leaders than his mother. Moreover, he bears a personal burden that might devitalize an ordinary man: He must go through life indebted to his sister-in-law for getting him a job.

The 46-year-old Governor of Pennsylvania, of course, is no ordinary man. Four years ago he was just cutting his teeth in politics as the Republican candidate for Congress from Pennsylvania's largely Democratic 10th District. This year, due less to his flare for politics than to the curious twists of fate, Scranton is an important Presidential contender.

His power base is the Keystone State itself, with its 29 electoral votes. But Pennsylvania governors have rarely been viewed as Presidential timber—because they are elected for one four-year term only (making them lame ducks immediately) and because Pennsylvania politics is so rugged it permits few survivors. On top of that, Pennsylvania has enjoyed the services of comparatively few outstanding governors (the most notable since the Civil War was conservationist Gifford Pinchot, and few people remember him today).

Scranton's name began to loom large when Southerner Lyndon Johnson succeeded Northerner John Kennedy as President. Only then did Scranton's vote-getting prowess in Pennsylvania cause GOP chieftains to look seriously in the direction of Harrisburg.

What they saw was a boyishly good-looking Ivy Leaguer who had a remarkable knack for getting his way in what had been a faction-ridden state party.

A Fortune From the Forge

Governor Scranton comes from a long line of Pennsylvania industrialists and Republicans. His great-great grandfather and two cousins started an iron works at a site in northeastern Pennsylvania that became the city of Scranton. Through the years the family diversified its interests and prospered.

Two of the Governor's forbears on his father's side were Congressmen. His father, Worthington, was one of Pennsylvania's leading contributors to the GOP. But it was his mother who was the real Republican power around the house.

Marion Margery Scranton, known throughout the Republican Party as the "Duchess," was the GOP national committeewoman from Pennsylvania from 1928 to 1951, and national vice-chairman of the party from 1940 to 1944. Governor Scranton is still referred to by some veteran Republicans as "the Duchess's boy."

The Duchess's boy was graduated from Yale in 1939. During his years there he became acquainted with a Harvard man named John F. Kennedy, and he occasionally dated Kennedy's sister, Kathleen. Scranton's career at Yale Law School was interrupted by

World War II in which he served as a captain in the Air Transport Command.

During the war he married his home-town sweetheart. Bill and Mary Scranton have three sons and a daughter ranging in age from 18 to nine. The family home is Marworth, a 22-room mansion set on a hilltop amid 140 rolling acres near Scranton.

Until 1959, when he took a job as a press aide to Secretary of State Dulles—a job he got through the social contacts of his sister-in-law, Mrs. Harold Coolidge of Washington—Bill Scranton's highest public office was chairman of the Lackawanna County United Fund Drive. He directed a successful fund-raising campaign and topped off his good work by dancing a lively Charleston at the victory dinner.

In Washington, he stayed with the State Department when Christian Herter took over for the dying Dulles, and soon he was given expanded responsibilities as Herter's liaison man with the White House. Today Scranton's aides like to stress the importance of that post but Scranton himself minimized its significance in newspaper interviews at the time.

Looking for Someone

In 1960, the Republican Party was looking around for someone to oppose the Democratic incumbent, Stanley Prokop, in the 10th District Congressional race. The prospect of entering the contest was hardly inviting; the Democrats had controlled Lackawanna County for 30 years.

After getting all the Republican leaders in the 10th District to support his candidacy—simply by saying he wouldn't run if they all didn't back him—Scranton hired several young political strategists.

In a particularly unorthodox move, the Scranton forces explained on television and in newspaper ads how to split a ticket; they knew they had to attract many Democratic voters to win. Republican regulars screamed, but Scranton was unmoved.

While Democrat Kennedy was carrying the district by 30,000 votes, Republican Scranton was sent to the House with a 17,000-vote plurality. The lessons in ticket splitting had paid off.

The freshman Congressman's voting record was generally liberal, except in fiscal policy where he took a conservative approach.

A breakdown is revealing: In 1962, Congressman Scranton's votes were 70% in favor of the Administration and 6% against in foreign policy matters, while the total Republican House score was 40% for and 47% against. On domestic matters in the same year, Scranton closely followed the party, 41% in support of the President, 45% in opposition, while the GOP composite was 43% and 47%.

In November of 1961, Pennsylvania resident Dwight Eisenhower urged Scranton to run for governor. After thinking about it for two weeks, the Congressman called a press conference in his home town and flatly announced "No."

Civil war followed in the state Republican Party, with particularly bitter feuding between conservatives

'All Things Come Round to Him . . .'

and the liberals led by Senator Hugh Scott. At stake were the gubernatorial and senatorial nominations. Republicans began to despair.

In this crisis situation, the party turned again to Scranton and pleaded with him to set his sights on the governor's chair. Scranton let the party leaders stew a little longer before telling them he would run for governor if he was given the party's united support. Almost as if by magic, other candidates withdrew and every county chairman in the state backed him. The pros went along because they were sure the young Congressman was their fastest horse.

Scranton ran against Philadelphia Mayor Richardson Dilworth, who had been re-elected mayor in 1959 by 207,000 votes and who had a reputation for being a tough fighter.

Bill Scranton is not a dynamic speaker, but he campaigned energetically, covering 150,000 miles between March and November. It was a typical Pennsylvania political brawl, with each candidate engaging in schoolyard name-calling. Dilworth called Scranton "Little Lord Fauntleroy" and "an Ivy League Dickie Nixon" (although Dilworth was a Yale man himself), and Scranton retorted that Dilworth was a "crown prince of failure."

The election wasn't even close. Scranton's margin was 486,000 votes, better than 55% of the total cast. He held Dilworth's margin in Philadelphia to 105,000 and carried Allegheny County (Pittsburgh) by 52,-

000, where Dilworth supporters had expected a 40,000 advantage for their man. Of 67 counties in the state, Scranton carried 62.

As Governor, Scranton worked quickly to make the state's revenues and expenditures balance. He launched an economy drive by lopping a flat 20% from departmental budgets, and he secured a boost in the sales tax to 5% from 4%. He failed to get a new constitution for the state, but the vote was close—closer than the five previous attempts to replace Pennsylvania's antiquated charter. Some 49% of the voters favored holding a constitutional convention.

As the 1964 Presidential contest got under way, William Scranton remained content to let others carry the ball for him. He would not say, for instance, how strong a candidate he thought Lyndon Johnson would be; he wouldn't give his opinions on the top Republican contenders; he wouldn't say how he thought the GOP convention would go; he declined to support any movements to "stop" any other candidate; he refused to say which other Republican Presidential prospect he feels philosophically closest to; and at the outset he wouldn't make any effort to win the nomination for himself.

At the outset, he scheduled several out-of-state speeches to let the pros have a look at him; otherwise, William Scranton behaved as if the Presidential nomination would have to come to him on a silver platter. And why not? Everything else has.

(Continued From Page 27)

Minnesota, 53, Senator Eugene J. McCarthy of Minnesota, 48, Peace Corps Director R. Sargent Shriver, 48, Attorney General Robert F. Kennedy, 38, Senator Edmund S. Muskie of Maine, 50, New York City Mayor Robert F. Wagner, 54, U.N. Ambassador Adlai E. Stevenson, 64, and California Governor Edmund G. (Pat) Brown, 59.

The Catholic Contenders

McCarthy, Wagner, Shriver, Muskie, Kennedy, and Brown are Catholics and this could be a factor one way or the other. Some Democrats are fearful of establishing a "Catholic spot" on the quadrennial ticket. Others think President Kennedy's assassination will prod more Catholics into the Democratic fold, especially if Johnson picks a Catholic for a running mate. For a similar reason there is some feeling that Robert Kennedy would be a good vote-getter, despite the bitter feeling toward his strong civil rights stand in the South and elsewhere. Too, he is an able diplomat.

Robert Sargent Shriver emerges as a possibility because, as the late President Kennedy's brother-in-law, he is a well-known member of the most publicized American family of recent years. But he is a member of the Kennedy clan without being a Kennedy and, according to some theorists, he represents the best of both worlds in a party with regionally disparate opinions about the late President.

On his own, Shriver has made a reputation as an effective administrator. It was he who got the Peace Corps program off the ground and who helped change the public notion of the Corps after its somewhat confused early days. He is a Northern liberal (from Illinois) who hasn't been on the national scene long enough to make many enemies in the Democratic Party. A sophisticated Ivy Leaguer (Yale, '38), he possesses an attractive, energetic personality. And, for those who care, he's tall, dark and handsome.

Senator Hubert Horatio Humphrey of Minnesota has undergone a definite transformation in the public mind since his unsuccessful attempt to win the Presidential nomination in 1960. Long considered—unfairly—just another talkative liberal, Humphrey has attained new stature as Majority Whip in the Senate and as a confidant of Presidents Kennedy and Johnson.

On Hubert Humphrey the liberal label is

Mayor Robert Wagner of New York City.

Sen. Eugene McCarthy of Minnesota.

Gov. Edmund (Pat) Brown of California.

Sen. Hubert Humphrey of Minnesota.

Sen. Edmund Muskie
of Maine.

U.N. Ambassador   Attorney General
Adlai Stevenson.   Robert Kennedy.

Peace Corps Director Sargent Shriver.

as comfortable as an old tweed coat. He believes in a strongly paternal Federal Government that, through more laws and more spending, will hopefully reshape society to the benefit of "the little man." He is extremely popular among union leaders, Negroes and other liberal groups whose votes the Democratic ticket in 1964 cannot afford to lose.

A Seminar-Room Manner

Humphrey's Minnesota colleague, Senator Eugene Joseph McCarthy, is a scholarly liberal who taught sociology (St. Thomas College) before being elected to Congress in 1948. As a product of Minnesota's Democrat-Farmer-Labor Party, McCarthy is Humphrey's philosophical twin, although he has a much more reserved personality.

Elected to the Senate in 1958, Senator McCarthy quickly gained popularity with liberal campus intellectuals who admire not only his ideas but his seminar-room manner. He is a polished speaker and an effective debater. McCarthy was a member of the Humphrey-for-President strategy board in 1960.

Maine's junior Senator, Edmund Sixtus Muskie is a strong Democratic vote-getter in what has traditionally been a Republican fief. He has been winning Republicans to his side ever since 1948, when he refused to marry his wife-to-be until she, a Republican, had registered as a Democrat. By 1954 he had made enough conversions to be elected Governor. He did it by promising a bigger state effort to boost Maine's lagging school system and faltering economy, and by waging a strenuous campaign that was a marked contrast to the listless Republican effort.

As Governor he started the largest road building program in Maine's history, spent more money to improve schools, fought a regulatory battle with local power companies, and sought to attract new industries to the state.

Down Easters found his performance in office to their liking. While Adlai Stevenson could only manage 29% of Maine's vote in the 1956 Eisenhower landslide, Muskie rolled up an impressive 59%. Two years later, he unseated an incumbent Republican Senator by a remarkable 61%. In the Senate, his voting record has earned him the liberal credentials that Lyndon Johnson is looking for.

Robert Francis Kennedy is best known as

his late brother's closest adviser who was on the inside during all of John F. Kennedy's foreign and domestic crises. As his brother's campaign manager in 1960, it was Robert who directed the Kennedy steam-roller, squashing many Democratic fingers in the process.

As Attorney General, Robert Kennedy directed Federal efforts to enforce racial integration in the South, where those efforts were met with resistance and violence. He is unpopular in the South and elsewhere because of his activities on behalf of Negro rights.

The Attorney General is reputed to see things in terms of absolute right and wrong, with little modification and has pursued his moralistic viewpoint with a sometimes ruthless determination. Still, since his brother's death, his name has led many polls in the North as a Vice Presidential possibility. He possesses a full measure of Kennedy energy and thrives on a good scrap. He is one of the shrewdest young politicians in the country.

Dalai Adlai

Adlai Ewing Stevenson has become, to many Northern liberals, the undisputed Dalai Lama of the Democratic Party. His two unsuccessful campaigns for the Presidency in 1952 and 1956 have, if anything, increased the esteem in which he is held by his partisans. Brilliant and urbane, Stevenson is a youthful elder statesman whose manner suggests a mixture of wisdom and world-weariness.

His political fortunes have gone awry partly because, for all his eloquence, he has been unable to communicate with grassroots America. His speeches and the published reports of his behavior as an adviser to President Kennedy during the Cuban crisis tend to mark him as something of a Hamlet. His major concern has always been foreign affairs; he is widely and deeply respected abroad. The bread-and-butter politicians of Democratic industrial strongholds have never really taken to him because he doesn't know how to speak their language—nor does he care about learning.

Despite his defeats, he has seen several of his foreign policy ideas adopted, and thus his supporters regard him as a prophet with too little honor in his own country.

Robert Ferdinand Wagner, Mayor of New York City, is the liberal overseer of countless political blocs which are polarized around diverse ethnic and economic interests. He sits in one of the great thankless hot seats of American politics. New York City is a community almost beyond the power of political man to run efficiently. Its administration has historically been stopgap measure piled upon stopgap measure.

Wagner, whose father gained fame in the Senate as a dedicated friend of organized labor, has built his power as most big-city mayors must build it—by catering to the wants and whims of minority groups. Thus he is popular among those groups, and they in turn supported him when he sought successfully to pry control of the state party away from his political enemies a couple of years ago.

Although a realistic politician who can fight when he has to, Wagner's style is generally given to speaking softly and carrying a small stick.

Edmund Gerald (Pat) Brown lost much of his prestige when, as governor of California, he was unable to control his own delegation at the 1960 Democratic convention. He regained some of that prestige in 1962, when he faced Richard Nixon in the gubernatorial race and was re-elected. California politics, partly because of the state's rapid growth, is rather chaotic and Brown has had a difficult time consolidating his position as party leader.

His biggest asset as a Vice Presidential possibility: He is governor of a state with 40 electoral votes.

These, then, are the popularly discussed contenders for the major parties' major nominations in 1964.

President Johnson is expected to head the Democratic ticket. The second spot could well be filled by Brown, Humphrey, Robert Kennedy, McCarthy, Shriver, Stevenson or Wagner.

Shaping up as Republican Presidential prospects are Goldwater, Lodge, Nixon, Rockefeller, Romney and Scranton. These six, together with Morton, Kuchel and Mrs. Smith, also fall within the wide circle of Vice Presidential possibilities.

Confronting them all are the issues of our time. And as events will influence these issues, so will the issues influence each candidate's star.

An issue becomes an issue when a politician seizes upon an event or condition and decides to make something of it. An issue may be big or small, public or personal, real or contrived. Issues are the yeast of politics.

The operating issues of the 1964 Presidential campaign cannot be known for sure until the battle is over; no one knows what turns history will take between now and election day. But there are some general areas of dispute which are certain to attract partisan volleys; there are also many potential targets that could pop up suddenly and draw the political fire.

Dominant is the issue of peace in a world bristling with atomic arms, and America's problems in containing the Communists.

At home, the drive for Negro rights is a double-edged sword that could easily cut down any contender for the White House. The seemingly inexorable growth of the Federal Government in power, size and budget will be appraised from opposite angles. So will the Johnson-Kennedy record. And President Johnson's medical history will be re-examined and wondered about.

Then, on November 3, 1964, the politicians will be silenced and the voters will decide.

☆　☆　☆

In the last two decades, the United States and Russia have had more than a hundred old fashioned reasons for going to war.

Communist hostility toward the Free World, a hostility which is apparently the balance wheel of Communist politics, is so basic and relentless that only the hellish consequences of a nuclear exchange have kept the Bear at bay and the globe intact.

But if the great missiles remain in their underground scabbards, the deadly rivalry between the two great powers still proceeds. Moscow and Peking, for all their differences in approach, are both committed to dominating the U.S.-led half of the globe. In between are the self-styled neutralist nations who believe that international relations in the atomic era can be a spectator sport.

Given the nuclear standoff, the Communists persistently press here and there, hoping to find a fault in the Western will. How the Free World, how the U.S. reacts to these challenges determines in large measure how the American electorate reacts to the incumbent administration. Foreign policy may, in a general

Part II: The Issues

way, be bipartisan in this country, but failure in foreign policy is never bipartisan.

Thus, any major U.S. setback in the foreign field between now and election day could be an insurmountable setback for President Johnson's effort to win the White House on his own. Moreover, the possibilities for trouble are many.

Some of those possibilities:

South Vietnam. America's fortunes in Southeast Asia have been steadily on the downgrade. The swamp and rain-forest countries that were cut out of old French Indochina (won for France by Napoleon III a century ago; lost to France in 1954 after an eight-year struggle with Vietminh rebels) have been whittled away from the West by the Chinese-equipped-and-directed guerrilla force known as the Vietcong.

These guerrilla actions snatched Laos from the West and forced the U.S. to agree to a nominally neutralist posture for that little patch of inland jungle. Neighboring Cambodia, desperately eager to wind up on the winning side, last year displayed the greatest form reversal since the Yankees lost the World Series in four straight. Cambodia told Uncle Sam to keep his foreign aid money and go away. Adjacent Thailand could get panicky at any time.

If South Vietnam falls—and less likely things have happened—Cambodia would jump into Peking's lap. The other countries in the area would proceed to make the best deal they could with China and U.S. influence in Asia would be nil. Even Japan would reappraise its policies, for Southeast Asia is Japan's second biggest market.

Thus, the loss of South Vietnam would give the Republicans an issue they could wield like an Indian club. And thus, President Johnson is likely to take extraordinary measures to achieve at least a face-saving Laos-like arrangement there.

Cuba. President Kennedy scored high with the American people when he told Khrushchev to get his big missiles out of Cuba or else. But thousands of Soviet soldiers remain and Fidel Castro still threatens the rest of Latin America.

Another Castro in this hemisphere, such as in British Guiana (now led by Marxist Prime Minister Cheddi Jagan) or in Chile (preparing for an election next fall that could see the Communists come to power through a coalition device), and all bets on the U.S. Presidential campaign would be off. U.S. prestige would plummet and the much-troubled Alliance for Progress could very well disintegrate entirely.

Latin America offers a wide variety of powder kegs, any one of which could go off in the face of the Democratic Administration. Communist-inspired anti-Americanism racks Panama. Labor unrest in Bolivia is setting the stage for further Red gains there, and leftist terrorism in Venezuela is threatening that country's stability. A roaring inflation is undermining the

economic and political structure of Brazil, and Haiti possesses a blood-soaked dictatorship. These conditions, plus the military governments of Ecuador, Honduras, Paraguay and the Dominican Republic add up to revolutionary and propaganda opportunities for the Communists.

Meanwhile, Americans grow tired of pumping millions into a continent that can't seem to get a grip on itself.

West Berlin. This is the perennial hot spot. The slightest Communist success in further tightening the noose about that half-city would shake the Atlantic Alliance, which is based on U.S. power and its will to use it. As it is, the Berlin Wall will be brought up in the U.S. Presidential campaign; it was built in the summer of 1961 and President Kennedy decided not to do anything about it.

And here is the ticklish part of the Republicans' problem in 1964. How far can they go in attacking the record of an assassinated President? Most observers don't think they can go very far. The criticism will have to be directed at an impersonal "Democratic Administration" or the GOP would risk an emotional boomerang. The Democrats will meanwhile be canonizing the late President and hoping President Johnson can make it until November without any serious reverses.

Other headaches for the U.S. could emerge from Pakistan's chummy attitude toward Red China, India's incomprehensible attitude toward everything, Indonesia's territorial ambitions in the Southwest Pacific, the persistent Arab-Israeli feud, the economic and racial imponderables in Africa, and the United Nations' difficulty in getting the world to pay attention and some of its members to pay their dues.

If President Johnson, pointing to the test ban treaty, can maintain the idea that U.S.-Soviet relations are improving, he will enjoy the special leverage in the campaign of a peace-keeping Chief Executive. But should something go awry, Republican fingers will be pointed at him.

At home, the gross national product—the total value of America's output of goods and services—and Federal spending steadily rise; and the Johnson Administration wants a $10 billion tax cut. Whether Congress passes a tax-cut bill before the elections or not, the arguments about the efficacy of the measure, its wisdom during a period of prosperity, and its

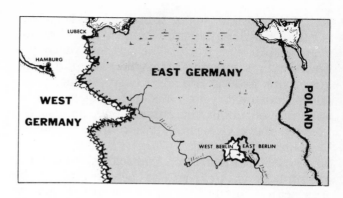

justification at a time of huge Government spending will be roundly rehearsed.

Economy. President Johnson has made some dramatic moves to steal the thrift-in-Government ball away from the Republicans. He has ordered the closing down of various obsolete military installations, clamped down on the Federal civilian payroll, and cut back production of nuclear weapons.

FEDERAL ADMINISTRATIVE BUDGET TOTALS
1954 TO 1963

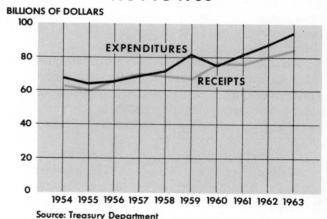

Source: Treasury Department

THE FEDERAL BUDGET DOLLAR
1964

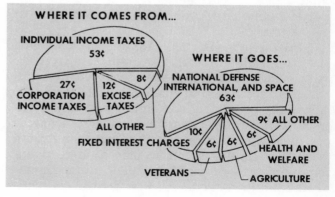

Source: Treasury Department

But LBJ isn't going to risk losing the Democrats' traditional liberal support by trimming welfare-state programs. The purpose of tighter purse strings in some areas, he says, is to provide more Federal aid elsewhere. While promising that next year's Federal budget will be $500 million under the current one, he also has pledged more Government action in a variety of fields.

Poverty in America. Politicians are playing a numbers game over the percentage of the American population that is inadequately housed and fed. Liberals are claiming 20% of the country's 190 million citizens are "poverty-stricken." Conservatives are pointing to the changing definition of "poverty" as the nation grows more prosperous.

The President plans to attack the poverty problem by expanding the area redevelopment program, by pushing special legislation to put jobless youths to work, by enlarging the Federal Food Stamp Program (which provides food for the needy), by creating a domestic Peace Corps (dubbed the National Service Corps) to help the "economically handicapped" in the U.S., by expanding minimum wage coverage to two million more workers, and by increasing Federal aid to slum dwellers.

Medicare. LBJ aims to step up the pressure for a hospital care program for the elderly financed through Social Security. Foes of the plan fear it would be a great boondoggle and a step toward socialized medicine. Proponents claim it would protect the elderly from destitution caused by mounting health costs.

Education. The President has promised to push for Federal aid to education below the college level (colleges already receive Government funds), especially in economically depressed areas. The whole question of Federal aid to schools—and of including or excluding parochial schools—and the danger of Federal control of public education will be loudly aired in the campaign.

Unemployment. The Administration plans to set up a Commission on Automation to study ways of alleviating joblessness caused by technological advances. It also will seek legislation financially penalizing companies that pay workers large amounts of overtime instead of expanding their work forces and thus providing more jobs. New emphasis will be placed on reducing the high rate of unemployment among non-whites and teen-agers. All Presidential contenders are against unemployment; the battle will come over alternative schemes to reduce it.

Balance of Payments. This problem has both foreign and domestic implications. For a variety of reasons, not the least of which is Uncle Sam's heavy expenditures around the world, the Government has been worriedly watching its supply of gold leave the country. The nation has been spending more dollars abroad than it has been taking in. Foreigners, unlike Americans, have the right to demand gold for their dollars. The resulting gold outflow threatens to undermine the value of U.S. currency. This issue, perhaps less well understood among the electorate than most other problems, will prompt a rash of pledges from both parties to reduce, or reverse, the outflow of the yellow metal.

Civil Rights. No domestic issue promises to be more inflammable than this one. President Johnson has allied himself with Negro aspirations; he has done this from conviction and because he needs the heavy Negro vote in the Northern industrial states.

This raises two questions: Will there be a backlash of anti-Democratic sentiment among whites who resent and fear Negro pressures for equal school, job and housing opportunities? Will the South stick with Johnson now that he has taken up the Negro's cause?

Much depends on the pace of integration the Negro leaders are willing to accept. If they decide to press hard in 1964, with more demonstrations and sit-ins, they will inevitably provoke a hostile reaction in the white community, especially in the lower-middle-income white suburbs and among job-conscious white blue-collar workers. The 1963 elections around the country gave an indication of this.

Signs of a Northern white reaction against Negro civil rights agitation was unmistakable. In Philadelphia's mayoralty race, perhaps the most widely watched barometer of white feeling, Democrat James Tate won re-election by 61,000 votes. This was considerably less than the 125,-000-vote and 207,000-vote margins scored by previous Democratic Mayors Joseph S. Clark and Richardson Dilworth.

Pre-election interviews found that white voters, especially in the working-class neighborhoods, widely felt that Mayor Tate had been too ready to yield to Negro demands for greater job opportunity, housing equality and school integration. And the voting substantiated these interviews. The GOP candidate, James McDermott, didn't openly oppose the Negroes' demands, but his talk about the need to restore safety to the streets and end fighting in the schools had an appeal for many white voters.

Precinct-by-precinct breakdowns of the Philadelphia vote showed that Mayor Tate carried Negro precincts by more votes than he won the election by. This means the Republican candidate outpolled Democrat Tate in the white precincts.

Similar white reactions to Democrat-backed Negro demands were apparent in the returns in Kentucky, Indiana, Boston and elsewhere.

The other side of this coin is that President Johnson, to win the Negro vote, must convince Negro leaders he means what he says. As a Southerner, he is automatically suspect in many Negro eyes. If he seems to lose his enthusiasm for their rights drive, Negroes could be persuaded to support a liberal Republican Presidential candidate.

If the President is successful in convincing Negroes he is their champion, can he hold the South for the Democrats at the same time? And this question leads to another that has long

perplexed many non-Southerners: Why does the South stick so close to the Democratic Party when that party, on the national level, has pursued policies many Southerners vigorously oppose?

To begin with, an intricate political pattern exists in the South today. Especially in the cities, the South has come a long way toward realigning itself politically with the rest of the nation. The growing urban middle class now votes heavily for the Republican Party. The white urban worker has been giving a majority of his votes to the Democrats, as has the urban Negro—for economic reasons.

While Southern cities develop national voting patterns, however, traditional ways persist in other areas. There is a hostility, for instance, between the people of the Appalachian uplands and those of the lowlands. And this hostility goes back at least to the early Nineteenth Century.

In 1861, when Virginia seceded from the Union, 46 mountain counties in the northwestern part of the state refused to go along with the decision; in 1863 these counties became the

The 1963 March on Washington: Negro militancy—and white reaction to it—will be important factors in this year's Presidential campaign.

Larry Stevens

State of West Virginia. In the Appalachian uplands, which stretch from West Virginia to Alabama, the Republican vote is much higher than it is in other rural areas of the South.

In the lowlands the Negro population is far greater and here segregationist feeling is the strongest. The farmers and, to a slightly lesser extent, the townsmen and urban workers are the most strongly opposed to the integration policies of the national Democratic Party.

Aside from the hard pull of tradition, both the farmer and laborer are drawn to the economic policies of the national Democratic Party. Locally that party is their instrument for perpetuating segregation.

Indispensable Local Party

For the townspeople the local party is indispensable. As creditors, major taxpayers and businessmen, they have a considerable stake in the local government. A sudden influx of new (Negro) voters would endanger the one-party dominance that is important to their prosperity. Another reason for not joining the Republicans is that the urban Republican middle class is the Southern group most inclined to be tolerant on the racial question.

Thus, the rank and file and the local leadership of the Democratic Party in the South find that leaving the party and going Republican, in protest against the national Democratic civil rights policy, involves too many compromises to be acceptable as a means for defeating the national party.

The alternative, then, is to form an independent party mechanism that will allow the protest against civil rights action to be demonstrated in national elections, without upsetting the important one-party dominance in local matters.

The device of the third party is being resorted to this year. Southern advocates of this device (Governors George Wallace of Alabama and Paul Johnson of Mississippi) insist they are not creating a third party. In terms of their own regional politics they may be correct: They expect their independent electors to be on the regular Democratic ticket. But in national politics, the creation of a slate of unpledged electors, designed to capture a part of the electoral vote, amounts to the formation of a third party.

The outcome of the Southern plan will not be known until November 3 (see Chapter VI for

SMOKE-FILLED ROOM

This term had its genesis in 1920, when Senator Warren G. Harding of Ohio was nominated for President by the Republican Party on the 10th ballot. In fact, Harding was selected by a group of GOP chieftains in a Chicago hotel room filled with cigar smoke late at night. The smoke-filled room that produced the Harding nomination, after the party's stronger contenders had split the convention, has come to be a political cliche describing back-room king-making.

The event was accurately predicted by Harry M. Daugherty, Harding's campaign manager, even before the convention began. In a widely publicized statement, that was roundly ridiculed at the time, Daugherty declared:

"Well, there will be no nomination on the early ballots. After the other candidates have failed, after they have gone their limit, the leaders, worn out and wishing to do the very best thing, will get together in some hotel room about 2:11 in the morning. Some 15 men, bleary-eyed with lack of sleep, and perspiring profusely with the excessive heat, will sit down around a big table. I will be with them and will present the name of Senator Harding. When the time comes, Harding will be selected, because he fits in perfectly with every need of the party and nation. He is the logical choice, and the leaders will determine to throw their support to him."

Daugherty was wrong on only one point. *He* did not attend the session in the smoke-filled room. He had predicted the meeting and the party leaders felt it might be embarrassing to ask him to sit in.

The smoke-filled room itself was the suite of George Harvey, a New York editor and one of the Republican party bosses, who had been an enthusiastic Wilson supporter but who had turned against Wilson during the war. It was the Blackstone Hotel's Room 404.

Presidential Preference Polls and Primaries

state	preference poll	delegates elected	consent of candidate	date	open or closed
Cal.	None	May Pledge	Required	June 2	Closed
Fla.	None	May Pledge	Unnecessary	May 26	Closed
Ill.	Advisory	Unpledged	May Decline	April 14	Closed
Ind.	Binding	None	Required	May 5	Closed
Md.	Binding	None	Required	May 19	Closed
Mass.	Advisory	May Pledge	Required	April 28	Closed
Neb.	Advisory	Unpledged	Required	May 12	Closed
N.H.	Advisory	May Pledge	Optional	March 10	Closed
N.J.	Advisory	May Pledge	Required	April 21	Closed
Ohio	None	Pledged	Required	May 5	Closed
Ore.	Binding	May Pledge	Unnecessary	May 15	Closed
Pa.	Advisory	Unpledged	May Decline	April 28	Closed
S.D.	None	May Pledge	Required	June 2	Closed
W. Va.	Advisory	Unpledged	Required	May 12	Closed
Wis.	None	Pledged	Required	April 7	Open
D.C.	None	Unpledged	Unnecessary	May 5	Closed

a discussion of third parties in American politics). The effort to counter the power of the Northern Negro Democratic vote by withdrawing Southern support from the national party may have the same result it did in 1948. Then the opposition of the Southern segregationists caused anti-segregationist voters to rally strongly to the national Democratic ticket.

Beyond all this, there is the fact of the New South that has been emerging in the last two decades. A region once hampered by reliance on tobacco and cotton has been rapidly diversifying, successfully competing with other areas for new industry. Meanwhile, many moderate Southerners are working quietly and effectively to change as painlessly as possible a pattern of race relations that is only less subtle than the pattern in the North.

As for the rest of the country, it has also been undergoing dramatic change. Millions of urban workers have moved to the suburbs since World War II. Cities are losing in total population while home-owning suburbanites increase by millions. New economic and social circumstances bring a change in political outlook. The old liberal Federal spending policies that seemed so attractive to their parents tend to lose their appeal when the new suburbanites find they are now paying more of the bill. In this situation the Republicans generally gain.

Meanwhile, the cities find themselves decaying, partly because feudal political machines have driven out the middle class by piling tax upon tax to accommodate the lower-income groups by whose votes the city machines are sustained.

All this adds up to a tremendous and tremendously complicated social and economic issue for both political parties. How can the Negro's cause be served without alienating the white newcomers who are jealous of their jobs, their schools and their neighborhoods? Many of them left the city just to be free of the racial tensions of the urban environment.

This is part of the civil rights dilemma. Never before has the question of Negro aspirations affected so many whites directly. Neither party will nominate for President a man hostile to the Negro's cause. But not all men who believe in that cause agree on methods and timing.

America's oldest, most vexing social problem will again be an issue in 1964.

President Johnson's Heart

Another campaign issue, less discussed but ever present, will be the President's health.

Nine years ago the six-foot-three LBJ weighed 220 pounds and had a 42-inch waist. His breakfast consisted of coffee and cigarets. He ate a sandwich on the run sometime in the afternoon, and ate a large meal late at night that typically consisted of fried steak and potatoes. By day's end he had consumed three packs of cigarets.

Johnson often worked 16 hours a day (he sometimes keeps longer hours now), almost all of them on Capitol Hill in endless conferences and taxing private talks. Restless, tense and given to sudden and often inexplicable explosions of temper, he was a locomotive with its throttle locked at full speed ahead.

On July 2, 1955, at the age of 46, Lyndon Johnson suffered a heart attack that nearly killed him. Doctors called it a "coronary thrombosis with myocardial infarction." A myocardial infarction is a loss of function of a part of the myocardium, or heart muscle, due to the absence of blood flow to it. The obstruction was a thrombus, a blood clot, in the coronary artery, the major artery serving the heart. A myocardial infarction is one of the most common forms of "heart attack."

Johnson's physicians described his attack as "moderately severe." Johnson himself later called it "as bad as a man can have and live."

After a period of recuperation, Johnson resumed his duties in Congress—without resuming his old habits. Instead he followed doctors' orders to be more conscious of his health. He slept at least eight hours each night, worked no more than nine hours a day.

During the 1960 campaign, in which Vice Presidential candidate Johnson's health was a minor issue, one of his aides declared: "His heart size, respiration, pulse are all normal. Recovery from his heart attack is so complete that doctors cannot now detect that he even suffered one."

After President Kennedy's assassination, Dr. George W. Calver, official physician to members of Congress stated: "You can give Lyndon Johnson a clean bill of health . . . his heart is in excellent condition."

Dr. Calver doubted that the strain of the assassination and the assumption of the burdens of office had an adverse effect on the new President's health.

Johnson's own verdict: "My heart attack saved my life. The heart attack slowed my pace, taught me to live more sensibly."

These, then, are the issues—the visible ones that can be mentioned and described with election day still in the distance. These are the issues the Presidential contenders must use for their own purposes as best they can. But there are also the invisible issues—those yet to be revealed by events—that hover above every candidate and intrude upon his dreams.

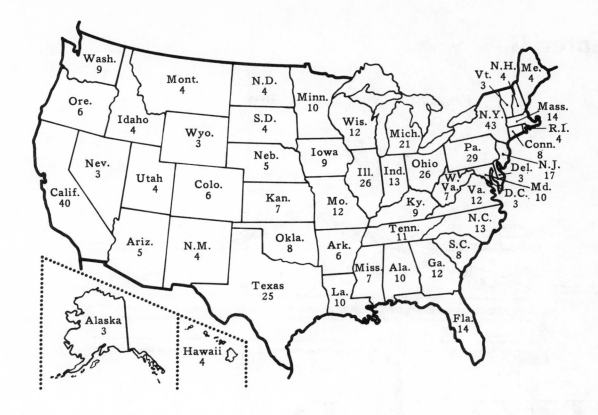

Election Night Tally Sheet

Write in electoral votes below when state results are reported. First candidate to get 270 electoral votes wins.

★ ★ ★ ★ ★ ★ ★ ★ ★ ★ ★ ★ ★ ★ ★ ★ ★ ★ ★ ★

STATE	DEM.	REP.	OTHER	STATE	DEM.	REP.	OTHER
Alabama				Montana			
Alaska				Nebraska			
Arizona				Nevada			
Arkansas				New Hampshire			
California				New Jersey			
Colorado				New Mexico			
Connecticut				New York			
D.C.				North Carolina			
Delaware				North Dakota			
Florida				Ohio			
Georgia				Oklahoma			
Hawaii				Oregon			
Idaho				Pennsylvania			
Illinois				Rhode Island			
Indiana				South Carolina			
Iowa				South Dakota			
Kansas				Tennessee			
Kentucky				Texas			
Louisiana				Utah			
Maryland				Vermont			
Massachusetts				Virginia			
Maine				Washington			
Michigan				West Virginia			
Minnesota				Wisconsin			
Mississippi				Wyoming			
Missouri							

Chapter II

When Presidents Die

It is one of the least acceptable facts of an unjust world that the life and work of a President of the United States can be cut short by the whim of a crank. And it is the sudden reminder of this fact that intensifies the nation's sorrow and momentary bewilderment when an American President is assassinated.

A cheap gun in the hands of a frustrated human cipher was sufficient to end John F. Kennedy's extraordinary career on November 22, 1963. This act of seconds, of incredible madness, finished the life of a man who had served in the Pacific war with gallantry, who had been a U.S. Representative and Senator, who had

written a Pulitzer-Prize-winning book, and who had worked long and hard to gain the Presidency.

Kennedy was 46 when he died, a young man whose greatest fascination as a historical figure was this very youthfulness which seemed to guarantee a long and distinguished career of national service. With such an early start, his record of accomplishment promised to be great. But in Dallas, Texas, that sunny day in November, there was a man who capped a remarkably futile life by putting the President's career to an end.

One hour and 39 minutes after Kennedy

died, Vice President Johnson was sworn in as 36th President. The order of succession is established and the vacancy was filled in an orderly way. The Office, unlike its occupant, is invulnerable to death. Whether the incumbent dies by the design of a crank, by accident, or from natural causes, the country carries on. History carries on, too, although a President's death jogs it onto another track. And politicians at home and abroad study the consequences of the event for them.

Since the nation began, eight Presidents have died in office. Four of these were shot to death by assassins. Each Presidential death has re-emphasized, rather than reduced, the continuity of American institutions. Each has occurred when a superior kind of man held the Vice Presidency, although in succeeding to the top job the newcomer often found the deck was stacked against him. Ironically, too, in the case of assassinations, the assassin's cause has never been served by his act.

Threats Were Routine

As they are with all Presidents, threats were routine in the life of President Kennedy. Threatening letters were numerous, and the authors of several were committed to mental hospitals. But it has long been clear that despite such precautions, the safety of the President cannot be completely guaranteed. The President, after all, cannot hide.

The political implications for the two major parties, and for their most ambitious leaders, stemming from President Kennedy's murder are discussed in detail in the foregoing chapter. But it is interesting, and perhaps instructive, to compare the current situation with the problems faced by politicians of other times who have seen the death of a President change the route of history and the destiny of White House hopefuls.

To begin with, the eight Vice Presidents who have succeeded to the Presidency were each selected more for the political "balance" he would bring to his party's ticket than for his own abilities. The Vice Presidency has traditionally been regarded with condescension by many politicians. Some, like John Nance Garner who served two terms in that office under Franklin Roosevelt, have regarded it with contempt ("The Vice Presidency isn't worth a pitcher of warm spit," said Garner to Lyndon B.

An incredible end to a remarkable life.

Johnson in 1960, shortly after John F. Kennedy had agreed to offer Johnson the number two spot on the ticket).

But even with this kind of reputation, the Vice Presidency has managed to attract some distinguished citizens. And luckily for the country, the men who have held the post when a President died have all been men of talent and character. Some, like Chester A. Arthur, have displayed in office an unexpected strength.

A Balm for Outrage

They have had need of strength, and not only because of the crushing nature of the job itself. The President must also be a political leader, and those who fail at this task seldom can be rated successes as leaders of Government. And in this political area, a Vice President who succeeds to the Presidency has a special problem.

When a Vice Presidential candidate is selected, he is usually picked to soften the outrage of a party faction that couldn't get the delegate support to put its own nominee in the top position. Thus, the President and the Vice President usually represent somewhat different points of view within the party and hail from different regions. So the new President must try to regroup his party around a new and different center. The first four men who tried this task—those who took over the Presidency in the Nineteenth Century—must be rated political failures.

The first of these was John Tyler, the running mate of William Henry Harrison in 1840. Tyler was a Whig and a man who often put his principles above his party, occasionally straying to support the ideas of the opposition Democrats. He was nominated for Vice President not because his ideas were shared by the Whig leadership; a main factor was the hope that Tyler, a Virginian, would help the Whigs carry the South.

The Whig Party was a Congressional party —its leadership was concentrated there and its ideas of government reflected this concentration. The Whigs believed that Congress would be better able than the Executive to set a middle course for the country and affect the compromises necessary to keep the Union strong. Therefore, the Whigs sought to elect a man who was likely to be a "weak" President, and Harrison was considered such a man.

John Tyler was not. He believed in a strong Executive and took no stock in his party's notion of Congressional superiority.

So when Harrison died one month after his inauguration and Tyler succeeded him, the new President had no real political base. Moreover, he was unwilling to compromise any of his principles to build such a base. He soon made it clear that he opposed the spoils system; he retained in office several of the abler men from the preceding Democratic administration.

Through much of Tyler's administration the Whigs were torn by dissension. The party did not have a large enough majority in Congress to pass measures over Tyler's veto, so legislation ground almost to a halt.

By the time of the 1844 convention, patronage had fallen into the hands of the Congressional Whigs; thus Tyler had little influence over the delegates. The Whigs snubbed the President to nominate Henry Clay as their standard bearer. Tyler was nominated by an irregular convention of Democrats but soon withdrew from the race.

Persuasion and Compromise

The second Vice President to move into the Presidency was Millard Fillmore, another Whig who took over after the death of Zachary Taylor in 1850. Fillmore's prime aim long had been to preserve the Union, an aim he sought to advance with his considerable skills of persuasion and compromise. Shortly after he was elected Vice President, he wrote a friend:

"I regard this election as putting an end to all ideas of disunion. It raises up a national party, occupying a middle ground, and leaves the fanatics and disunionists, North and South, without the hope of destroying the fair fabric of our Constitution."

But Fillmore had underestimated the passions that were building. Slavery—where it should be permitted and where not—was an issue wearing through the bonding tape that held the parties and the states together.

In 1852 the Whig politicians passed over Fillmore in favor of General Winfield Scott. The Whigs were strong on nominating popular heroes because they felt such a personality could better lead the party to victory in the Congressional elections. As it turned out, Scott was defeated and the Whigs were about to perish as a party.

War between the states came, and it would take a man of moderation and political shrewdness to bind the nation's wounds. Abraham Lincoln, who seemed designed by fate for just that job, was assassinated even as he began the work of restoring the Union. And that work seemed headed for success as Southern states started electing new legislatures and revising their old constitutions.

Throughout the nation in those days was a general longing for an end to the bitterness that had been stirred up by years of bloodshed

The pistol ball that crashed through Lincoln's head ended the best chance that moderate policies toward the South would prevail. The assassination produced not only grief but an almost hysterical rage in the North. This was a rage that Andrew Johnson himself at first shared, but he was soon to recover. Few others came to their senses so quickly.

Johnson moved almost at once to continue reorganization of governments of the Southern states, as well as to provide for those states to send representatives to the U.S. Congress. Con-

John Tyler

Millard Fillmore

and war propaganda. There was a yearning for a return to peaceful conditions under which men could pursue their private lives and livelihoods.

But against this hope for an early restoration of a fraternal spirit, for lenient policies toward the South, ran a counter force. Many Americans, still deeply disturbed by the South's act of secession, wanted to make sure the Union would not break apart again. And, too, there were those who, not having seen what the ravages of war had already done to Dixie, rubbed their palms in anticipation of punishing the South still further.

gress, though, led by Radical Republicans, rapidly upset much of the President's program and instituted far more severe Reconstruction measures of its own. The break was so complete that Johnson, in a public address, attacked Republican leaders as working to destroy the principles of Government. The party leaders later were to try, unsuccessfully, to remove President Johnson from office.

Bitterness begets bitterness and the South responded in kind. After regaining political control of their own region in 1877, the Southerners moved further from the moderation of Lincoln.

Segregation was established as a way of life in the South, a way of life the nation was to learn many years later is not easily changed. No one can know if the long story would have been different had Lincoln lived, but with his death the fanatics were rid of their greatest foe.

Only 16 years after Lincoln's murder another President of the United States, James A. Garfield, was assassinated, elevating Chester A. Arthur to the White House.

Garfield was not a spectacular President. He was a Republican compromise candidate to succeed Rutherford B. Hayes. On July 2, 1881, as President Garfield waited for a train in

get Arthur's past record. Thus the Republicans in 1884 nominated not Arthur but a lesser man, James G. Blaine.

Seventeen years later, as the dull summer of 1901 wore on, there was little news. The United States was a comfortable nation, having just won a war with Spain, and the country settled into confident prosperity. In May the Pan-American Exposition opened at Buffalo and President William McKinley telegraphed his congratulations: "May there be no cloud on this grand festival of peace and commerce."

Then the President and most of his cabinet toured the Pacific Coast. In September he went

Andrew Johnson

Chester Arthur

Washington, he was shot by an unsuccessful office seeker. In the furor over the assassination and the assassin's motives, President Arthur supported Congressional efforts to revamp the Federal civil service. The result was the Pendleton Act of 1883, which made merit rather than political partisanship the chief qualification for Federal officeholding.

But Arthur's newly articulated principles, like the principles of Tyler, Fillmore and Andrew Johnson, contributed to his political downfall. His support of civil service reform naturally did not endear him to party regulars, and the liberal reform element in the party was unable to for-

to the Exposition at Buffalo, and on September 5 he delivered a speech.

As the President stood as guest of honor at a reception in the Temple of Music on the Exposition grounds the next day, two shots were fired and he slumped over. A young anarchist, Leon Czolgosz, had fired at close range with his revolver. One bullet penetrated the President's abdomen but physicians assured the press the patient would recover.

Early in the morning of September 13, Vice President Theodore Roosevelt was informed that there was no hope for the President's survival. At 2:15 a.m., Saturday, September 14, as

Mr. Roosevelt's carriage met a train that would carry him to Buffalo, the Vice President learned that McKinley had died shortly after midnight.

The tragedy of President McKinley's assassination went far beyond his death. The speech he had delivered in Buffalo, forgotten in the excitement of the shooting, was a great "might-have-been" of history.

McKinley had announced a change in his views on the tariff, and his speech was a call for liberalizing American trade policies through the use of reciprocal trade agreements. In the spirit of international trade cooperation and optimism that characterized the Buffalo Exposition, McKinley had made his most significant public utterance—but it was overlooked as the nation worried about its President's survival.

The United States stuck to its high tariff walls, and even raised them higher. Economic liberals criticized the barriers, ironically attributing them to the "protectionist" philosophy of the "businessman's President," William McKinley. It would be almost 35 years before reciprocal trade agreements came into being.

An Anarchist's Motive

Leon Czolgosz, the assassin, bore McKinley no personal malice. He was an anarchist, believing that a social paradise could be created only after all existing forms of government were destroyed. So Czolgosz tried to move the country toward anarchy by killing its President.

Under the leadership of Theodore Roosevelt the nation entered a period of change, but it was not the kind of change that would have been understood by a Czolgosz. Orderly and moderate reforms were introduced; accommodation and gradual adjustment, not anarchism, were to be the mode of social reform in America.

If, at the moment he was sworn in as President, Teddy Roosevelt cast about for inspiration and solace, he probably did not ponder long on those Nineteenth Century predecessors who also came to the White House through the death of an incumbent. Tyler, Fillmore, Johnson and Arthur had all had a nasty time of it. And whatever Roosevelt thought, few Americans believed he would fare much better than those four.

It was rumored that financier J. P. Morgan had collapsed when he heard of McKinley's death, and that GOP king-maker Mark Hanna became almost hysterical when he realized "that damn cowboy" was the new President.

Like all Vice Presidents who suddenly find they have to go to work, Roosevelt assured the country the policies of his predecessor would be maintained. This is standard procedure and, in the context of funereal gloom, it is appropriate. But when, as one observer put it, the Vice President "suddenly finds he's holding all the marbles," he rather quickly loses his reluctance and sets about putting his own stamp on the Presidency. Certainly Teddy Roosevelt did that and was easily returned to office on his own in 1904. In 1912, when he tried to make a comeback after a break with William Howard Taft, Roosevelt himself was shot—although not seriously—during the election campaign.

The next on the list of eight Vice Presidents is Calvin Coolidge, who was a distinct improvement over the man he succeeded, Warren G. Harding, who died in 1923. Through the Teapot Dome and other scandals of the early 1920s, Coolidge's New England simplicity and utter integrity provided something the people could trust. It was a time of prosperity and Coolidge was readily elected for a full term in 1924.

Death in Miami

During the Twenties, when gangsters were shooting at police and each other with unprecedented enthusiasm, no one took a shot at the President of the United States. But in 1933, as President-elect Franklin D. Roosevelt, Chicago Mayor Anton J. Cermak, and Secret Service agents rode in an open car in a Miami parade, an anarchist named Joseph Zangara fired at the President. His bullets missed Roosevelt but killed Mayor Cermak.

Until November 22, 1963, the most recent Vice President to succeed to the Presidency was Harry S. Truman, who took over for FDR in 1945—in the midst of world war. The public knew little of Truman and many expected little.

Yet he carried the war through to its conclusion and was later to prove himself a politician of surpassing skill.

The political tides seemed to be running against him. The Republicans won control of Congress in 1946, and many Democrats would have preferred a more liberal candidate in 1948. Yet to the surprise of almost all politicians except Harry Truman, he won election in that year.

His terms of office witnessed the Marshall Plan, the Truman Doctrine, the Berlin air lift, the decisive move into Korea. A President who seemed lacking in promise accomplished much. And Truman, too, once found himself the object of assassination.

In 1950, while Truman was staying at Blair Mansion across Pennsylvania Avenue from the White House, Puerto Rican nationalists tried to shoot their way into the building. Guards killed one gunman and the other is now serving a life term in prison.

The motive of the assassins was to kill the man they thought responsible for withholding freedom from their home island. The independence they sought has not been gained, but by remaining a part of the United States, Puerto Rico has benefitted from large injections of money from the mainland; it is now one of the most prosperous areas of Latin America.

After John F. Kennedy was killed, his body lay in state in the rotunda of the Capitol. Perhaps a few of the many thousands who passed by the catafalque remembered that that rotunda was the scene, in 1835, of an attempt on the life of Andrew Jackson. The would-be assassin's pistols misfired and Jackson was spared. The culprit was committed to an institution for the insane for life.

The unpretty truth is that the President's life is always in jeopardy. And so, therefore, are the best laid plans of men and parties.

Lyndon B. Johnson: The eighth man to become
President through the death of a predecessor.

In August, 1944, FDR and Vice Presidential
candidate Truman lunched on the White
House lawn and discussed campaign strategy.
In eight months, Truman would be President.

Calvin Coolidge was sworn in as President by
his father, John Coolidge, a justice of the
peace, in a rustic Vermont farm house. Coolidge spoke the oath quietly, but he spoke it.

Chapter III

Intra-Party Warfare

Primaries and Promises, Delegates and Deals

The Presidency of the United States is a job like no other, and a man must apply for it as he would for no other.

The Presidency can be won only through a collective effort, by many people working together. Thus, the first concern of the candidate is to build a team. If his early efforts at rallying supporters are successful, he may go on to make his whole party his team—at the national convention—and then he and his party battle the rival candidate and party for the biggest prize in the land.

The first major task for an aspirant, then (along with raising money—no great problem for 1964 hopefuls), is to expand his team until it includes practically all the members of his party, and he must do this at a time when other candidates are also trying to expand their teams within the same party. The resulting warfare among the teams points up the peculiar structure of the American party system —a system that foreigners have long looked upon in wonder.

Many nations determine their leadership by pitting party against party, but in no other country does each major party contain so wide a diversity of opinion. Convinced conservatives and burning liberals battle each other in both camps, and it is a marvel of the American system that both the Democratic and Republican Parties have developed the elasticity to contain their most extreme elements most of the time.

Imperfect Institutions

When Americans vote every fourth November they are given a real choice between but two candidates. But in the battles for the nominations they are free to choose among several, enjoying all the while the pleasure of witnessing the world's noisiest family fights.

And these family fights are often stormiest during the Presidential primaries, state-wide contests that are supposed to show which candidate for his party's nomination has the most pull with the voters. But primaries are imperfect institutions, as we shall see later, and there is at least one fellow who hates them with a passion. He is the professional politician, the local party leader who much prefers to settle things by getting various heads together, and occasionally knocking them together, instead of flapping the dirty linen in public.

Presidential primaries — there are 16, including the District of Columbia's, scheduled for

1964 — are elections in which the public indicates who it would like to see be the standard bearer for each party. In all states but one, the primaries are "closed," meaning that only registered Republicans can cast ballots for one of the Republican aspirants, and only registered Democrats can vote in the Democratic contest. In Wisconsin, however, a Democrat can, if he chooses, vote in the Republican race—and vice versa, thus adding to Wisconsin's reputation as one of the most difficult states to analyze politically.

Cosy Little Meetings

Although primaries at the state and municipal level originated prior to the Civil War, Presidential primaries are a relatively recent development; the first one was held in Florida in 1904. They are theoretically designed to give the people a larger voice in the selection of a party nominee than is possible under either the caucus or state convention system.

In the early days of the country, party leaders got together in cosy little meetings, or "caucuses," and decided among themselves who their party's candidate would be. More democratic is the state convention method, now used by 35 states. In general, the convention system works like this: Each precinct (the lowest political unit) holds a caucus and picks delegates to the county convention, which in turn chooses delegates to the state convention. The state convention then selects the "at large" delegates to the national convention. Some delegates, because of each party's rules of apportionment, will represent Congressional districts and county delegates within each such district decide who these will be.

The convention system is preferred by professional politicians because it permits them much firmer control of nominations than does a primary. In a primary the ballots are secret and all registered voters are entitled to participate. The old weapons of the political boss—reward and retribution—cannot be used as they can in a convention where delegates must stand up and be counted.

Aside from the ammunition they afford the rival party and their freedom from organization control, Presidential primaries vex politicians because they can be enormously expensive—using up funds that could have been employed against the opposition party.

Moreover, primaries are expensive to the

states that hold them. (The most famous example of this is the 1916 Iowa primary, in which each party had only one candidate on the ballot. The meaningless election cost the state $200,000, and the following year Iowa repealed its primary law.)

From the voter's standpoint, too, the primary system is less than perfect. Frequently, the voter is denied a real choice between major candidates. A Presidential hopeful may decide for any of a number of reasons not to enter a given primary. The consequences of a primary defeat can be grave, so the aspirant will not be anxious to run in a doubtful state. Or, the candidate may be so widely regarded as a shoo-in in a particular state that a victory there would not advance his cause.

Oregon's Trail Blazing

The State of Oregon, much to the extreme displeasure of many campaign managers, has tried to improve this situation. In 1959, it passed a law directing the Oregon secretary of state to put on the primary ballot the name of a candidate if his "candidacy is generally advocated or recognized in national news media throughout the United States." A candidate can have his name deleted from the ballot only by "stating without qualification that he is not now and does not intend to become a candidate."

Should Oregon's idea catch on in other states, more people will get a chance to judge more candidates—and more candidates will get grayer sooner.

Some Presidential aspirants have good reason for not wanting their names entered in any primaries at all. These are the candidates—like Lyndon B. Johnson, Stuart Symington and Adlai E. Stevenson in 1960—whose only chance for their party's nomination lay in a convention deadlock. It was their basic strategy to sit tight until the delegates split over two initially favored candidates, and then step forward as the compromise choice.

In 1960, of course, John F. Kennedy was nominated on the first ballot and the three sit-tighters were left sitting. Another major Democratic possibility, Hubert H. Humphrey, had been eliminated in the West Virginia primary—the same primary that permitted Kennedy to come into the convention with the momentum of a freight train.

And here we have the most important feature of Presidential primaries. While only about

In the 1948 Oregon primary, Thomas E. Dewey let his hair down.

THE VERB, "TO RUN"

One of the curiosities of the language of American politics is the word "run." While we have taken over some words from British politics, such as polls, hustings and ballot, we have thrown over others. Politicians still "stand" for election in Britain, as they did in the Eighteenth Century. In America they "run." The dictionary tells us that both words mean the same thing—"to be a candidate." Americans, perhaps, are just more urgent about it.

There's no known cure for Harold Stassen's White House bug.

ELECTION OF 1952

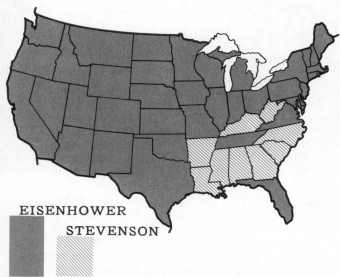

EISENHOWER
STEVENSON

55.14   44.38 % OF POPULAR VOTE

40% of each party's delegates to the national conventions are chosen in the primaries, the influence of these preliminary contests on political thinking in every state is enormous. Thus it was that Wendell Willkie, trying for a second Republican nomination in 1944, failed to win a single delegate in the Wisconsin primary and was forced to bow out of the race.

In 1948, Harold E. Stassen looked for a time as if he would crush Thomas E. Dewey's bid for a second GOP nomination. Stassen won in Wisconsin and Nebraska and the Gallup Poll showed him to be running ahead of Dewey throughout the nation. The two met in a life-or-death struggle in Oregon and, although Stassen had had a head start, the usually reserved Dewey campaigned mightily, not passing up the corniest baby-kissing trick.

Stassen got worried as Dewey continued to make inroads. It was becoming clear that the Oregon primary could very well be decisive. Then Stassen made a mistake that was to be the beginning of the end for him. He challenged Dewey to a radio debate.

Forensics Fortissimo

Tom Dewey was a tough trial lawyer who had made his reputation as a rackets-busting special prosecutor in New York City. But for years he had considered becoming an opera singer, and in the Oregon debate against Stassen he combined a brilliant lawyer's way with argument with a formidable voice to completely out-class his opponent. With more than 200,000 votes cast, Dewey beat Stassen in Oregon by 9,000 votes.

With this comeback after his earlier primary defeats, the New York Governor gained the leverage he needed to cop the party nomination on the third ballot. Although he had behaved prior to the Wisconsin and Nebraska primaries as if the nomination were his for the taking, those preliminary elections forced Dewey to fight. The Oregon campaign, by the way, cost Dewey and Stassen about $100,000 each.

Adlai Stevenson exhibited a similar burst of energy in 1956 after Estes Kefauver had won the primaries in New Hampshire and Minnesota. Stevenson, despite his 1952 loss to Dwight Eisenhower, fully expected to be his party's candidate a second time; and he expected to carry Minnesota in the primary because he had campaigned there and had the backing of popular Minnesota Senator Hubert Humphrey.

So, startled by his Minnesota defeat, Stevenson worked hard to win the Florida, California and Oregon primaries—and win he did. Kefauver, finally withdrew from the race in favor of Stevenson, thus ending not only Kefauver's chances but the chances of those candidates, such as New York Governor W. Averell Harriman, who hoped for a deadlock.

Though Presidential primaries have been the route to a second nomination for Dewey and Stevenson, and were responsible for the 1960 success of John F. Kennedy, primary victories have turned out to be hollow ones for not a few aspirants.

When Primaries Are Secondary

Ex-President Theodore Roosevelt, seeking to replace incumbent President William H. Taft as the Republican nominee, lost out at the convention after winning a string of primaries. Senator Albert Cummins in 1916 and Senator Hiram Johnson in 1920 finished first in the primaries but were passed over at the national conventions.

Many times candidates who shied away from all primaries were victorious in the end. Thus Wendell Willkie, a political unknown and a Democrat two years earlier, captured the GOP nomination in 1940, thanks to an extraordinary campaign by a group of so-called amateurs who set up Willkie Clubs around the country and capitalized on their man's unusual assets. Not only was Willkie a successful businessman who supported much of the New Deal, he also was a Midwest-born internationalist who lived in New York City. Thus he seemed to have a diverse enough background and outlook to be appealing to a variety of Republicans. Beyond that, he had a flamboyant personality and charm to spare. And his chief opponents in 1940—Robert A. Taft and Thomas E. Dewey—were still too inexperienced to block his nomination.

In 1944, Dewey, now Governor of New York, similarly steered clear of primary fights and, against little competition, walked off with the nomination. Willkie had been undone by the Wisconsin primary, General MacArthur's candidacy never got off the ground, Stassen was in the Navy, and Taft had yet to attain leadership stature. Senator John Bricker of Ohio was held in high esteem by party regulars but Dewey seemed to be the better vote-getter. So Dewey it was on the first ballot.

On May 13, 1956, Senator Estes Kefauver bumped into a cowboy in Los Banos, California. Both were seeking the state's 68 Democratic convention votes in the June 5 Presidential primary. Stevenson roped in the primary—and his second nomination.

The hottest intra-party battles generally occur when the issue is not only between two men, but between two distinct points of view as well. The Republican Party, for instance, has been portrayed since the Willkie era as having two great wings—one tending to be Midwest-based and conservative and the other Eastern and more liberal. Like most attempts to categorize in politics, this division of the GOP is an oversimplification, but it is a useful one.

Rise of "Mr. Republican"

Through the 1940s the Republican Party polarized about two men—Taft of Ohio and Dewey of New York. The forces these two represented collided with a bang in 1952.

In 1940, 1944 and 1948, Bob Taft and his fellow conservatives in the GOP had watched the national conventions repeatedly pick as standard bearers liberal-leaning Easterners. These "me-too" candidates, as they were contemptuously called by the Taftites, did not dislodge the long-reigning Democrats, and the conservatives of the party were convinced that the people strung along with Franklin Roosevelt and Harry Truman because they were denied a real choice. In 1952, the Taft wing was ready to make its strongest try for the nomination.

Taft's stature had grown enormously in the late 1940s and by 1950 he was conceded by both parties to be the most distinguished member of the Senate. Dubbed "Mr. Republican," he stood head and shoulders above any other GOP politician, and for a time it looked as if he would have a clear field in 1952.

But the Ohio Senator's hope for an easy victory was suddenly dashed in October of 1951, when New York Governor Dewey, while declining to go after a third nomination himself, proposed Dwight D. Eisenhower as the man to head the ticket. At the time of Dewey's statement, Eisenhower was president of Columbia University, but before long he would be back in uniform and back to Europe as commander of the NATO forces.

For the anti-Taft camp the choice boiled down to Ike. They believed that for a Republican to win the Presidency he would have to attract the kind of people for whom the Ohio Senator was thought to have little appeal—the middle-of-the-road independents and Democrats who were unhappy with Truman's handling of the stalemated Korean War and the revelations of Communists and corruption in Government. The man they felt most likely to win such voters to the GOP column was the extraordinarily popular General.

Thus, Senators James H. Duff of Pennsylvania, Frank Carlson of Kansas, and Henry Cabot Lodge of Massachusetts—and Dewey—started a "Draft Eisenhower" campaign to press the reluctant Ike into making a decision. Finally, in January, 1952, General Eisenhower permitted his name to be entered in the primary that most often carries the greatest psychological thrust. Because it is the first primary scheduled in the Presidential election year, the eyes of the nation are fixed on the early-March balloting in New Hampshire.

Helped by political legmen under the direction of New Hampshire Governor Sherman Adams, General Eisenhower—even though he remained at his post in Europe—won the primary over Taft and the still-hopeful Harold Stassen. It was a serious, though by no means fatal, blow to the Taft cause.

LAME DUCK

Eighteenth Century Englishmen used "lame duck" to refer to a man gone broke, a bankrupt. It spread to America, and in the 1830s the word first turned up in the nation's political vocabulary. Referring to a politician who could not deliver his state, William Henry Harrison called him a lame duck.

During the Civil War the expression came into use as a description of a politician who had been voted out of office but who had not yet formally relinquished his position—sort of a political bankrupt.

In the 1920s this epithet was applied to the President, Vice President and the entire Congress during the campaign to amend the term-of-office clause of the Constitution. The Constitution provided that the incumbents remain in office until the first week in March—four months after election day. The Founders had provided for this time lapse in an era when travel was measured in terms of weeks rather than hours.

The 20th Amendment advanced the inauguration and the meeting of the new Congress from March to January.

Direct clashes between Taft and Eisenhower were avoided in most of the other primary states, and the results were indecisive. But in Minnesota something happened that rocked the Taftites.

Just Plain "Ike"

The Eisenhower strategists decided against entering the Minnesota primary in deference to Governor Stassen, the favorite son. But three days before the voting on March 18, the state ruled that write-in votes would be counted.

Scribbling in such variations as "Isenhowr" and sometimes just plain "Ike," the people of Minnesota gave the General 106,000 write-in votes—only 20,000 less than the total received by Stassen whose name was on the ballot and who was a Minnesota boy. Taft's write-in vote was 24,000.

But Taft captured the Wisconsin primary over Stassen and Governor Earl Warren of California, and he defeated Eisenhower in a write-in vote in Nebraska; it began to look as if the General could be beaten. The partisan passions that were being aroused in the two wings of the Republican Party exploded in Texas, where a furious battle for delegates by supporters of the two major candidates made chaos of the state convention and resulted in two separate contingents of delegates going to the national convention in Chicago.

An example of how politicians occasionally use primaries to stop one candidate rather than directly promote another is the ironic experience of Oregon Senator Wayne Morse in his state's 1952 primary. In order to cut down the strength of General Eisenhower, some backers of Senator Taft, without his consent, filed Senator Morse's name in the primary, also without Morse's consent. The result was that Senator Morse had to campaign throughout the state pleading with voters not to vote for him. This campaign against himself is said to have cost Morse $10,000.

Eisenhower resigned from the Army and returned home in early June. Unlike Douglas MacArthur who had long been identified with the ideology of Taft conservatives, Ike had remained silent about his political convictions (Senator Paul Douglas of Illinois even suggested Eisenhower be named the candidate of both parties, with each party then running a different Vice Presidential candidate). This clean

Ohio Senator Robert A. Taft (above) gets to know the voters of Wisconsin in March of 1952. Shortly thereafter, Taft (below) was politicking at Town Hall Square in Clinton, Massachusetts. Meanwhile, General Eisenhower remained at his post in Europe. Paul Hoffman (on the left), co-chairman of the Citizens for Eisenhower movement, and John J. McCloy, U.S. High Commissioner for Germany, discuss international and domestic politics at Eisenhower's headquarters near Paris. A few months later, in June of 1952, Ike would return to the U.S. to snatch the Republican Presidential nomination away from Taft.

slate meant that nobody could point critically to his stand on anything because Ike had never declared himself publicly on political matters.

Because the Taft forces controlled the Republican National Committee, they were able to pick the keynote speaker (MacArthur) and decide which rival delegations would be recognized. This was important because the contesting delegations represented the balance of power. Moreover, every convention committee was loaded with Taft men (Herbert Brownell, a former national chairman and a Dewey Republican, wasn't even permitted to sit on the platform). For a time it looked as if the Taft people had the convention, and the nomination, wrapped up and tied with a bow.

The Governors Intervene

Then 23 of the nation's 25 Republican governors tore into that neat package with a pick-ax. The governors issued a statement urging that no delegate whose credentials were in doubt be allowed to vote on the legitimacy of the credentials of any disputed delegate. This the Taftites could not agree to, because they needed the votes of 68 disputed delegates who would be barred by such a rule change.

There could be no question that what on the surface was a procedural wrangle was really a crucial confrontation of the Eisenhower and Taft forces. The side that won would almost certainly win everything. The adoption of the governors' so-called fair-play amendment by a margin of 110 votes staggered the Taftites and, as it developed, assured the nomination of the General.

How was it that the Eisenhower camp was able to get the governors' amendment passed? It was a simple matter of patronage. The Republican governors, who tended to be more liberal than the Taftites, controlled patronage in their states and were thus able to keep their delegations in line. Rare was the delegate from a Republican-controlled state who was anxious to lose favor at the statehouse. Senator Taft himself attributed his defeat in part to the governors' control of state jobs. But the power politics employed by the Eisenhower people did not stop there.

Governor John S. Fine of Pennsylvania found it to his advantage not to commit his delegation for either candidate. To entice Fine

Sam Rayburn stands by as an old friend announces his candidacy for the Democratic nomination in 1960. Lyndon B. Johnson lost the Presidential nomination that year, but he took the second spot.

into the Eisenhower camp, Ike's supporters reportedly made him an unusual offer. If the General became President, Governor Fine would be given the privilege of dispensing all Federal patronage due the State of Pennsylvania. This was a privilege traditionally given to Republican Senators—not the governor—and it was not the kind of offer Fine was inclined to turn down. The Governor delivered the delegates to Ike and their votes wrecked Taft's hopes.

Given the formidable leverage of promised control of Federal patronage in his state, it was a simple enough matter for Governor Fine to make his delegates do what he wanted them to do. But even this exercise in power politics tended to pale next to Governor Dewey's handling of the New York contingent.

At the start of the convention, Dewey reminded his delegates that he would still be in Albany for more than two years and that he was blessed with "a long memory." He further reminded the delegation of the jobs that had been allocated to each delegate's district; he

added without subtlety that there could be new appointees two days after his return to Albany. This meant that the delegate who was prepared to disobey Dewey had to be prepared also to see his brother or some friend lose his state job. There is no resisting this kind of pressure.

Ike won on the first ballot.

While the primaries were not decisive for the Republicans in 1952, they *were* decisive for the Democrats in 1960. For John F. Kennedy knew that if he didn't prove his vote-getting power before the convention, his candidacy would be scuttled in the back rooms at Los Angeles. Circumstances dictate strategy in American politics and Kennedy realized that for him the primary route was the only way.

The youthful Senator from Massachusetts wound his way around and over a variety of hazards with rare agility. In the beginning there weren't many people who thought he could do it.

A wealthy, handsome, personable war hero, John Kennedy had achieved little of note as a member of the House and Senate.

Kennedy, too, was a Catholic and nobody was quite sure how the largely Protestant American electorate would feel about having a Catholic in the White House.

Nor did organized labor immediately cotton to the Senator who had been a member of the McClellan Committee which had put the public spotlight on evil-doing union leaders. And the candidate's brother and campaign manager, Robert Kennedy, had been the Committee's aggressive special counsel.

Still another handicap was John Kennedy's youth. When he announced his intention of seeking the Democratic nomination in January of 1960, he was 42 years old. He would be 43 on May 29. No man so young had ever been elected President (Teddy Roosevelt took office at the age of 42, after McKinley's assassination). What's more, Kennedy looked years younger than he was.

Yet with all these supposed barriers to his ambition, John F. Kennedy copped the Democratic nomination on the first ballot. How did he do it?

Ways of a Winner

He did it by building a vast political organization, by assembling a huge file on practically every party leader in the nation down to the municipal level, by making hundreds of speeches across the country, by winning — thanks partly to his pretty, fashion-wise wife— enormous publicity in national newspapers and magazines, by turning some "liabilities" to his own advantage, by scoring a convincing victory in the West Virginia primary, by utilizing an attractive, open-faced manner on television, and by spending millions.

He also did it by starting early.

Shortly after losing the Democratic Vice Presidential nomination to Estes Kefauver in 1956, John Kennedy decided to try for the top spot on the ticket in 1960. The 1956 convention had brought him to national attention; now he had to maintain and increase that attention. In the period between 1956 and January, 1960, no party figure addressed more Jefferson-Jackson Day dinners, spoke in behalf of more Democrats seeking election, or shook more rank-and-file hands than did the junior Senator from Massachusetts.

And during it all, in that vital, sub-surface area of American politics, key Kennedy aides were working on state and local party leaders.

Thus, when Kennedy tossed his hat into the ring, elaborate groundwork had already been laid. By January, 1960, Kennedy was the front runner because he had had the foresight, and the means, to get a running start.

Government as Guardian

The situation was altogether different for Hubert H. Humphrey of Minnesota. A poor boy who made good in politics (he was elected mayor of Minneapolis in 1945 at the age of 34), Senator Humphrey throughout his career has possessed an almost mystical faith in "the people." Out of this faith has sprung an extremely liberal philosophy which views government at all levels—but especially at the Federal —as the economic and social salvation of farmers and working men.

Although he had been a Senator since 1949, Humphrey had attracted little national attention prior to his 1958 call on Nikita Khrushchev. This widely-publicized interview won him speaking invitations throughout the country and soon the press was making the people aware of the friendly, garrulous man from Minnesota.

Unlike Kennedy, Hubert Humphrey could not afford to send squads of workers around the country to cultivate grass-roots party support. Nor could he begin to solicit campaign funds seriously until he could convince enough people that he indeed had a chance for the Democratic nomination. To do this he first had to become known, to broaden his appeal both to the voters and to the big-city bosses who are interested chiefly in a candidate with demonstrated appeal—someone who, in leading the ticket, could sweep in the local machine candidates along with him.

The choice of strategy was made for Senator Humphrey by the circumstances. He would have to enter the primaries against Kennedy, but he would have to do it selectively. A win in the District of Columbia, for instance, would be useless; most residents of the nation's capital are Negroes and the Negroes were already partial to the Humphrey brand of liberalism. Agrarian South Dakota, too, could be won handily but it's adjacent to largely agrarian Minnesota, so a win there might not mean much.

But there was one state that, although close to Minnesota, possessed a diverse population and both an agricultural and industrial base. Humphrey would take on Kennedy in Wisconsin.

In a different situation from either Humphrey or Kennedy was the Senate Majority Leader, Lyndon B. Johnson of Texas. Johnson, a one-time school teacher, had risen to power in Congress under the tutelage of the late Sam Rayburn. He had shown himself to be a master parliamentarian, an expert at maneuvering legislation through the traps and bunkers in the upper house. His was the art of tit for tat, and many political leaders in practically every state were in his or Rayburn's debt for one favor or another.

Johnson decided that 1960 would be the year to call the debts.

Sam Rayburn and Johnson himself believed that their one hope was in a convention deadlock, and in the latter days of 1959 a deadlock appeared likely. At the right moment, when the party was divided between, say, Kennedy and Humphrey (or perhaps Stevenson), the old master would cash in the many Johnson-Rayburn chips and carry off the nomination. Given this strategy, entering the primaries would be unnecessary as well as very likely suicidal.

One man who has always regarded Presidential preference primaries as unwise—because they divide the party and often assure the winner of nothing—is former President Harry Truman. And in 1959, Truman's choice for the Democratic nomination was the distinguished-looking Senator from Missouri, Stuart Symington.

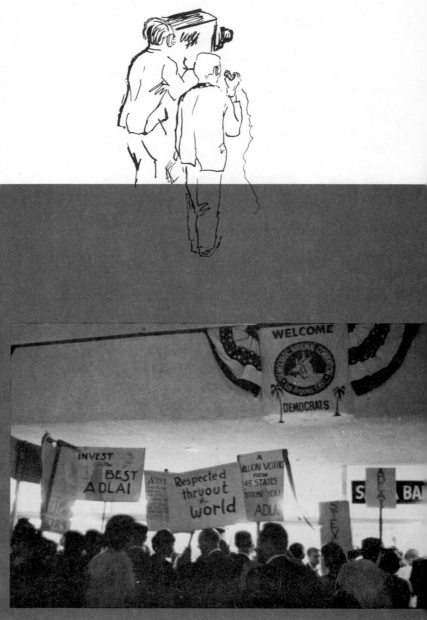

Two things catapulted Symington into contention. The most important was his landslide re-election to the Senate in 1958, capturing 66.4% of the vote; this was the most important because it convinced Symington himself that he had a chance for the Presidential nomination. Secondly, Symington had made a reputation as a leading critic of the Eisenhower defense program at a time when, in the wake of the Soviet space feats, the efficacy of that program was being questioned. Thus, the Symington name was well known, even if the man himself was not.

Aside from a handful of Symington intimates, relatively few Democrats regarded the Missouri Senator as the "best man" for the country's top job. He was looked upon, instead, as an able executive with a consistent liberal voting record who, in the event of a deadlock, would be generally acceptable. He had been a successful businessman and Senator, and he came from an industralized border state.

The Symington candidacy wasn't announced until March 24, 1960. The Senator from Missouri had waited too long.

He did not, however, wait as long as Adlai E. Stevenson, who did not really become an "active" candidate until a day before the nominations.

While Humphrey and Kennedy were bracing for the primaries, Adlai Stevenson left on a business trip to South America. His supporters

were perplexed. Their man refused to lift a finger to win the nomination again; they could do nothing but raise funds, make very tentative plans, and watch John F. Kennedy pull away from the pack.

In contrast to the wide open Democratic race, on the other side of the fence Richard M. Nixon was consolidating his position. Since he was elected Vice President in the Eisenhower victory of 1952, Nixon had meticulously courted the favor of GOP regulars throughout the country, lending his presence and oratory to the campaigns of numberless Republican candidates. These efforts would not be forgotten at the 1960 convention.

But Nixon had far more than the traditional political quid pro quo going for him. In eight years as Vice President he had shown that his could be a functional office, and he used it to build his stature. He made frequent trips abroad, often making front page news. He showed raw physical courage, for instance, by remaining unflustered when Red-instigated mobs attacked his car during a visit to South America.

Poking Khrushchev

On his most famous overseas journey, to Moscow, Nixon engaged Nikita Khrushchev in a public argument (the so-called kitchen debate) and pictures of the Vice President poking an emphatic finger into the Soviet leader's chest brought joy to Americans—and popular acclaim to Nixon.

And, while playing a statesmanlike-role in helping to settle a key labor dispute and other domestic controversies, the Vice President was taking advantage of a peculiar situation caused by President Eisenhower's dislike for party politics. Eisenhower never really wanted the job of party leader and was content to have his Vice President assume those duties. Nixon assumed them with a relish, thus greatly increasing his leverage within the GOP.

But while Vice President Nixon had shown himself to be an effective personality on the national and international scenes, and while he was extremely popular with Republican leaders in most parts of the country, his path to the GOP Presidential nomination was not entirely clear.

His biggest obstacle was Nelson A. Rockefeller, an heir to the country's most famous private fortune and the popular governor of

New York, the nation's most politically important state. (Between the Civil War and 1948, there were 21 Presidential elections; 13 times one, or both, of the major parties nominated a governor or former governor of the Empire State.)

A Generous Family

Yet Rockefeller's potential power in Republican politics did not end with his governorship. Since long before the turn of the century the Rockefeller family has been a foremost financial backer of the GOP. It was not a family the Republican professionals were anxious to treat with discourtesy.

In personality, Nixon and Rockefeller could hardly be more unalike. Nixon was born poor and made his own way, learning in the process that a man without the insulation of family wealth must be prepared to take a battering if he seeks high goals in politics. The Vice President, intensely ambitious, took the battering; but in the effort he developed a suspicious attitude toward all but his closest friends. In the process, too, he learned how to dish it out, and few modern politicians have aroused the animosity of other politicians (especially Democrats) as has Nixon.

Rockefeller, for his part, grew up a child of enormous privilege but somehow managed to avoid the extraordinary shyness that is common to many in his family. Instead he has a buoyant personality ("I've never found it a handicap to be a Rockefeller," he has said) and a zest for public affairs.

In 1959, Governor Rockefeller expanded his private and official staffs to hundreds of paid and volunteer workers—to "explore" his chances for the Republican Presidential nomination in 1960. He was to find the party regulars suspicious of his liberal attitudes and, more importantly, long since committed to Richard Nixon. Still, what influence in the party he had, Rockefeller intended to use.

Thus was the political situation early in 1960 as the nation prepared for the primary elections. The Republicans appeared certain to choose Nixon in any event. But for the Democrats the race was anybody's—or so it seemed.

With Johnson, Symington and Stevenson eschewing the primaries, the Democrats' center ring was left to Kennedy and Humphrey who fought their first battle in April in Wisconsin.

The 1960 Republican convention: Nelson A. Rockefeller is not in this picture.

FAVORITE SON

The exact source of this term is unknown. After 1835 it was applied to the leading statesman from a particular state (Henry Clay was Kentucky's favorite son for 30 years). Gradually the meaning of nationally-known hero was modified by applying the phrase to state politicians who ostensibly seek a national nomination at the convention. A state delegation's backing of a state leader, a "favorite son," is a stop-gap maneuver used to keep the delegation uncommitted to a major candidate and therefore free to jump in any direction when the time is ripe.

The outcome was inconclusive in every respect. Kennedy carried the heavily Catholic areas plus one district with an about even Catholic-Protestant population. He lost the predominantly Protestant areas, but whether this was because they were largely Protestant or because they were agrarian and therefore more likely to be sympathetic to Humphrey could not be known. Kennedy won the primary six-districts-to-four.

On to West Virginia

It was not enough of a victory to impress anybody, least of all Senator Kennedy himself. He knew he needed not only to win in the primaries but he needed to win decisively. Humphrey, for his part, was pleased with his respectable showing in Wisconsin and, against the advice of many in his party, decided to continue the battle with Kennedy in West Virginia. And it was there that the issue was all but decided.

If it takes anything to mount a national political campaign it takes money. Thanks to the money-making success of Joseph P. Kennedy, his son had at his disposal one of the largest family fortunes in the country. Whatever else it did or didn't do, such a sizeable bankroll permitted Senator Kennedy to conduct a campaign that was to doom the aspirations of Senator Humphrey.

Kennedy flew about in his own airliner, going where and when he wanted, never dependent on the vagueries of public transportation. His money, and the social position that money brought, afforded him the services of scores of old Ivy League chums whose talents were not for sale but whose voluntary labors in commanding thousands of paid and volunteer workers were of inestimable value. Kennedy money, too, bought television time and all the other political advertising his strategists thought wise.

Over the Bumps by Bus

Senator Humphrey, by contrast, traveled by chartered bus. His staff of managers were largely part-timers, his corps of workers relatively small. He could afford little political advertising (much of his Eastern financial support, never large anyway, was sharply reduced after his Wisconsin defeat). His lack of more than a few aides with top-level organizational talent cost him dearly.

In West Virginia, the issue was all but decided.

In Milwaukee, as elsewhere, the youthful Bostonian found his way to the people.

But it would be an error to ascribe the Kennedy success only to money—as many of his critics enjoyed doing. Kennedy beat Humphrey in West Virgina because he artfully transformed a popularly advertised "liability" into a powerful asset.

West Virginia has long been regarded by many Americans as a great pile of coal populated by feuding mountain folks—people who prefer their politics, religion and whisky plain and simple. If this ungenerous stereotype were true or even half true, how would West Virginians look upon a Roman Catholic Presidential candidate?

An Oath Before God

Kennedy had two choices. He could either play down the religion issue or he could meet it head on. He chose to meet it. He told crowd after crowd that the man who was elected President was required to swear an oath before God to uphold the Constitution, the Constitution which absolutely bars an alliance between church and state. Any man who violated this pledge, added Kennedy, would not only be violating the Constitution, but would be committing "a sin against God, for he has sworn on the Bible."

In cold print four years later, this appeal to the fundamentalist instincts of the people has a theatrical ring. But at the time, delivered as it was in a manner of deep reverence and sincerety, it was an appeal that drew thousands of responding nods. Soon the issue was no longer Kennedy's Catholicism; it was tolerance versus intolerance. A West Virginia Protestant could show his open-mindness by voting for Kennedy; a vote for Humphrey might carry the implication of prejudice.

Humphrey saw the way the Kennedy forces were manipulating the question of religion and it angered him. He stepped up his attacks on his opponent's wealth and elaborate organization but he continued to lose ground. When the vote was counted on May 10, Hubert Humphrey's Presidential campaign was over.

Kennedy's 60-40 victory was decisive, and no Democratic politician could fail to understand its meaning. If he could win under the circumstances in West Virginia, could he fairly be expected to lose in Los Angeles? The bandwagon was now in high gear.

Interestingly, Kennedy might never have won the Democratic nomination had Humphrey decided to give up after Wisconsin. In the absence of competition, West Virginia would have meant nothing, and Kennedy would have been without effective proof of his power as a vote-getter. History often turns on small hinges.

No Contest

Similarly, in a dissimilar way, Richard M. Nixon was far out in front in the contest for the Republican nomination, and in truth, there was really no contest. Nixon's claim to the prize was challenged only by that strong-minded newcomer to politics, Nelson A. Rockefeller. And Rockefeller had sounded out the party leaders in 1959 and concluded sadly, and publicly, that the party leaders' hearts belonged to Nixon.

In the spring of 1960 there occurred a series of events on the world stage that complicated the task of the party that was seeking to be returned to the White House. A remarkable high-altitude spy plane flown by an American named Francis Gary Powers was shot down deep in the Soviet heartland. President Eisenhower, to the surprise of the world, admitted that the plane had indeed been on an espionage flight. The event was grasped by Khrushchev as an excuse to torpedo the Paris summit meeting a short time later. The deterioration of U.S.-Russian relations, and especially the bureaucratic bungling immediately following the U-2 incident, gave the Democrats something to holler about.

In the months leading up to the ill-fated summit meeting in May, the Governor of New York had kept silent about his misgivings over Administration policy, hoping thereby not to rock the boat during a period when very sensitive diplomatic negotiations were being undertaken. But after Khrushchev's volcanic explosion in Paris, Rockefeller decided to speak his piece.

On June 8 he released a remarkable statement in which he charged the leadership of the GOP with failing "to make clear where this party is heading and where it proposes to lead the nation."

He went on: "I find it unreasonable—in these times—that (Nixon) has firmly insisted upon making known his program and his policies, not before, but only after nomination by his party. . . .

"I find it reasonable—and urgently necessary—that the new spokesmen of the Republican Party declare now, and not at some later

Senator Hubert Humphrey, wearing a miner's hat, hears about the hard time West Virginia was having. Humphrey was having one too.

Kids don't vote, but their relatives do.

date, precisely what they believe and what they propose, to meet the great matters before the nation. . . .

"I can no longer be silent on the fact. We cannot, as a nation or as a party, proceed—nor should anyone presume to ask us to proceed—to march to meet the future with a banner aloft whose only emblem is a question mark. . . ."

With this blast at Nixon and the Republican leadership generally, Rockefeller effectively removed any outside chance he might have had for the nomination. To the Republican pro, this kind of outburst on the eve of a Presidential election campaign smacked of party disloyalty, however much it said for Rockefeller's courage.

But the Rockefeller forces had only begun.

Impotent Remedies

Campaign platforms are part of America's quadrennial madness; each party draws one up supposedly to relate party principles to vital issues, thereby giving the voters a handy guide to the policies the candidates would follow if elected. In reality, platforms do not always mean too much. They are almost always vaguely worded to attract the most voters while infuriating the fewest. They are almost always forgotten after the election as the victor comes to grips with problems for which slogans and generalizations are impotent remedies.

Though there was no reason to believe the 1960 Republican platform, as written in Chicago, would be taken with any more seriousness than its predecessors—of either party—the Rockefeller people decided to make an issue out of it. They would carry their views to the floor of the convention, if necessary.

What Rockefeller wanted, among other things, was a stronger civil rights plank and a promise that defense spending would be increased by at least $3 billion. He believed, as did John F. Kennedy, that America was on the weak side of a "missile gap" and that only large, new defense expenditures could close it. The GOP platform-writers resisted the Rockefeller argument because it amounted to an admission that President Eisenhower had neglected the country's defenses.

A floor fight threatened that might well have left the Republican Party in pieces. This, in the eyes of Richard Nixon, would be intolerable.

On Friday, July 22, Nixon telephoned Rockefeller and requested a private meeting between the two in New York. The Governor agreed, but on his own terms. It would have to be announced later that Nixon had asked for the meeting and the rendezvous would have to take place at Rockefeller's apartment, rather than at a neutral site Nixon would have preferred. Nixon agreed to all Rockefeller's conditions and, without notifying his strategists in Chicago or even his press secretary in Washington, the Vice President flew secretly to New York.

There Rockefeller laid down the law. The key planks in the platform were to be written the way Rockefeller wanted them or, implied the Governor, all hell would break loose in Chicago. Except for some minor modifications that Nixon was able to coax from the Governor, Rockefeller had his way.

When the Republican Platform Committee, which had been working long and hard at its job, heard about the secret meeting in New York, its members were on the verge of apoplexy. Immediately the cry went up: Nixon has sold out to Rockefeller.

Whatever one's view of Nixon's visit to the Governor's apartment that fateful night, rarely has one man undercut his own strategists as effectively as the Vice President did. Never was Nixon's cardinal rule in better evidence: Trust thyself—and, preferably, only thyself.

Lingering Echoes

To the more conservative members of the party, here again was the insidious New York liberal influence exerting itself. Here again was a surrender to "me-tooism."

Arizona Senator Barry Goldwater declared that the Nixon-Rockefeller "agreement" assured "Republican defeat in November."

Nixon himself saw his capitulation another way: He had avoided a messy floor fight and preserved party unity. Let Rockefeller take this round; he, Nixon, might soon be President.

Rockefeller, while pleased with his success, still had little to be happy about. He knew he had alienated the leaders of his party, and a man he disliked professionally and otherwise was to be the Republican standard bearer.

The sounds of this intra-party battle are, four years later, still reverberating. And they may well be amplified many times before 1964 is history.

Joy abounds as two rivals meet to close party ranks just before the 1960 Republican convention. Nixon's aides were less joyful.

the Conventions

Rules and Rulers, Harangues and Hurrahs

Because of their diversity, the two political parties have long defied absolute philosophical classification. This is a wide country and within each party the range of opinion is also wide. But occasionally a party, like a person, will reveal itself unwittingly, and in that brief moment of revelation the voter can see what it is that separates Democrats from Republicans.

The Republicans are holding their 1964 convention in a building used for measuring farm animals; the Democrats are holding theirs in a building used for measuring girls in bathing suits.

No longer, perhaps, will the difference between the parties be described simply as one of emphasis.

Even so, the similarities between the parties persist; nor are they less apparent when the national conventions are held every four years. These massive meetings, during which the delegates choose a Presidential and Vice Presidential candidate, follow pretty much the same book of rules, with a few important exceptions. And they are a great show not only for the politicians, but for the millions of Americans who follow the acts on television and in the press.

And "acts" is the word, because more and more in recent years the important business of a national convention is settled before the delegates have even found their seats, and far more of substance is accomplished backstage than is ever witnessed on the home screen.

Indeed, the noise and color of a convention can be misleading; it's not a circus. In the words of Alistair Cooke, it is a "chess tournament disguised as a circus."

Choosing a Site

But before the chess tournament can begin, the party must make the basic decision of where it will be held. Deciding upon a city is one of the many convention jobs of the national committees and their choice is based on a variety of factors.

San Francisco, where the Republicans will meet July 13 at the livestock exhibition hall known as the Cow Palace, and Atlantic City, New Jersey, where the Democrats will meet August 24 at Convention Hall (home of the annual "Miss America" contest) were picked because each city satisified the respective parties of its physical ability to handle a convention, of the importance of the state's electoral votes, of its recreational facilities, and of the minimal danger of adverse publicity resulting from possible civic disorder.

Then too, each city had to come up with a sizable chunk of cash.

It is not a simple job for a city to host a national political convention. Delegates and their families, politicians and their staffs, newsmen and tourists temporarily swell a city's population by between 15,000 and 25,000. There must be adequate, high-quality hotel and restaurant accommodations for this influx, and transportation facilities must be able to rise to the occasion.

Elaborate communications arrangements have to be made to handle thousands of extra telephone calls and the many requirements of a huge press corps. Finally, the convention hall must be big enough and adaptable enough to accommodate the big show.

Both San Francisco and Atlantic City have guaranteed 12,000 to 14,000 hotel or motel rooms, with the former having the more modern facilities. The newest hotel in Atlantic City was built in 1928, although the seashore resort has added several dozen new motels in the last decade.

And while San Francisco can offer newer hotels, Atlantic City can offer greater convenience. All the Democratic delegates will be housed within a mile of Convention Hall and within a mile of the railroad station. Most politicians and newsmen will be able to walk to work.

The Cow Palace is about eight miles from downtown San Francisco where the hotels are located. There are very few Republicans or newsmen who are known to favor that long a walk. By taxicab they can make it in 25 minutes most of the time, although it can be done in under 20 minutes at three in the morning.

Getting to Atlantic City in the first place, however, will be more difficult for most people than getting to the Golden Gate City. Unlike San Francisco, the New Jersey resort lies off the nation's main transportation routes. Two local railroad lines connect with Philadelphia and the trains that ordinarily run on these are older than Atlantic City's hotels. An airport four blocks from the beach can handle nothing but small planes and large sea gulls. The city claims it is the world's oldest municipal airfield, built in 1919.

Proximity of Other Cities

Atlantic City does possess, however, a newer municipal airport 11 miles out of town that, according to a spokesman, "can handle anything." It regularly accomodates only a few feeder flights a day, however. Major airports, at Newark and Philadelphia, although linked to Atlantic City by modern highways, are well over an hour away.

San Francisco, a key transportation terminal, has a first-class airport 15 miles from the center of the city.

Communications people on the West Coast will be working with facilities that are elaborate to begin with. San Francisco is a major metropolitan area (area population: 3,275,000; city population, 743,000).

By contrast, Atlantic City is off the main long-distance telephone routes and its needs normally are modest (area population: 130,000; city population, 60,000).

The biggest communications job the resort has ever tackled before is the annual "Miss America" television show, a one-station transmitting operation. A New Jersey communications expert called this event "child's play" when compared to the electronic preparations for a national political convention.

The communications arrangements in both cities are, of course, temporary, but they must be first-rate. A list of the gadgetry includes about 30 television circuits, 350 teleprinters, 2,500 telephones, and 20 switchboards.

In San Francisco this installation will cost $3 million, most of which will be paid by the TV networks and the rest by the telephone company. In Atlantic City, the installation will cost $8 million—because $5 million will have to be spent just to bring the resort's communications to metropolitan-area capability. That extra $5 million includes the cost of 200 additional public telephone booths in Convention Hall and nearby locations, as well as a micro-wave tower to handle the telephone, TV, radio and other signals pouring out of Atlantic City.

The television networks have good reason to invest heavily in such an operation, aside from the importance of the conventions themselves. Attracting a large audience during the conventions and the ensuing campaign can yield important dividends in the next four years. Viewers' preferences since 1960 indicate that the network winning the greatest following during the campaign is the one that will dominate the TV news field for the following four years. In a sense the networks are also running for election in 1964.

The recreational facilities in and around San Francisco and Atlantic City are many. The former is noted for its exotic neighborhoods, its hills and scenery, its waterfront, and a remarkable cultural climate.

Walking the Planks

Atlantic City has the most famous boardwalk in the world—originally constructed in 1870 and running for eight miles along the beachfront, well beyond the city limits. Along with the usual seashore attractions, the city has a race track that will be in operation during the convention—although this is not expected to prevent the Democrats from producing a quorum. Beyond that, Atlantic City is only 100 miles from New York where the World's Fair will be in progress.

Both cities advertise paradisaical climates, with San Francisco claiming that its natural air conditioning makes the mechanical variety unnecessary. Atlantic City says its weather is great, too, but it doesn't like to take chances. Some 70% of the hotel and motel rooms are air conditioned, and the city is spending $2.5 million to refrigerate Convention Hall. The space where the delegates will assemble is the largest room ever to be air conditioned. (It also may be, as the city boasts, the largest room, period. New York City's Madison Square Garden would fit inside it, leaving plenty of room for several average-size business conventions. It's big enough to house a regulation football field plus seats for 12,000 spectators; and the home run has never been hit that would reach from one end of the hall to the other).

Cars and Bars

San Francisco's Cow Palace is a cavern of similar dimensions, and is used more for conventions than for the livestock shows from which it got its name. Along with a main meeting hall it includes various exhibition halls, four restaurants, four bars, and 67 acres of grounds with parking for 6,500 cars. It is less than five miles from the Pacific Ocean, although not as close to the Pacific as Convention Hall is to the Atlantic. If the Atlantic City building were any closer to the ocean the delegates would have to wear life jackets.

Once, or perhaps before, a national committee is satisfied a city can accommodate its party's convention, the political situation of the state is considered. California and New Jersey both possess sizable electoral votes and both are within reach of either party. A national convention can interest and inspire enough people in the state in which it is held to help swing the state accordingly.

For this reason, the Democrats would gain nothing by holding their convention in Vermont, even as it would be futile for the Republicans to convene in Georgia. Nor would either party be likely to hold its convention in a sparsely populated state like Nevada.

The danger of adverse publicity is another factor in picking a site. Neither party, for instance, would benefit from a civil rights demonstration or a "free-Cuba" march. Such demonstrations for special treatment in a party's platform could embarrass the party and result in bad publicity. Thus, the selectors try to find a city where such disturbances are considered less likely.

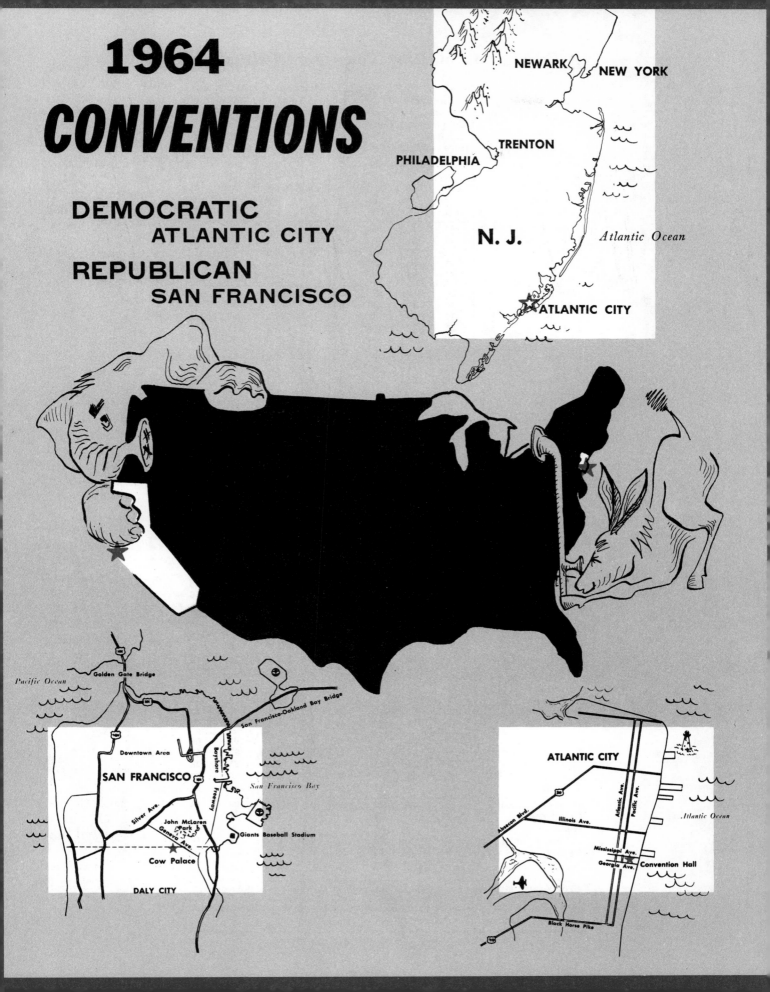

A Comparison of 1964 Convention Delegations

State Delegation	Number of Convention Votes		Rank, By Number of Convention Votes		Portion of Total Convention Vote (in %)		Maximum Number of Members in Delegation	
	Dem	Rep	Dem	Rep	Dem	Rep	Dem	Rep
Alabama	38	20	22	23	1.6	1.5	94	40
Alaska	12	12	50	44	0.5	0.9	28	24
Arizona	19	16	39	29	0.8	1.2	51	32
Arkansas	32	12	28	44	1.4	0.9	84	24
California	154	86	2	2	6.7	6.6	314	172
Colorado	23	18	36	27	1.0	1.4	63	36
Connecticut	43	16	19	29	1.9	1.2	84	32
Delaware	22	12	37	44	1.0	0.9	42	24
Florida	51	34	13	9	2.2	2.6	107	68
Georgia	53	24	12	17	2.3	1.8	117	48
Hawaii	25	8	33	50	1.1	0.6	48	16
Idaho	15	14	45	33	0.7	1.1	39	28
Illinois	114	58	4	4	4.9	4.4	250	116
Indiana	51	32	13	11	2.2	2.5	117	64
Iowa	35	24	25	17	1.5	1.8	85	48
Kansas	27	20	30	23	1.2	1.5	67	40
Kentucky	34	24	27	17	1.5	1.8	94	48
Louisiana	46	20	17	23	2.0	1.5	96	40
Maine	16	14	42	33	0.7	1.1	44	28
Maryland	48	20	16	23	2.1	1.5	94	40
Massachusetts	69	34	9	9	3.0	2.6	149	68
Michigan	92	48	7	7	4.0	3.7	192	96
Minnesota	50	26	15	15	2.2	2.0	110	52
Mississippi	24	13	34	43	1.0	1.0	68	26
Missouri	58	24	10	17	2.5	1.8	134	48
Montana	17	14	41	33	0.7	1.1	47	28
Nebraska	19	16	39	29	0.8	1.2	49	32
Nevada	22	6	37	51	1.0	0.5	50	12
New Hampshire	15	14	45	33	0.7	1.1	35	28
New Jersey	77	40	8	8	3.3	3.1	157	80
New Mexico	26	14	32	33	1.1	1.1	58	28
New York	179	92	1	1	7.7	7.1	405	184
North Carolina	58	26	10	15	2.5	2.0	130	52
North Dakota	15	14	45	33	0.7	1.1	35	28
Ohio	99	58	5	4	4.3	4.4	225	116
Oklahoma	30	22	29	22	1.3	1.7	86	44
Oregon	24	18	34	27	1.0	1.4	56	36
Pennsylvania	125	64	3	3	5.4	4.9	285	128
Rhode Island	27	14	30	33	1.2	1.1	59	28
South Carolina	38	16	22	29	1.6	1.2	78	32
South Dakota	15	14	45	33	0.7	1.1	35	28
Tennessee	40	28	21	14	1.7	2.1	104	56
Texas	99	56	5	6	4.3	4.3	219	112
Utah	16	14	42	33	0.7	1.1	40	28
Vermont	12	12	50	44	0.5	0.9	28	24
Virginia	42	30	20	12	1.8	2.3	106	60
Washington	35	24	25	17	1.5	1.8	87	48
West Virginia	37	14	24	33	1.6	1.1	85	28
Wisconsin	46	30	17	12	2.0	2.3	106	60
Wyoming	15	12	45	44	0.7	0.9	41	24
Dist. of Columbia	16	9	42	49	0.7	0.7	32	18
Canal Zone	5	..	53	..	0.2	..	11	..
Guam	3	..	55	..	0.1	..	9	..
Puerto Rico	8	5	52	52	0.3	0.4	20	10
Virgin Islands	5	3	54	53	0.2	0.2	11	6
TOTAL	2,316	1,308	*	*	100.0†	100.0†	5,260	2,616

*There are 55 Democratic delegations and 53 Republican delegations.

†Because the data in these columns are rounded off their sums are not exactly 100.0.

The last—and certainly not least—item considered by the party leaders is the amount of cash each city baits the hook with. This money is used by the parties to defray the costs of the convention itself, and it's not supposed to be used for partisan activity—that is, the campaign.

San Francisco put up $650,000. Of this, $400,000 was contributed by the city itself with the additional $250,000 coming from local businessmen and sales of an illustrated convention program.

Atlantic City offered $625,000 in cash and free rental of Convention Hall, worth $25,000, making the offers from both cities the same. The contribution of the city itself and local businessmen amounted to $175,000. The State of New Jersey put up $200,000 and the New Jersey Democratic Committee contributed $250,000.

Who Gets to Go?

Sponsors are happy to spend $650,000 to get a national political convention, because a convention brings from $5 million to $7 million into the city and its environs.

Having decided where the big event is to be held, the national committees must determine how the convention votes will be apportioned among the states. The parties use differing, and complicated, systems.

The Democrats apportion their votes according to the states' populations, as reflected in their electoral votes, and according to the states' performances in the 1960 Presidential election. Each state is given three convention votes for each of its electoral votes.

A bonus of 10 votes is awarded to each state that contributed its electoral votes to the Democratic column in 1960. Alabama, however, only gets five of these victory votes because only five of its 11 Democratic electors actually voted for the national ticket in 1960. (The other six were cast for Senator Harry Byrd by unpledged electors running on the Democratic slate.) Another bonus is distributed according to the popular vote performance in 1960. Each state gets an extra convention vote for each 100,000 popular votes, or major fraction thereof, cast in 1960 for the national Democratic ticket. Again, Alabama is an exception: Its popular vote bonus is determined on the basis of 5/11ths of the popular vote cast for the Democratic slate in 1960.

When the Democratic National Committee looked in the record books it found that every state except Alaska had earned at least one of these popular vote bonuses in 1960. Rather than slight the biggest state—in area—in the Union, the committee decided that every state, including Alaska, would get at least one of these extra votes.

If, when a state party counts up the votes it deserves, it finds that the total is less than its 1960 total, it need not fret. The national committee has also decided that no state shall have fewer convention votes than it did in 1960.

Party regulars do not have to worry over another stipulation that each state shall pick one delegate and one alternate for each convention vote. As it stands this ruling would cut back the delegations from 46 of the 50 states. The national committee has allowed the states to send as many delegates as they did in 1960, but the number of alternates may be no more than the number of 1964 convention votes that the state is assigned.

As in the past, the states which did well in the previous election, and which showed a population growth, have been rewarded, both with more convention votes and with more convention seats. At the same time these gains have not been subtracted from the delegations of the states that have not done as well.

The More the Merrier

The result is a gigantic Democratic convention. When each state's two members of the national committee—each with a vote—are thrown in, the total convention vote will amount to 2,316 and the total number of official convention-goers will be 5,368.

Because the total number of a state's delegates is often more than its total vote, a state may divide some or all of its votes in half so that a delegate may have only a one-half vote. The assignment of votes on a district or at-large basis is a matter to be decided within each state in accordance with state election laws and/or the rules of the state Democratic committee.

Arbitrary allotments are made to the District of Columbia, the Canal Zone, Puerto Rico, Guam, and the Virgin Islands.

The Republican system is different but equally complicated. There are no half votes; just one delegate for each vote. The basic delegate allotment is four delegates-at-large from each state and two delegates-at-large for each U.S. Representative at large from each state.

The Republicans also use a bonus system. Six at-large delegates are awarded to each state that either cast its electoral votes for Nixon in 1960, or elected a Republican governor or senator in 1960 or later.

One district delegate is awarded for each Congressional district which cast 2,000 votes or more for Nixon in 1960, or for the Republican candidate for the House in 1962. Another district delegate is also assigned for each Congressional district which cast 10,000 votes or more for Nixon in 1960, or for the Republican candidate for the House in 1962.

Like the Democrats, the Republicans assign one alternate for each delegate vote, and arbitrarily assign the number of delegates to the District of Columbia, Puerto Rico, and the Virgin Islands at the GOP convention. Guam and the Canal Zone are not represented.

The bonus system of apportionment was originally designed to reward the states where a party's performance was strong. Before the turn of the century delegates were assigned entirely according to the states' electoral votes. But under this system, weak state parties were represented disproportionately.

Power of Postmasters

By 1912 this fault was especially troublesome to the Republicans. Southern delegations to the national convention possessed almost no popular following, yet they held a strong block of votes for which candidates eagerly competed. Thus, the Southerners were able to decisively influence the convention choice without representing any significant popular support in the party.

This Southern block, largely made up of Federal appointees, was relied upon by William Howard Taft to win the nomination. Thus, the power of the "postmaster vote" became notorious.

The party rank and file were not able to win the nomination for the man of their choice, Teddy Roosevelt. Roosevelt's subsequent bolt from the party led to a reform in the delegate apportionment system, and the bonus system was introduced.

Since its introduction, the bonus allowance has been increasingly liberalized so that the existing system now permits practically every district in the nation to be eligible for all the bonus Republican votes.

The GOP sends about 1,300 delegates and the same number of alternates to its national conventions. Because they split delegate votes, the Democrats send about 3,000 delegates plus 2,200 alternates. (See page 82.)

A national convention is the official governing body of the party but because it meets only once every four years and has so unwieldy a number of participants, the authority of the convention is delegated to the national committee. Thus the committee is the permanent agency which acts on behalf of the party between conventions.

Limited Authority

The convention's authority, however, is not very great because it has full power only over its own actions. And the power of the national committee is confined to national matters. Neither can control other party groups, state and local organizations, Congressmen and other officeholders. Party membership is largely controlled at the state and local levels by the rules of the state parties and the state laws. Thus, American politics is highly decentralized.

To do its work the national committee has a number of powers. It organizes, finances and directs the national campaign in cooperation with the House and Senate Campaign Committees. The national committee has the power to fill vacancies in the national ticket when they occur between the conventions and the election.

In order to organize and direct these activities, the national committee of each party maintains a headquarters in Washington. Here the permanent committees of the national committee have offices, and here the official party publicity originates.

A national committee has exercised its power to fill a vacancy on a ticket just once. In 1860, the Democratic convention, depleted by a Southern walkout, picked a Southerner, Senator Benjamin Fitzpatrick of Alabama, to run with Stephen Douglas on the moderate platform of the regular Democratic Party. Fitzpatrick later declined the nomination and the Democratic National Committee named Herschel V. Johnson, a former governor of Georgia, as a replacement.

Along with its pre-convention duties of site selection and delegate apportionment, the national committee makes tentative decisions on the officers and committee chairmen of the convention. The principal officers are the temporary chairman, the keynote speaker (the

THE CONVENTIONS

Democrats combine these two jobs), and the permanent chairman. There is usually no contest over these selections when they are submitted to the convention for approval, because they are selected after negotiation among the party leaders.

The national committee also tentatively selects the chairmen of the four major convention committees—Rules and Order of Business, Permanent Organization, Resolutions and Platform, and Credentials—long before the convention opens. These positions are largely honorary and do not give significant power to the man in the chair. Thus, opposition to these choices from the convention floor is unlikely.

Nor are the actions of the Rules and the Permanent Organization committees frequently challenged. While it's true that each convention is self-governing and adopts its own rules, over the years the manner in which the convention operates has evolved from the practices of past conventions. The system is based on the rules of parliamentary law and the rules of the House of Representatives.

A convention is governed by the rules of the preceding convention until the Rules committee has made its report and it has been adopted by the delegates. As a matter of practice, conventions for many years have adopted the rules and procedures of the preceding convention with little variation.

The actions of the other two important committees, Credentials and Platform, are often contested and sometimes reversed in the floor debate. This frequently occurs because of the different representation in the committees from that in the whole convention.

In the committees each state is represented equally, as in the Senate. In the convention the representation reflects the population and, to a lesser degree, party strength, as in the House.

Because of this difference, the Democratic Platform Committee in 1948 recommended a mild civil rights plank, yet the convention rejected it and adopted a more liberal proposal. In a like manner in 1952, the Republican Credentials Committee favored seating a number of Taft delegates from the South; however the Eisenhower strength on the floor was so great

Atlantic City's Convention Hall:
In Miss America's chambers, 5,000 Democrats.

San Francisco's Cow Palace:
In the livestock arena, a rogue elephant.

Saturation advertising.

that the Taft men were ousted in favor of delegates who preferred the General.

The national convention, which is four years in preparation, usually lasts four or five days during the summer, beginning on a Monday. It is many things: An elaborate series of party rites, a television extravaganza, a rally of loyal party workers, a week of tourists' merrymaking, an appeal to the voters, and a time to make decisions on the vital matters of policy and leadership.

Until the platform is presented to the convention, most of the important activity takes place backstage, with many issues settled in the committee meetings. State contingents caucus often to resolve differences in the delegation and determine the delegation's position on the primary matters before the convention.

Behind-the-Scenes Politicking

In these meetings, most of the power politicking takes place. The delegates are wooed here, sometimes by the White House aspirants themselves. There are more deals in such meetings than in a statehouse poker session. The caucuses are sandwiched in between press conferences and numberless social functions.

The purpose of this backstage activity is the same as that of the program on the floor: To assemble a policy and leadership that will win popular support without upsetting the consensus of the party.

But there is an important distinction between the open convention seen by the public and the unannounced convention that takes place off the floor. One is a place of display; the other is a place of action.

On the floor the convention is unwieldy, apparently disorganized, first energized and then enervated by loud, long speeches, and looking like anything but a civilized parliament about to make vital decisions. The real work is being done elsewhere.

As the convention moves on, more and more important activities move out of the back rooms to the convention hall. The climax comes with the balloting for the Presidential nomination.

The first day of the convention floor program is taken up with opening ceremonies, temporary organization of the convention, various speeches and presentation of party dignitaries. The party itself is depicted throughout as an organization of noble spirits whose wisdom is matched only by its virtue. The delegates are welcomed by the host city, county, and state in generally non-partisan greetings because the welcomers may belong to the opposing party. This year, for example, a Democratic governor will greet the Republicans in San Francisco, and in Atlantic City a Republican state senator will welcome the Democrats.

Every other item in the convention program, except the *Star Spangled Banner,* has a partisan significance. Even the invocation serves the party's political purpose, although in an indirect way. Religious leaders are chosen from many faiths to offer the appropriate opening and closing prayers, and thus no major religious group's feelings are hurt.

After saying its prayers, the convention almost automatically approves the temporary convention rules proposed by the national committee. The various convention committees then retire to prepare their reports and no further business is done until they do. Floor activity continues, however, as some of the party's leading nominees are presented on the speakers platform, and a file of candidates for the House, Senate and governorships are given the spotlight briefly.

Nor is there a shortage of speeches. Chief among them is the keynote address, in which an attempt is made to combine the inspirational gifts of Thomas Paine, Demosthenes and Knute Rockne. Because the consensus of the convention has not yet been measured by decisions on platform and candidates, the keynoter is forced to stick to high-flown generalities calculated to arouse the delegates and appeal to the electorate.

As Will Saw It

Many observers have said many things about keynote speeches, and Will Rogers was among them. He picked out the Republicans for his target, but his barbs would have been no less true if aimed at the Democrats. Said Will:

"A Keynote Speech is Press notices of the Republican Party, written by its own members.

"Here are just a few things that I bet you didn't know the Republicans were responsible for: Radio, Telephone, Baths, Automobiles, Savings Accounts, Law Enforcement, Workmen living in houses, and a living wage for Senators.

"The Democrats had brought in War, pestilence, debts, Disease, Bo Weevil, Gold Teeth, need for Farm Relief, suspenders. . . .

Nixon accepting the GOP nomination. His last hurrah?

"He told of so much money that we had saved that I think if he talked another hour he would have paid us a dividend.

"Once I thought sure he was referring to 'Our Savior' till they told me, 'No, it was Coolidge'. The way he rated 'em was Coolidge, The Lord, and then Lincoln.

"It was an impromptu address that he had been working on for only six months. He made no attempt at Oratory, he just shouted."

On the second day, while the speeches and the carnival atmosphere prevail, some committee reports are usually heard. The committees on Rules and Permanent Organization rarely provoke any floor debate, and an occasional restless delegate has been known to duck out for a beer during these recitals.

Shaping the Platform

The Credentials committee, however, can very well stir up discord and the ensuing battle is sometimes an early test of the strength of various factions. The uproar over the reports of the Credentials committee in the 1912 GOP convention is one of the best known examples of these floor fights. The refusal of the Roosevelt delegates to accept the Credentials committee's determinations led to a split in party ranks, which is described in detail in Chapter VI.

The proposed party platform is presented to the convention in the second or third session, immediately before the nominating speeches for President. If there are serious disagreements about platform content, they usually originate in the committee's discussions and, if unresolved, are expressed in the form of minority reports by the dissident factions. If the convention decides to modify the platform, it customarily does this by adopting the minority report as an amendment.

Platforms are frequently criticized as meaningless because they are vague and not binding on the candidates. Yet a successful candidate who does not attempt to carry out the mandate of the platform can find himself in political hot water when the next campaign begins. The platform is, after all, a campaign document designed to have as broad an appeal as possible.

Ultimately, the many compromises that are needed to create a platform that will attract wide support result in considerable vagueness. And while most planks end up in a limbo of ambiguity, parties do take definite stands on specific issues. Thus, the Democrats clearly favored the unlimited coinage of silver in 1896, and the Republicans affirmed their belief in a balanced budget in 1956.

Once the platform is adopted, the next order of business is a roll call by states for placing candidates for the Presidency in nomination. States are called alphabetically and may nominate or second a nomination, may yield to another state, or pass. A good deal of negotiation is involved in deciding who will nominate and second the various hopefuls. These are honors that many covet and the candidates try to achieve a favorable geographical balance in selecting the politicians who speak in their support.

Years ago nominating speeches were very short. It took just 27 words to place Lincoln's name in nomination in 1860; and his chief rival, William Seward, was nominated in 26 words. But brevity, while the soul of wit, is rarely found in the soul of the politician. The nominating speech has gradually become more elaborate and more boring.

It May Knock But Once

The fellow chosen to do the nominating may well be a political figure of little renown, a man who feels he must make the most of this chance to address the entire universe lest the opportunity not come his way again. With millions watching him on television, if a man has any ham in him at all it will be revealed at such a moment. He quickly goes into a long list of the candidate's virtues, but does not mention his name until the very end of the speech. Some people are often surprised at the name that follows the list of virtues. When the magic name is spoken, the candidate's supporters burst into a kind of frenzy not seen very often between conventions—save, perhaps, in the rural areas of New Guinea.

Once the fertility dance is over, the balloting begins. The ballots are cast by each state delegation as a body, with the delegation chairman announcing the result. Although delegates are usually permitted to vote for their own choice, they tend to vote as a bloc, thus enhancing the state's power in the convention.

In the Democratic convention, unanimous agreement within a state delegation is sometimes enforced by the "unit rule." Under this system the majority of a state's delegates may cast the entire vote of the state regardless of the will of any dissident delegates.

THE CONVENTIONS

This arrangement is similar, but not identical, to the system of the Electoral College, where the entire electoral vote of a state goes to the man with the most popular votes in that state, whether or not they amount to a majority. In the case of the unit rule, it is only binding where an absolute majority of the delegation decides in the favor of one candidate. The unit rule can be imposed on a delegation by the party's state convention or by the delegation itself.

The unit rule, however, cannot apply to delegates who are elected directly by the voters in a primary, and it may be abrogated by a two-thirds vote of the entire national convention. Where a delegation has imposed the rule on itself, it can be removed by a vote of those members of the state delegation present on the floor at the time.

Politicians rarely make anything simple if they can think up a complicated alternative.

For 100 years—between 1832 and 1932—the Democrats required that a candidate could not be nominated without the vote of two-thirds of the convention. The two-thirds rule was adopted in the very first national Democratic convention at the behest of Andrew Jackson to insure the nomination of his protege, Martin Van Buren, for Vice President.

Ironically, this rule was the instrument that prevented Van Buren's nomination for President in 1844. After eight ballots, Van Buren had achieved a majority but could not win the necessary two thirds. There followed the first compromise on a "dark horse" in convention history, when James K. Polk, a Vice Presidential aspirant, was chosen.

On two other occasions the two-thirds rule prevented the nomination of the front runner. In 1860, Stephen Douglas was denied the Democratic nomination. But after the Southern delegates left the convention, Douglas was chosen by the remaining delegates.

In 1912, House Speaker Champ Clark lost out in the Democratic convention to Woodrow Wilson in the same manner that Van Buren lost out to Polk.

When a Presidential candidate is not selected on the first ballot, the carefully arranged convention schedule is forgotten. The crucial matter of party leadership is at stake. The value of accommodating the timetables of the broadcasting networks and the deadlines of the press now becomes secondary.

Decorations will be worn.

The real sign went up in West Virginia.

What follows depends on the tactics of the several factions. In such uncertain situations the ability of a delegation to vote as a bloc demonstrates its importance. When a leader of a delegation can speak for all his state's delegates, he can wield considerable power, especially if he represents a larger state.

But the likelihood of the Presidential balloting going beyond the first roll call has been reduced in recent years. In past party history, state party leaders had sole influence over the nomination and thus the way to win the nomination was to form a coalition of state party organizations.

Since the turn of the century the state parties have lost their monopoly over the selection of Presidential candidates. The state parties still make the final choice through the casting of the delegations' votes at the convention, but there are now a number of factors that limit this choice. These are the appearance of more powerful national leaders within the parties, the expansion of pre-convention campaigning, and the pressure of popular preference.

Overwhelming Influence

The influence on conventions of key party leaders, especially an incumbent President, in this century has been overwhelming. Since 1900, no incumbent has been denied the nomination, nor has any incumbent refused to serve a second term. When contrasted with the Nineteenth Century record, these facts indicate the political power of the modern Chief Executive. In the Nineteenth Century, five incumbents were refused the nomination and three others declined to run for a second term.

While recent Presidents have been able to have their own way in seeking party approval for a second term, they cannot fix their party's choice of a successor. But they do seem able to veto an unacceptable one. In the Nineteenth Century, retiring Presidents had no such authority. Stephen Douglas and William Jennings Bryan, for instance, were nominated over the opposition of Presidents Buchanan and Cleveland.

Special interest groups began to influence convention choices late in the 1890s. Mark Hanna, William McKinley's political mastermind, was a leading innovator in this field. By pledging the continuance of the protective tariff and the gold standard, Hanna was able to collect heavy contributions from financial and industrial interests in the East and Midwest. Businessmen have continued to exercise their influence on nominations by offering or denying funds, rather than by intervening directly through the selection of friendly delegates.

The business community, chiefly in the East, aided in the Republicans' surprise selection of Wendell Willkie in 1940 and the defeat of Robert Taft in the 1952 GOP convention.

The leading special interest group on the Democratic side for years has been organized labor. In 1952 the unions opposed Vice President Alben Barkley as a successor to President Truman, despite Truman's endorsement of Barkley. And here pops up an almost forgotten bit of political lore.

Truman orginally had backed Adlai Stevenson for the 1952 Presidential nomination but early in the year, after Stevenson had expressed disinterest in the nomination, Truman, in Barkley's words, "had decided to back me for the nomination. . . . Furthermore, he would personally ask his own alternate, Thomas Gavin of Kansas City, to vote for me."

"MONOPOLY"

Thousands of Democrats visiting Atlantic City, New Jersey, for the first time this summer may find the street names curiously familiar. The reason is simple: Atlantic City is the original "Monopoly" board.

Names like St. James Place, Park Place, Pacific Avenue and Boardwalk are part of the real estate complex that is the basis of the parlor game, "Monopoly."

When Charles Darrow was out of a job during the Depression, he decided to invent a game to create the illusion of wealth for himself and his unemployed friends. Darrow had often vacationed in Atlantic City when it was a favorite summer retreat of the rich, and so he thought that the city's street names would be appropriate for his toy-money pastime.

Darrow's illusion of wealth didn't last long; reality replaced it. He has made more than $1 million in royalties on the game and now lives in pleasant retirement—caring not a whit whether he ever again passes "Go".

Gavin corroborated this, saying in an interview in 1960, that he had been directed in a sealed message from the White House to support Barkley. But at the convention, Gavin voted for Stevenson, indicating that he had received a switch in signals shortly before the first nominating ballot. By that time the Stevenson bandwagon was rolling fast and President Truman jumped aboard. Truman's own claims that he was responsible for Stevenson's winning the nomination are in conflict with the testimony of the other principals involved.

Reuther's Role

A key reason the Stevenson bandwagon accelerated so quickly was that Walter Reuther, president of the United Auto Workers, controlled more than 100 delegates from various states who caucused as a group and who persuaded the Northern delegations to back Stevenson.

Aside from strong national leaders and the growth of special interest groups, conventions have been taken more and more out of the hands of the state leaders by the Presidential primaries. Some 48% of the GOP convention votes at San Francisco will belong to states where Presidential preference primaries are held, and some 49% of the Democratic votes will be chosen in the same way.

Since 1924, there has been no case of a minor figure nominated. In that year, John W. Davis, who had only 31 votes on the first ballot, or 3% of the total, was finally named after 103 ballots and 14 days. During the long 1924 harrangue, one delegation leader is reported to have told his people to consider "moving toward a more liberal candidate or into a cheaper hotel."

Once the nominee is assured of enough votes to guarantee his victory, a leader of an opposition faction usually moves to make the nomination unanimous. After the convention has united behind the new leader and let out a big hurrah, the next order of business is the selection of a running mate.

Although the second spot on the ticket has frequently been disputed in the past, the trend now is toward less commotion. Vice Presidential nominees have usually been picked with an eye on offering a sectional balance and a broader range of policies, as well as soothing the feelings of a faction defeated for the top prize.

Recently, however, the importance of the office has grown and men of considerable stature have been chosen. That the U.S. Ambassador to the United Nations and the Majority Leader of the U.S. Senate were not only willing but anxious to run in the second position in 1960 indictates the new prestige of the office. The story that Lyndon B. Johnson hemmed and hawed before accepting John F. Kennedy's "offer" of the second spot is disputed by some insiders who were on the scene. They contend privately that Johnson got the Vice Presidential nomination because he demanded it. In any case, it didn't take long for LBJ to make up his mind.

With the selection of the Vice Presidential candidate—a decision hammered out by the Presidential candidate, party leaders and special interest group leaders—the last substantive act of the national convention is accomplished.

No Rubber Stamp

From all this one may infer that there has been a decline in the independence of the delegates assembled, but this decline has hardly made the convention a rubber stamp. The convention still exercises a choice, although now it is a more limited one.

The changes that have occurred in recent decades make ever more remote the nomination by either party of an inoffensive compromise candidate, a mediocre man picked wearily and desperately by party bosses in a hazy hotel room. The external forces working on a convention are such that secret, cynical kingmaking is no longer a significant possibility.

The national political conventions are good and bad, obvious and subtle, sensible and absurd, cumbersome and efficient. Many contradictory adjectives can be found to fit, even as they fit the whole two-party system—a system that, at its worst, still permits a democratic country of 190 million to decide upon one man to lead them all.

Chapter V

Campaign Techniques
Money, Manpower, Media
and Perpetual Motion

Robert La Follette, 1897 (Wisconsin Historical Society).

It's not a circus, although there are tricks and pretty girls and marching bands. It's not a funeral, although the praise is thick. It's not a hanging, although laments are many. It's not a trial, although a verdict will come. It's not a revolution, although there are urgent cries for a change of power.

It's an American Presidential campaign, and under the sun and the moon there's nothing else quite like it. From the national conventions in summer to election day in November, the country is witness every fourth year to an oratorical explosion that would daunt the North Wind.

In recent times, the quadrennial campaign has increased markedly in size, impact, and cost as candidates have sought to exploit the opportunities presented by jet travel and electronic communications. Long gone are the days when Presidential aspirants thought it too undignified (and too much work) to stump the country themselves, preferring to remain aloof while their lieutenants and party recruits waged the fight for them. Barely believable in 1964 is the historical fact that Lincoln made not a single speech in his 1860 campaign, or that McKinley in 1896 asked delegations of voters to come to *him*—so that it would be unnecessary for him to leave his home in Ohio.

Today, Presidential candidates are less reluctant, and their first goal is to be seen and heard by as many people as possible. Thus, in 1960, John F. Kennedy and Richard M. Nixon flew tens of thousands of miles, visited scores of cities (Nixon went to all 50 states), spoke millions of words, and in four joint television appearances attracted an audience each time averaging 70 million people.

Twisting Roots

But even these figures pale when one considers the size and the activity of the great party structures on top of which the standard bearers are themselves borne. Thousands of paid and volunteer workers distribute campaign literature, ring doorbells, hold rallies, and raise money for their cause. The Democratic and Republican Parties possess long roots that have worked their twisting way deep into the soil of American society, and every four years these roots stretch and flex to serve the organism that stands so high above them.

The man-hours and the money that go into a Presidential campaign are incalculable. In 1960 the Republican Party officially spent $12,950,232 and the Democratic Party $11,800,979. In the long and honored history of bookkeeping, few figures are as deceptive or as meaningless as these. Unreported campaign spending, money that did not go through the parties' official committees, boosts the actual campaign spending totals by many millions—just how many millions can never be known. The laws that require disclosure of campaign spending are masterpieces of legislative futility. They are narrow in scope and broad in ambiguity.

But whatever it costs, and it costs more every four years, a Presidential race provides a service as vital as it is expensive. One of the two principal candidates will be President of the United States, with all the power free men dare give a leader, with power enough to blow up the world. Under the circumstances it behooves the voters to look over these two rivals closely, to hear their views, to test their composure and stamina during the long grind of travel and speech-making.

In an era of electronic marvels, when a reporter's story can be transmitted across the country with the speed of summer lightning, when great newspapers are circulated throughout the nation, when television cameras can transport the candidates into millions of living rooms, the voter's involvement in a campaign is infinitely more intimate than it was just a couple of generations ago. And such intimacy serves the democratic process.

The high point in campaign drama was probably reached four years ago, on September 26, 1960, when an event took place that was a milestone in campaign history.

In a television studio in Chicago, John F. Kennedy and Richard M. Nixon engaged in the first of four "great debates." In fact, the encounters were neither "great" by oratorical standards, nor were they "debates." They were a kind of two-headed press conference in which a small group of reporters asked each candidate in turn his views on a given issue. There was a moderator, who didn't have much moderating to do, and both candidates tended to repeat the general statements they had been making for months.

Measuring the Men

But the show—and a show it was—was significant because it permitted 70 million Americans to study the reactions of the two hopefuls under conditions of intense pressure. In such a situation the men could be compared and measured—and the voter could do his comparing and measuring in the quiet and privacy of his own home.

As it turned out, Kennedy had the better of it in the first debate, sitting rock-calm while his rival was speaking, and then rising to address his replies to the television camera with force and frankness. Nixon, an expert debater, chose to direct his remarks more to his adversary than to his unseen audience, the audience that was also his judge. And Nixon's effectiveness was further diminished by his physical appearance at the time.

The Republican candidate was just recovering from a cold. And this illness, together with his heavy campaign schedule, had left him several pounds below his normal weight and looking weary. His shirt collar sagged, the studio lights exaggerated his pallid complexion and the dark circles under his eyes, and the TV camera exposed the roots of his beard under his light skin—even though he had just shaved.

Nixon came back strong in the three subsequent dabtes; his health returned and more complimentary lighting and facial makeup were used. But that first encounter had served

The first TV debate between Kennedy and Nixon in 1960. It wasn't viewed as a close shave.

★★★★★★★★★★★★★★★★★★★★★★★★★★

to show the youthful-looking Kennedy as his rival's equal, and Nixon's previous advantage of being better known to the people was erased.

Asked after the election if he could have won without the television debates, Kennedy replied: "I don't think so."

Thus, a new and dramatic feature has been added to Presidential campaigning, one that is likely to figure in some form in all future races for the White House. There are proposals now for even more debates between the candidates in 1964, beginning soon after Labor Day with the final encounter on Election Eve.

Unlike 1960, when neither candidate was an incumbent President, the 1964 debates would see a President of the United States sharing the aura of his office with an antagonist who can only gain by standing on the same stage with the Chief Executive. But so far, President Johnson has indicated little interest in thus accommodating an opponent.

Campaign techniques have come a long way since 1789, when George Washington was elected, or since 1840 when the Whigs conducted a campaign consisting of little more than songs and slogans, or 1860 when Lincoln made no speeches because he feared anything he might say would aggravate rifts within the country. Even so, barnstorming politicians are not peculiar to the Twentieth Century, nor are campaign buttons and banners.

One of the most memorable early stumping demonstrations didn't occur in a Presidential election year at all. In 1866, President Andrew Johnson campaigned about the country in behalf of his moderate policies. This trip completely failed to set a style. Johnson was continually heckled and, unwisely, he attempted to reply to his hecklers—thereby making indiscreet statements that were quickly picked up by the radical press and other proponents of stiff retaliatory measures against the de-

* * * * * * * * * * * * * * *

feated South. After seeing what happened to Johnson, few politicians were inclined to try whistle-stopping during Presidential campaigns or between them.

It wasn't until 1896, when William Jennings Bryan led the Democratic Party against Republican William McKinley, that a standard bearer stumped the nation. And stump Bryan did, covering more than 18,000 miles and making 600 speeches to five million people.

Bryan's best weapon was a tremendous voice that could reach to the farthest corner of a hall, and it was this weapon that determined his strategy. His aides lived in constant dread of laryngitis stilling that great voice at a key moment, and so Bryan was regularly plied with compresses, gargles and cough drops. Gargling is a tiresome sport, however, and Bryan finally told his lieutenants he would forego the treatments and take his chances. Not once did his heavy-duty larynx fail him.

McKinley, for his part, employed a strategy that was the exact opposite of Bryan's. Not only did he not budge from his home in Canton, Ohio, but he requested the people to come to Canton if they wanted to hear what he had to say. McKinley, billed as the "Advance Agent of Prosperity," concurred in the generally held belief that a Presidential candidate should remain in dignified waiting until election day, although McKinley himself had actively pleaded his cause when he was running for lesser offices.

A Few Choice Words

Under the supervision of McKinley's political mastermind, Mark Hanna, special trains carrying thousands of people chugged into Canton. The delegations, representing farmers, merchants, Civil War veterans, railroad workers, and racial and religious groups, came in a continuing pilgrimmage to hear a few choice words from McKinley (McKinley not only required all questions to be submitted in advance, but he often had the questions rephrased to his advantage). The mass arrivals in Canton and the candidate's carefully-prepared speeches, questions, and answers provided continual—and favorable—copy for McKinley in the nation's press.

Meanwhile, Mark Hanna was also overseeing the distribution of millions of pamphlets and leaflets, some of them printed in eight languages, and aimed at practically every group in the country. Billboards bearing McKinley's likeness sprang up by the hundreds and tens of thousands of school children were given brightly colored McKinley buttons.

Between them, the hard-traveling Bryan and the well-organized McKinley had introduced the basic features of a modern Presidential campaign.

William Howard Taft, a man whose judicial temperament did not take naturally to stumping, found that campaign procedures had undergone such a change by 1908 that, like it or not, he had to go to the people. His opponent was the traveling man, W. J. Bryan.

Four years later Teddy Roosevelt traveled far and wide to assemble a string of convention victories as he sought in vain to block Taft's renomination.

Library of Congress

Organizer Marcus Alonzo Hanna.

Culver

Orator-Traveler William Jennings Bryan.

But until the 1920s, it was still impossible for a candidate to reach a majority of the voters directly. The advent of radio changed this, permitting a man to speak at once to thousands, and later millions, without so much as raising his voice. It was a boon to politicians with resonant tones and educated enunciations. But for the 1928 Democratic candidate, Alfred E. Smith, with his New York Lower East Side accent, radio was no friend at all.

It took a New York aristocrat to show how the wireless could be used for maximum effect. Between 1928 and 1932, hundreds of thousands of American homes acquired radios for the first time, giving candidates Herbert Hoover and Franklin Roosevelt a far wider radio audience than Hoover and Smith had had in 1928.

And if Hoover's radio manner had been superior to Smith's, then in 1932 Roosevelt's radio manner was far superior to Hoover's. President Hoover was articulate but flat-sounding. FDR possessed a mellow voice and an actor's instinct. Roosevelt recognized that radio required a more intimate delivery; the audience, after all, was scattered in countless living rooms, and appeals to crowd psychology did not apply in the same way.

Reach Not for Relief

What was true of radio three decades ago, is even more true of television today. Now not only a man's voice but his every mannerism is bared by the TV camera. By campaign's end, an observant voter should have a good picture of a candidate's stock of suits and neckties. A candidate, emotionally at ease but perspiring under the lights of a hot TV studio, will think twice about reaching for his handkerchief to mop his brow. Such a movement could suggest to millions of voters that the candidate is feeling the pressure. And, of course, if the White House aspirant has an itchy scalp, he dare not see to it lest the gesture be construed as one of puzzlement.

In 1952, two things happened that presaged important changes in campaign techniques. Richard Nixon, then the GOP candidate for Vice President, was accused of benefiting from a private fund set up by some California businessmen. There was talk of dropping Nixon from the ticket.

At this moment of crisis in his career, Nixon demonstrated his shrewd political instincts. He replied to the charge by going on

Alfred E. Smith: The mike was no friend.

television—with his wife, his two young daughters and the family dog—to narrate the story of his humble beginnings and to protest his honesty. The Democrats screamed that the Nixon performance was soap opera. Whatever it was, it worked. Thousands of telegrams and letters poured in from sympathetic viewers; Nixon had changed an almost fatal liability into an asset in a few minutes on television.

That same year a Democratic Senator from Tennessee tried to win his party's Presidential nomination by capitalizing on a Congressional investigation into organized crime. Estes Kefauver had directed the investigation and had become widely known because the crime hearings were televised. Senator Kefauver's biggest obstacle in gaining the nomination was his unpopularity with the party leadership.

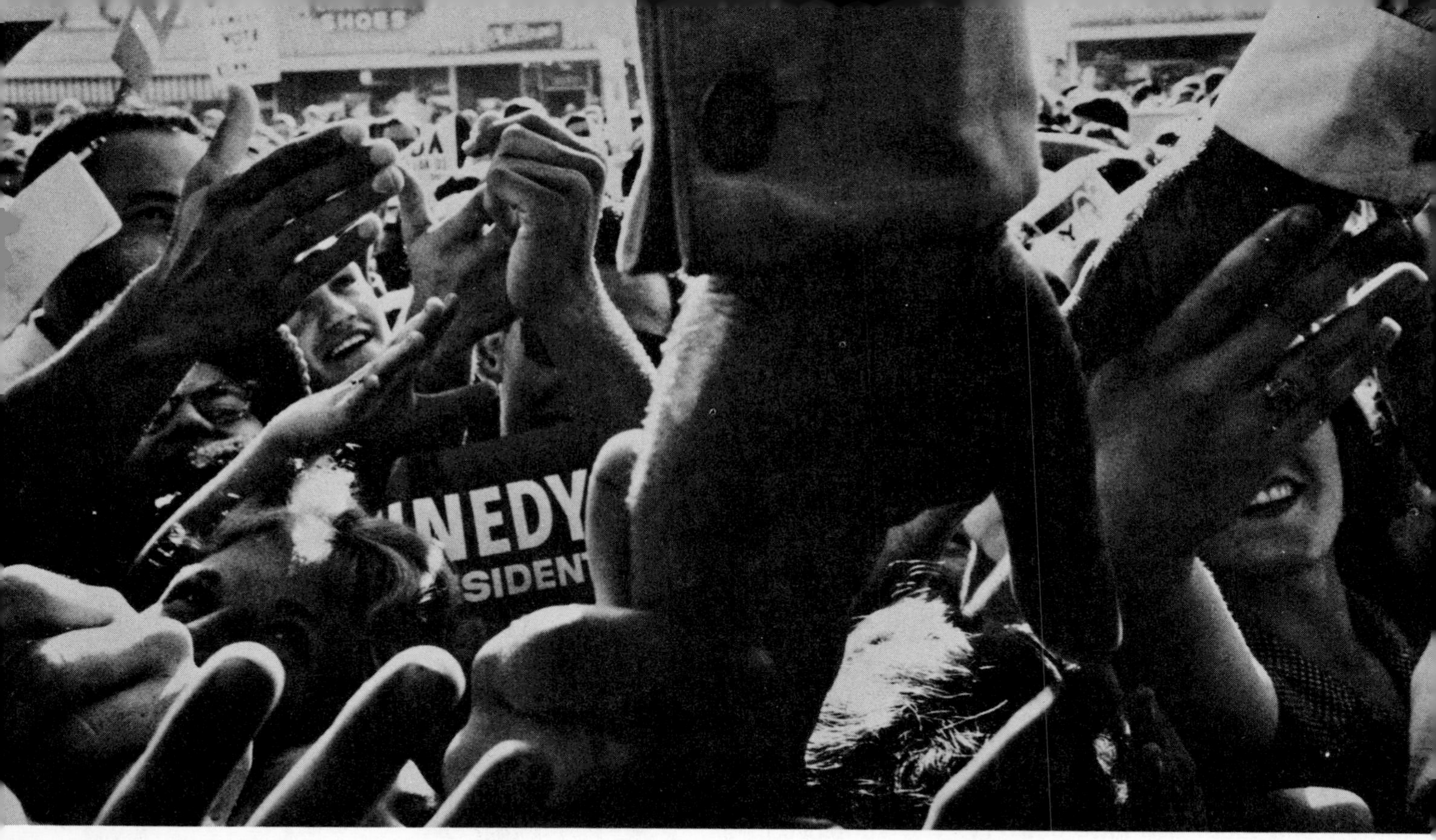

IPS

John F. Kennedy, campaigning for President, extends his hands to the source of power.

Kefauver decided to remove this obstacle by winning a string of state primaries, and this he did. He did it by campaigning like one running for county sheriff. In the New Hampshire primary alone, Kefauver walked miles through snowy village streets and shook hands with thousands of people ("Hi. I'm Estes Kefauver. I'm running for President of the United States.").

So energetic was his handshaking assault that his hand became swollen and raw. Once he got his arm stuck in a bank teller's window as he reached through the bars to shake hands with a flattered employe. To the surprise of nearly everyone except the delighted people of New Hampshire, Estes Kefauver won the primary with ease.

It was not enough to convince the party chieftains, however, and the Tennessee Senator tried the same tactics in 1956. Again he was successful in the primaries, so successful his victories forced his more reserved adversary, Adlai Stevenson, to plunge into the primaries with the same kind of hand-to-hand fighting.

Americans apparently love to shake hands. Senator Kefauver was a far wiser and far more effective campaigner than he has been given credit for. One reason he beat out John F. Kennedy for the Democratic Vice Presidential nomination in 1956 is that for years he had sent Christmas cards to thousands of party members—party members who would likely be national convention delegates. In his travels, too, he would often stop by the homes of lower-ranking Democrats, and these friendly, intimate visits were not forgotten.

John F. Kennedy and his high command borrowed many of these Kefauver tactics in their bid for the Presidential nomination in 1960.

But Kennedy added many fillips of his own. Aside from organizing his campaign with an efficiency surpassing even James A. Farley's great efforts for Franklin Roosevelt, Kennedy himself skillfully developed a public personality more winning than that of any contemporary public figure except Eisenhower.

Nor did he develop this public presence overnight. As recently as 1958, two years after he decided to try for the Presidency, Kennedy was often visibly nervous as he addressed a party gathering; nor did he then possess the wit and facility for extempore speaking that marked his Presidential news conferences. But Kennedy understood the art of seeming artless; he understood that no two qualities were more important for a political personality than the seemingly contradictory ones of discretion and frankness. These are qualities that journalists are quick to spot and which the electorate gradually comes to know.

Candid and Considerate

The Washington press corps, a group that plays a key role in any Presidential campaign, was extremely friendly to the Kennedy candidacy because he was candid and considerate.

One veteran Washington reporter put it this way: "Jack Kennedy was exactly the way Jack Kennedy appeared on television or anywhere else. In a fight there was nobody tougher. But he went out of his way to avoid making a malicious crack about a political enemy. He believed that people were either 'civilized' or 'uncivilized,' but he could be as gracious to a man he regarded as 'uncivilized' as he was to someone he really respected.

"Kennedy's best campaign weapon was the Kennedy personality. He knew that reporters could spot a phony fast, and that their readers would soon get the hint. Kennedy was designing all right—he wouldn't have won the Presidency if he hadn't been—but his design was to be on the level. He knew an open-faced manner would pay off in an age of mass communication. And I guess he was right."

Some students of modern politics lament the heavy injection of public relations techniques in Presidential campaigns. These critics often charge that such techniques promote a "cult of personality" in which the candidate's charm or lack of it is given too much weight by the voters.

"The truth is," said one unhappy observer, "that what the American people want in a President is a famous smile."

Said another, "Let's face it. Nobody had talked sense to the American people since Adlai Stevenson first said: 'Let's talk sense to the American people'."

There are many ways for a candidate to use a campaign to become popular. In a time of mass communications, for instance, Harry S. Truman resorted to old-fashioned, Bryan-like stumping to get his message to the voters. Whether or not they liked his message, many voters couldn't help but admire Truman's courage in battling the heavy odds against him in 1948.

Supposedly, too, Nixon didn't have the "right" personality to attract wide support. But he lost the 1960 election to Kennedy by the slimmest of margins.

Also, there is a point of diminishing returns in political advertising as well as any other kind. Declared one 1960 Republican strategist: "The secret is to know when you're overdoing it. People can get damn tired of a singing commercial, and they can get just as tired of a candidate who is always on TV or a billboard saying the same thing."

There are cases, however, when a single sentence has won or lost an election.

In 1884, Republican James G. Blaine was running against Democrat Grover Cleveland. For a variety of reasons it was viewed as an extremely close race. Then a Presbyterian minister named Samuel D. Burchard greeted the GOP candidate in New York with one of the most potent remarks in U.S. political history: "We are Republicans," Burchard declared, "and don't propose to leave our party and identify ourselves with the party whose antecedents have been rum, Romanism and rebellion."

The Voters' Response

Blaine—poor Blaine—didn't catch the remark and made no reference to it in his reply. A reporter, however, had heard it and quickly passed it along to the local Democratic organization. Within hours, newspapers and handbills were carrying the minister's remark and the fact that Blaine had apparently been content to let this insult to Roman Catholics pass undisputed. Enough Irish votes were believed lost by Blaine to give New York—and the election—to Cleveland.

One sentence worked just the opposite way for Dwight D. Eisenhower in 1952. It was a short sentence: "I will go to Korea." Some analysts claim Ike won the election the first time he uttered the line to a people tired and frustrated by the bloody Korean standoff.

In 1916, Woodrow Wilson won re-election with the slogan: "He kept us out of war." In 1940, Franklin Roosevelt promised: "Your sons are not going to be sent into any foreign wars."

Public opinion polls have shown that millions of Americans don't make up their minds about whom to vote for until just before election day. Therefore, any serious change in the

President Truman was expected to lose his bid for a full term in 1948. The pollsters apparently spoke to the wrong people.

world situation can have a decisive effect upon the results.

On the weekend before the election of 1956, the Israeli-Egyptian war exploded and for a time it appeared that America's security might be in danger. The voters supported the Commander-in-Chief—while at the same time giving the opposition party, the Democrats, majorities in both houses of Congress. This hadn't happened in 100 years, and it was probably due to Ike's personal popularity as much as to the trouble abroad.

But, as one 1960 Kennedy strategist put it: "You never know how things are going to break toward the end of a campaign, at a time when you really don't have enough time before election day to recoup. All you can do is go after all the votes you can and hope you have enough of a cushion if something happens."

Certainly if Thomas E. Dewey had run scared in 1948, he might well have overcome Harry Truman's effective campaign. It doesn't do to be half safe in politics.

A main—and risky—standby of any political campaign is the campaign promise. Both Franklin Roosevelt in 1932 and Dwight Eisenhower in 1952 promised mightily to reduce Federal spending. They wound up increasing it by billions.

Such form reversals after a candidate is elected often have honorable explanations, but their effect is to make people increasingly skeptical about politicians' integrity—a skepticism that doesn't need any increasing. Beyond that, unfulfilled promises can come back to spook the promiser.

Exactly what kind of campaign a candidate decides to mount, and what he decides to say, is determined by his own and his opponent's strengths and weaknesses. Basically though, because a President is elected by a majority of the electoral vote, rather than the popular vote, candidates campaign hardest in the more populous states that have large electoral votes. When they don't, they don't succeed.

In 1960, Richard Nixon promised a cheering convention he would go to all 50 states, and so he did. No doubt the people of Alaska were happy to see the Vice President drop in shortly before the election; certainly the Alaskans gave Nixon all the electoral votes they had: Three.

Richard M. Nixon went whistle-stopping in his 1952 campaign for the Vice Presidency. His real locomotive was called the General.

WHISTLE-STOPPING

A whistle stop is another term for a small town, the kind of town that railroad trains stop at only on signal, to which the engineer responds by tooting his whistle.

In political parlance, whistle-stopping refers to a candidate's traveling from small town to small town to bring his message to the voters. Harry S Truman made this kind of campaign famous in 1948, when he won thousands of votes from the rear platform of a "whistle-stopping" train, and won the election as well.

While Nixon was in Alaska, Kennedy was beating his way back and forth across New York, New Jersey and Illinois. On election day, those three states gave Mr. Kennedy 88 electoral votes.

An interesting fact about the American electoral process is that a candidate need carry only 12 states—providing they're the right ones—to win the Presidency. Putting it the other way, a candidate could carry 38 of the 50 states and still lose the election. For this reason White House aspirants get a special gleam in their eye when they contemplate such grand old names as California, New York, Ohio, Pennsylvania, Michigan, New Jersey, Texas, Massachusetts, and Illinois.

It's not that politicians have anything against the people of a sparsely populated state like Alaska. As a Democratic strategist put it: "Alaska is a nice place to live, but with three electoral votes I wouldn't want to visit there."

Political Pollsters

Unless a candidate wants to rush blindly about the country, speaking whatever thoughts pop into his head, he must begin with a good idea of what various groups of voters are thinking about. He will want to know, too, what various groups of voters think about *him*. To get this information, John F. Kennedy hired a professional pollster, Louis Harris, who took samplings of opinion in areas of particular interest to the Democratic candidate. By election time, 1960, Harris' firm had polled more people throughout the nation than any political analyst ever did.

There is little doubt that Harris' reports contributed importantly to Kennedy's success, and 1964 will almost surely see both major candidates adopt the same intensive research methods.

But there are other public opinion polls, independent of the political parties, that have had a growing influence on Presidential campaigns. These are polls such as those conducted by Dr. George Gallup and Elmo Roper. Based on a sampling of opinion, scientifically taken, the pollsters claim they can figure out what millions of Americans are thinking. Such opinion-sampling has been going on for decades, but it was the 1948 election, when all the polls were dead wrong, that brought them wide public notice.

Despite respectable records of accuracy in predicting elections, the public opinion polls have not won universal trust.

The skepticism is usually put something like this: "A Republican dentist in Tenafly, New Jersey, can't speak for a Republican dentist in Detroit."

The argument against the polls is based on the idea that countless factors determine a man's voting decision, and that it's erroneous to project a sampling so that the findings are represented as the national sentiment. But the success of the pollsters in recent elections has tended to give them increased prestige and their tabulations are now given great weight in plotting campaign strategies.

Some pundits don't like polls during a campaign whether the polls are right or not because, it's alleged, they exert an unhealthy influence on the voter. According to this argument, a pollster's report that the people favor a certain candidate is in itself a great boost for that candidate, and therefore tends to unfairly influence the decisions of other voters.

Mounting Expenses

Nevertheless, public interest in a candidate's chances is so great there's little likelihood the pollsters will be out of work soon. And especially since Kennedy's success with polling in 1960, all major candidates in the future will probably rely on pollsters' findings.

Hiring opinion samplers, though, is just one of many additional expenses a candidate and a party must reckon with. Thus, money in large amounts is exceedingly important to a campaign, and politicians regularly must pass the hat around. But large donations from "interested" supporters can themselves be a headache.

In 1936, labor leader John L. Lewis saw to it that his unions contributed $500,000 to FDR's war chest. Lewis naturally expected that after kicking in such a sum he might reasonably expect to have some influence around the White House. When President Roosevelt refused to go along with Lewis' plans, the labor chief complained loudly about the ingratitude of those who had "supped at Labor's table." And in 1940, Lewis refused to support FDR's bid for a third term.

Wealthy party contributors, of course, often expect glamorous Government jobs in return, especially ambassadorial appointments. Efforts have been made by both major parties to increase public participation in campaign financing by soliciting many small contributions. The success of these efforts has not been great.

Ancient Passions

Since 1910 bills have been offered in Congress from time to time to have the Government pay campaign costs. Such bills have never gotten very far because it's believed few taxpayers would like the idea and the candidates would continue to spend additional funds anyway.

The Republicans are often said to have the bigger purses to work with. But when the amount spent on "political education" by organized labor is added to the Democratic total, the figures are very close. The Democrats and unions together in 1960 accounted for 50.7% of all funds reported spent on the 1960 national campaign. The Republicans accounted for 46.1%, with miscellaneous groups making up the remainder.

Campaign costs continue to go up, and campaign techniques become ever more complicated and sophisticated. But the campaign's basic idea—winning votes—hasn't changed since the days of the Founders.

The Smithsonian Institution houses the fascinating Ralph E. Becker collection of campaign memorabilia, including buttons and ribbons dating back to George Washington. In these mementos the ancient passions of American politics, many long cold, come alive again. And they are useful reminders.

They remind us that the right to disagree with one another is part of our heritage, and that a hot Presidential campaign, far from being a threat to national unity, serves our common cause. Controversy is not the foe of freedom. It is the forge.

1956

CLEVELAND THURMAN

1888

FOR PRESIDENT
JOHN F. KENNEDY

1960

NIXON LODGE

1960

Keep Cool-idge

1924

DEWEY WARREN

1948

A GALLANT LEADER

FRANKLIN D. ROOSEVELT

1932

GENERAL GRANT PRESIDENT

1868

MARTIN VANBUREN

1836

VOTE
TRUMAN
FOR PRESIDENT

1948

STEVENSON ADLAI ALL THE WAY

1952

Chapter VI

the Third Party

After the Last Straw, the Last Resort

The fabric of America's two major political parties is similar to the fabric in women's stretch pants: There is enough "give" to accommodate almost anyone, but in some cases the strain in crucial areas finally leads to a dramatic parting.

When this happens—in politics—the result is the third party, an exercise in outrage that has historically complicated the affairs of Democrats and Republicans alike. While three's a crowd in a two-party system, and therefore a third party has scant chance of victory, it can and often has functioned as a spoiler, splitting the vote of a major party and thereby giving the prize to the other major party. In 1964,

the threat of a party schism is spooking both Democrats and Republicans.

For the Democrats the threat comes from the South where, since the 1940s, there has been a growing disaffection with the national party leadership. The thorny issue is the two-headed one of Negro rights and states' rights, with many Southerners embittered by what they view as unwarranted Federal intrusion in the life and customs of the South. These customs include the segregation of Negroes and whites, an arrangement which the Government has sought to destroy through friendly persuasion, legislation, Supreme Court decisions, and the use of Federal troops.

Since 1961, this Federal pressure on the traditionally Democratic South has been directed by a Democratic Administration—a fact that has brought an angry response from the most determined segregationists in Dixie.

Governors George Wallace of Alabama and Paul Johnson of Mississippi are leading a movement to run slates of electors in Southern states who are pledged to neither party's candidate. Instead, the electors would be pledged to the idea of preserving racial segregation.

Emphasizing Deep Feelings

The plan's supporters expect to accumulate at least enough votes for the unpledged electors to emphasize to the nation how deeply many Southerners feel about preserving racial segregation. Secondly, and more ambitiously, these strategists hope to capture the electoral votes of enough Southern states to hold a balance of power in the Electoral College. In such an advantageous position, the segregationists believe they would win important concessions to their point of view.

The Republicans, too, may find that in 1964 they are no longer able to contain the warring factions within their ranks. The liberal Eastern faction, led by New York Governor Rockefeller, has indicated it would not support a conservative candidate, such as Senator Goldwater, running on a conservative platform. GOP conservatives, for their part, say they've had enough of Eastern Republican "me-tooism." Because the ideological gap between the Goldwater and Rockefeller contingents is so wide, an agreement such as the one reached by Nixon and Rockefeller in 1960 may not be possible this year.

Thus, on paper at least, the Republicans possess the classic conditions for a party split —two large camps with viewpoints so incompatible as to try the ingenuity of Solomon. Indeed, perhaps only the implications of a party schism, which could well scatter the Republican vote to the winds, will force the antagonists to remain under the same banner. Politicians, after all, have long memories, and both parties have bloodied these battlefields before.

The battlefields of Negro rights and liberal Republicanism have been the scenes of continual sniping and skirmishing between elections. Usually though, faced with the job of fighting the other party, the factions will arrange a truce before or during the convention.

Thus, intra-party strife is most often settled by compromise, although sometimes an issue is "compromised" simply by dodging it. The offending question is sugared over with vague statements designed to repel as few party members as possible.

When Andrew Jackson was President, for instance, his supporters were divided over the tariff issue. The South, producer of large, staple crops, preferred a low tariff for revenue only. In the Northeast, the new industrial interests favored a higher protective tariff. To avoid losing the support of either area, the Democrats took the suggestion of the artful New York politician, Martin Van Buren.

Instead of presenting a definite stand on the tariff to the electorate, the party concentrated on other issues. This technique prevailed for more than 50 years, until Grover Cleveland injected the question into the campaign of 1888.

But when the leaders of a party cannot resolve their differences—or avoid them—their battling breaks the party apart. This kind of split, at the top of the party, has been a major source of third party efforts in past Presidential elections. One such experience, the 1912 Republican rupture that produced the Bull Moose Party of Teddy Roosevelt, quickly comes to mind. Less well known is the Republican schism of 1872. The impetus of this earlier break came from a reform element that grew up in the Republican Party during its post-Civil War supremacy.

A Radical Doctrine

Even before Appomatox, the pre-Civil War anti-slavery sentiment in the GOP was converted into a radical and severe doctrine of governing the defeated South, and Republican moderates were increasingly alienated by this policy.

These dissatisfied moderate groups, who were especially strong in the border states, not only opposed the Grant administration's Reconstruction program in the South, but they also vigorously attacked the corruption and favoritism of Grant's political proteges. To this anti-Grant group was lent the support of several leading newspapers, along with some important politicians who sought revenge for Grant's erratic distribution of patronage.

After leaving the party, they organized a separate convention, adopted the name Liberal Republicans, and picked the editor of the New York *Tribune,* Horace Greeley, as their candidate. Greeley was a discouragingly poor choice as a Presidential candidate because he had a wide reputation for eccentricity, a quality almost always fatal in politics. His appearance was certainly curious. He habitually wore a long linen duster, white hat and socks, and a fringe of white chin whiskers. During his long editorship of the *Tribune,* moreover, he frequently contradicted himself. Too, he advocated a number of generally unappealing causes such as vegetarianism.

A Vulnerable Candidate

In his essential goodness, his surplus of ideas, and ceaseless experimentation, Greeley was not unlike Ben Franklin. As a Presidential candidate, however, he was extremely vulnerable. Under the circumstances, the Democrats endorsed him, but without enthusiasm.

The campaign quickly degenerated into an exchange of smears by the opposing machines; the sincere and outspoken editor was more vulnerable to pitiless lampoons of his eccentricities than the hero General was to the attacks on his blunders and permissiveness. Despite the support of nearly the entire Democratic vote (the official candidate of the war-weakened Democrats was a non-entity), the Liberal Republicans were decisively beaten.

The reform element in the GOP had failed as party organizers, and they did not try to form a third party again. Like the conservative Republicans of today, however, they did continue to make themselves felt within the party. In 1876 they had the satisfaction of seeing their party nominate Rutherford B. Hayes, who represented their lenient attitude toward the South. And they were active in the subsequent compromise of 1877 that put Hayes in the White House and ended Republican political coercion of the former Confederate States.

With the Reconstruction issue settled, the Republican independents turned to the problems of civil service reform and honesty in government. Under Hayes, and during the subsequent Garfield-Arthur administration, progress was made in these areas.

But the Republican nomination of James G. Blaine in 1884 was viewed as a setback by GOP reformers, who were now called Mugwumps. They announced they would not support Blaine and called for the Democrats to select a reform ticket. The Democrats obliged. Their candidate, Grover Cleveland, backed by the Mugwumps, won a narrow victory.

Twenty-eight years later, after a period of relative peace within the party, Republicanism was split as if by an ax. But the 1912 schism was a good deal more than an updated rehearsal of the Mugwump fight for clean government. Now the discontented faction of the GOP was agitating for such things as direct primaries, woman suffrage, unemployment insurance, a graduated income tax, and a lower tariff.

During the Congressional sessions before the 1912 conventions, this "progressive" wing allied itself with Democrats to try to legislate such innovations. President Taft and his Congressional lieutenants resisted these efforts, and the differences between the GOP factions were widened further when ex-President Roosevelt began speaking out on the issues of the day. Roosevelt's speeches outlined a sweeping program that offered the liberal group guidance and leadership in the areas of Federal action and reform.

President Taft upheld most of Roosevelt's earlier policies. The difficulty was that what was called "progressive Republicanism" in Roosevelt's hands in 1908, became "Taft conservatism" by 1912. And the country wasn't in a mood for conservatism; the reformers were rushing ahead with a comprehensive program that seemed to have the approval of large sections of the population.

A candidate again, Teddy Roosevelt rolled into the national convention in Chicago with support so widespread it had the makings of a bandwagon. The direct Presidential primary had come into use in a number of states, and during the spring the voters had given T.R. an overwhelming endorsement. He was clearly the choice of the party's rank and file.

MUGWUMPS

"Mugwump" is an Algonquin Indian term for "big chief," and it was used, at first chidingly, a century ago to describe a reform element in American politics. Occasionally the name is dusted off today to label any reform movement within a party. Less respectfully, a Mugwump has been described as a fellow "who has his mug on one side of the fence and his wump on the other."

THE THIRD PARTY

Where the state convention method of selecting delegates prevailed, the Republican machine operated effectively for Taft, and he came into the convention with almost half the delegates on his side. Roosevelt had more than a quarter of them and nearly that many were contested.

When the Republican National Committee, dominated by Taft men, seated only a scattering of Roosevelt delegates, T.R. ordered his men to sit on their hands. The refusal of the Roosevelt forces to participate made Taft's renomination a formality—and meant that no compromise was possible between the two wings of the party.

The Roosevelt followers (dubbed Bull Moosers because their leader had proclaimed himself as strong as one) later held an emotional convention of their own, to give their blessing to their leader, to take the official name of Progressives, and to adopt one of the most detailed platforms ever drafted by an American party.

No Time to Organize

The platform demanded direct primaries, direct election of Senators (they were still elected by state legislatures in many states), recall of state judicial decisions, woman suffrage, unemployment insurance, sick pay, old age insurance, a business regulatory commission, income tax, inheritance tax, parcel post, a department of labor, a lower tariff, a broader conservation program, and a more elastic currency.

It was tall order.

Although the Progressives marshalled considerable zeal and had substantial backing, they faced a serious problem in organizing a national party between the time of their defection from the Republican Party in June and the election in November. The Progressive policy makers decided to concentrate on the head of the slate, and to make terms with the regular Republicans on the lesser offices, or simply let them go by default. This decision explains the relatively poor showing the Progressives made in the 1912 Congressional elections in comparison with their Presidential vote (see map).

The failure of the Bull Moose Party illustrates some of the problems of the third party in American politics. Even with substantial financial backing and the broad appeal of its program and leadership, the Progressives' lack of thorough organization proved an insuperable

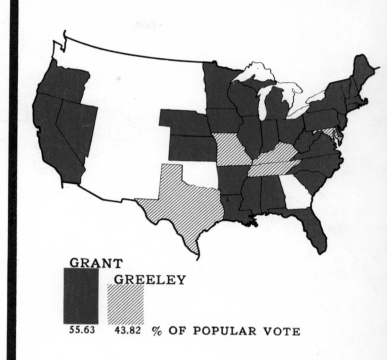

ELECTION OF 1872

GRANT
GREELEY
55.63   43.82   % OF POPULAR VOTE

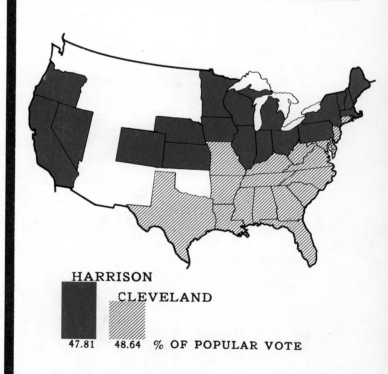

ELECTION OF 1888

HARRISON
CLEVELAND
47.81   48.64   % OF POPULAR VOTE

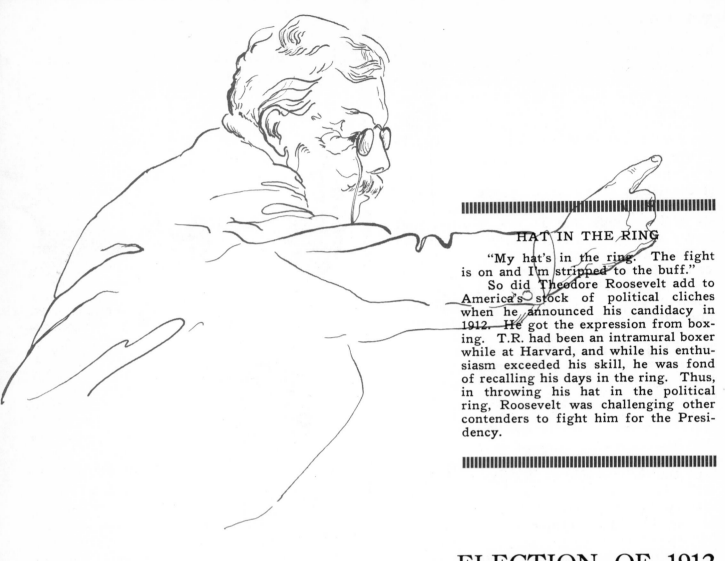

HAT IN THE RING

"My hat's in the ring. The fight is on and I'm stripped to the buff."

So did Theodore Roosevelt add to America's stock of political cliches when he announced his candidacy in 1912. He got the expression from boxing. T.R. had been an intramural boxer while at Harvard, and while his enthusiasm exceeded his skill, he was fond of recalling his days in the ring. Thus, in throwing his hat in the political ring, Roosevelt was challenging other contenders to fight him for the Presidency.

ELECTION OF 1912

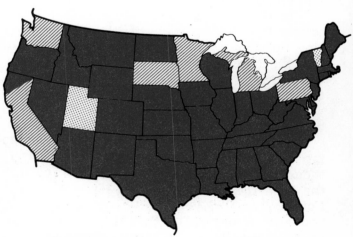

WILSON

T. ROOSEVELT

TAFT

41.85   27.42   23.15 % OF POPULAR VOTE

handicap. The need for these three ingredients in combination—organization, money and popularity—are evident also in the careers of three pre-Civil War third parties: The Know-Nothings, the Republicans and the Unionists.

A Party Perishes

The breakdown of the Compromise of 1850 after the election of 1852 signaled the collapse of the Whigs as a national party. The Compromise had been worked out by moderate leaders of both parties for the purpose of permanently settling the divisive issue of slavery's status in the new territories acquired from Mexico and Britain in the 1840s.

In 1852, however, the Democrats won overwhelming control of Congress. An exceptionally large number of Southern Democrats gave the pro-slavery advocates tight control of the party. Under these conditions, the Southerners were able to force through the Kansas-Nebraska Act which repealed certain moderate features of the Compromise of 1850 and the similar Compromise of 1820.

As the sectional crisis continued, more and more voters—North and South—abandoned the idea of compromise and moderation that had kept the sections and parties together before 1852. The great Whig leaders, Webster and Clay, were dead; in their place no one had emerged to rally the electorate to repudiate the immoderates and to re-establish compromise as the method of dealing with national problems. This erosion of the center—in the electorate and the leadership—was fatal to the Whigs, and almost fatal to the Union.

In the Old Northwest, from Ohio to Iowa, former Free Soilers and abolitionists were stirring up emotion against the Kansas-Nebraska Act, which extended slavery into previously free territories. The Whigs of the Old Northwest turned to this "anti-Nebraska" movement in wholesale lots. Thus was the Republican Party born.

In the East, meanwhile, Whigs were defecting to another new political movement. Although there was anti-Nebraska sentiment in the East, the anti-foreign, anti-Catholic Know-Nothings were more important in the confused two years before the election of 1856. By 1856, so little was left of the Whig Party, that no national convention could be held. The only significant remnant, New York's conservative Whigs, joined with the Know-Nothings in nominating Millard Fillmore, who had been the last Whig to live in the White House.

The campaign proved to be the turning point for the two aspiring young parties. The Know-Nothings did not take a strong stand on the slavery issue, and as a result lost much of their Northern support. Other than nativism, there was little to distinguish the Know-Nothings from the Democrats, with whom they competed for votes. Because nativism was not a popular issue, the Know-Nothings trailed the better-organized Democrats and the more popular Republicans. The infant Republican Party carried 11 free states, including giant New York, and a third of the popular vote.

The Republicans became a major party after the election of 1856 because they combined the important elements of popularity, organization and financial backing. Only the Republicans offered a definite stand—the Wilmot Proviso—against extension of slavery into the western territories. With this emotional weapon in their arsenal, the Republicans made themselves popular. And, the Republicans expanded their popularity by skillfully including ideas to attract support from doubtful areas and wavering groups. Then they worked on organization.

Filling the War Chest

The Whigs of the Old Northwest, a minority party since 1844, went over to the anti-Nebraska cause almost unanimously, taking with them the entire Whig political machinery. The Republicans usurped most of the Eastern Whig organization in the same manner; thus, much of the Republican organization was born full-grown.

Having made themselves popular and acquiring the abandoned machinery of the old Whig Party, the Republicans then filled their war chest—chiefly by attracting former Whig businessmen.

The carefully drawn Republican platform of 1860 indicates the broadened interests of the party. It opposed slavery in the territories and thus pleased the abolitionists, yet it soothed the moderates by avoiding open advocacy of abolition. The platform also pledged to enact a homestead law for the many immigrants, laborers, and pioneers who could not buy farms at existing prices. Here, as the organization comes to include several interests, is the crucial point at which a crusading protest group becomes a political party.

The other important third party of the period, the Union Party, had a brief and unsuccessful history. The leaders of the Union effort were conservatives who opposed the sectionalism that was overtaking both major parties. After John Brown's raid in October of 1859, the sectional hostility seemed to many to be irreconcilable.

In 1860, the Democrats split over the sectional issue. A majority of the Southerners bolted the convention, nominated John Breckinridge of Kentucky, and wrote a platform endorsing the positive protection of slavery. Meanwhile, the Northern rump had chosen Stephen Douglas of Illinois, who wanted the slavery issue to be left to the residents of the states and territories for solution.

If they won the election themselves, the Union Party supporters reasoned, they would prevent the dangerous possibility of the victory of one sectional group and the resulting secession of the other. They were a stop-gap party, seeking to hold the Union together until the divisive issues could be resolved. Their principal strength was in the areas of the South where the slave population was small. There, in the upland regions and in the border states, the defense of slavery was not a paramount issue, and it seemed that the election of Lincoln would certainly cause the Southern radicals to lead the South out of the Union.

Three States for Bell

The Union Party candidate for President, John Bell of Tennessee, won the electorial votes of Virginia, Tennessee and Kentucky. In the other slave states he ran second, capturing 38% of the Southern vote. But, having failed in their purpose to prevent the dissolution of the Union, the Unionists ceased to exist as a party.

Thus, the 1850s had produced three new parties, but only one—the Republican—was able to put together the essential combination of financial support, broad popularity and party machinery reaching down to the grass-roots.

Another Nineteenth Century third party, the Populists, developed not from the top down, but from the grass-roots up. This "People's Party" was an expression of the resentment that spread across America's farmlands after the Civil War. Agrarian discontent had found vent in minor third party movements in the elections after 1872, as the cities grew and a new industrial economy forced painful personal and social readjustments on the rural American.

The farmer felt himself an outcast in the new society where revised values and changing economics seemed to alienate the agrarian life from the rest of America. The stereotype of the farmer changed from that of the industrious yeoman to that of the unmannered "hick"— reflecting a hostility toward the farming classes that was new in America.

Elusive Prosperity

At the same time, prosperity became elusive. Men were aroused; they were being deprived of their share in the growing wealth of the country. From the farmer's emotional reaction to the "hick" stigma, and his discontent with declining crop values, came an impulse to gain back the respectability and prosperity that the farmer thought were rightly his.

The political form of this impulse was the Populist movement.

From a base of local farm societies, the Populists developed into a national party. They attempted to expand their support throughout the debtor classes by endorsing the "soft" money idea at their convention of 1892. In the campaigns of 1892 and 1894, the People's Party adopted the tactic of fusion with the Democrats. Fusion and soft money helped the Populists win the popular vote in six Western states, gain successes in several Congressional races, and capture enough seats in the Senate to hold the balance of power there.

The Populists, too, were the first serious threat to the one-party rule that the Democrats had fixed on the South in 1877. There, the Democratic leaders cut the ground from under the People's Party by taking over Populist ideas for their own.

By 1896, the agrarian sentiment overtook the entire Democratic Party. In their platform, the Democrats endorsed many Populist proposals including the soft money plank. The Populists faced a dilemma. They could throw their support to the Democrats and thus lose their political identity, or they could go it alone and force a split in the agrarian "reform" vote. They decided on the former.

The Populists' dilemma illustrates yet another problem to be added to those faced by a third party: The third party that develops a

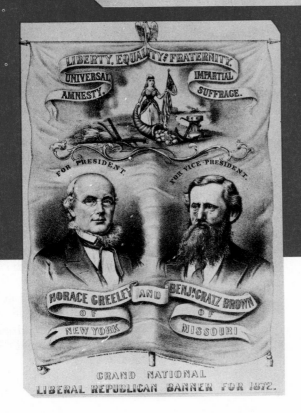

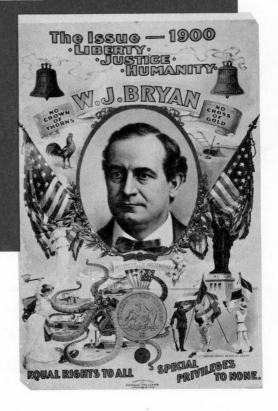

ELECTION OF 1892

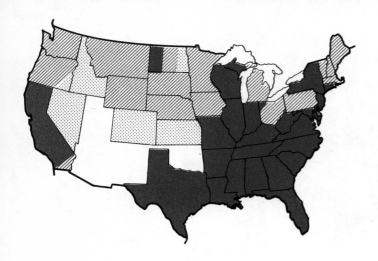

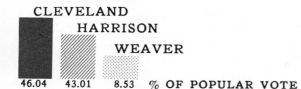

CLEVELAND
HARRISON
WEAVER

46.04   43.01   8.53   % OF POPULAR VOTE

ELECTION OF 1948

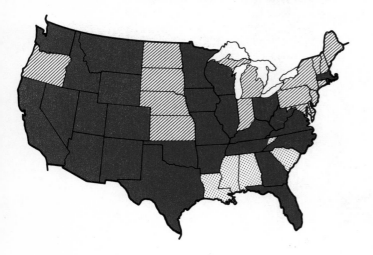

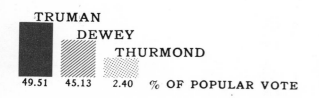

TRUMAN
DEWEY
THURMOND

49.51   45.13   2.40   % OF POPULAR VOTE

popular program runs the risk of having that program usurped by one of the major parties.

Shift of Sentiment

This same difficulty harassed the Progressives during and after the campaign of 1912. The Progressives seemed to be correct in identifying the mood of the country. Had the Democrats also selected a conservative like Taft, Roosevelt's more liberal position would have given him a decided advantage.

Instead, the Democrats picked the best man for the situation. Once a conservative, Woodrow Wilson had come to the reform movement at a time that coincided with the shift of political sentiment in the country. As Governor of New Jersey, Wilson had won the admiration of liberals, and the endorsement of the party's titular leader, William Jennings Bryan. By accepting some progressive ideas as a campaigner, and more as President, Wilson won enough of the liberal support to deprive the Progressives of any chance of attracting a majority of the voters.

Even when a third party has the additional blessing of a glamorous leader, it still needs the other ingredients. Teddy Roosevelt's leadership qualities could not overcome the Progressives' shortcomings in organization.

And, in 1948, the mixture of radicals, extreme liberals, and Communist sympathizers who made up a very different Progressive Party thought that Henry Wallace, the ardent old New Dealer, would make a wonderful leader. So did the ardent old New Dealer.

The Wallace people believed that, in the revolutionary post-war world, only radical changes would allow America to become the master, rather than the victim, of global upheaval. But the Progressives quickly got the reputation for harboring crackpots and Communists, and Henry Wallace himself drew far more fire than votes.

The radical Wallace platform called for immediate unilateral disarmament, immediate racial integration, and immediate destruction of nuclear weapons—three planks that made the Progressives immediately unpopular. In the election of 1948, Wallace served as Harry Truman's lightning rod; Wallace rather than Truman attracted the thunderbolts of the conservatives. Thus the regular Democratic nominee was freed of the stigma of excessive liberalism that had driven conservative Democrats in the

Grover Cleveland did not win a majority of the popular vote when he was elected in 1892, because a third party—the Populists—cut down the Democratic total.

Henry Wallace, the Progressive Party candidate for President in 1948, failed to hurt the Democrats. Wallace's third party attracted more fire than votes.

farm states out of the party in the Congressional elections of 1946.

Each of the third parties discussed so far has tried to build a national party. But since 1948, distinctly sectional third party movements have occurred in the South. In that year Southern Democrats, repelled by the civil rights plank in the national party platform, formed their own States' Rights Party in an effort to defeat the national Democratic ticket. But the Southern opposition was really not so much a bolt from the national party as it was an uprising of local Southern Democrats. Few Southern leaders of national importance were attracted to the movement.

In the four states where the sectionalists were able to control the state organizations, they could compel the Democratic electors to vote for their candidate, Governor Strom Thurmond of South Carolina. Elsewhere in the South, they had to run their electors on an independent slate. This tactic split the vote against Truman; some voters backed the independent ticket and some went Republican. Thus in Virginia, Tennessee, and Florida, Truman captured only a plurality of the vote but was able to carry these states (see map).

The issue that led to the formation of the States' Rights Party in 1948 is, if anything, hotter than ever in 1964. And, on the Republican side the emergence of Senator Goldwater, a conservative leader with vast popular appeal, may make it extremely difficult for liberal Republicans to dominate this year's national convention as neatly as they have every convention since 1940.

Whatever happens, any third party movement in 1964 would face the inevitable problems of organization, financing, popularity, and the ability to resist annexation by a major party. These problems can also be summarized as one problem—that of victory.

Teddy Roosevelt accurately identified this need for success shortly after his defeat on the Progressive ticket in 1912. Having few officeholders and little patronage, the party was in sorry shape. Although Roosevelt had made optimistic declarations about the eventual success of Progressivism, in private he was without illusions.

"There is only one thing to do," he told a friend, "and that is to go back to the Republican Party. You can't hold a party like the Progressive Party together. There are no loaves and fishes."

Chapter VII

the Various Americans 1789-1964

We the People of the United States, in Order to form a more perfect Union, establish Justice, insure domestic Tranquility, provide for the common defence, promote the general Welfare, and secure the Blessings of Liberty to ourselves and our Posterity, do ordain and establish this Constitution for the United States of America.

Article I

Section 1. All legislative Powers herein granted shall be vested in a Congress of the United States, which shall consist of a Senate and House of Representatives.

Section 2. The House of Representatives shall be composed of Members chosen every second Year by the People of the several States, and the Electors in each State shall have the Qualifications requisite for Electors of the most numerous Branch of the State Legislature.

No Person shall be a Representative who shall not have attained to the Age of twenty five Years, and been seven Years a Citizen of the United States, and who shall not, when elected, be an Inhabitant of that State in which he shall be chosen.

Representatives and direct Taxes shall be apportioned among the several States which may be included within this Union, according to their respective Numbers, which shall be determined by adding to the whole Number of free Persons, including those bound to Service for a Term of Years, and excluding Indians not taxed, three fifths of all other Persons. The actual Enumeration shall be made within three Years after the first Meeting of the Congress of the United States, and within every subsequent Term of ten Years, in such Manner as they shall by Law direct. The Number of Representatives shall not exceed one for every thirty Thousand, but each State shall have at Least one Representative; and until such enumeration shall be made, the State of New Hampshire shall be entitled to chuse three, Massachusetts eight, Rhode Island and Providence Plantations one, Connecticut five, New York six, New Jersey four, Pennsylvania eight, Delaware one, Maryland six, Virginia ten, North Carolina five, South Carolina five, and Georgia three.

When vacancies happen in the Representation from any State, the Executive Authority thereof shall issue Writs of Election to fill such Vacancies.

The House of Representatives shall chuse their Speaker and other Officers; and shall have the sole Power of Impeachment.

Section 3. The Senate of the United States shall be composed of two Senators from each State, chosen by the Legislature thereof, for six Years; and each Senator shall have one Vote.

Immediately after they shall be assembled in Consequence of the first Election, they shall be divided as equally as may be into three Classes. The Seats of the Senators of the first Class shall be vacated at the Expiration of the second Year, of the second Class at the Expiration of the fourth Year, and of the third Class at the Expiration of the sixth Year, so that one third may be chosen every second Year; and if Vacancies happen by Resignation, or otherwise, during the Recess of the Legislature of any State, the Executive thereof may make temporary Appointments until the next Meeting of the Legislature, which shall then fill such Vacancies.

No Person shall be a Senator who shall not have attained to the Age of thirty Years, and been nine Years a Citizen of the United States, and who shall not, when elected, be an Inhabitant of that State for which he shall be chosen.

The Vice President of the United States shall be President of the Senate, but shall have no Vote, unless they be equally divided.

The Senate shall chuse their other Officers, and also a President pro tempore, in the Absence of the Vice President, or when he shall exercise the Office of President of the United States.

The Senate shall have the sole Power to try all Impeachments. When sitting for that Purpose, they shall be on Oath or Affirmation. When the President of the United States the Chief Justice shall preside: And [illegible] shall be convicted without the Concurrence of two thirds of the Members present.

Judgment in Cases of Impeachment shall not [illegible] to removal from Office, and disqualification to hold and enjoy any Office of honor, Trust or Profit under the United States: but the Party [illegible] nevertheless be liable and subject to Indictment, Trial, Judgment and Punishment, according to Law.

Section 4. The Times, Places and Manner of holding Elections for Senators and Representatives, shall be prescribed in each State by the Legislature thereof; but the Congress may at any time by Law make or alter such Regulations, except as to the Places of chusing Senators.

[illegible] Congress shall assemble at least once in every Year, and such Meeting shall be on the first Monday in December, unless they shall by Law appoint a different Day.

Section 5. [illegible] the Elections, Returns and Qualifications of its own Members, and a Majority of each shall constitute a Quorum to do Business; [illegible] from day to day [illegible] provide.

Each House [illegible]

Member.

Each House shall keep a Journal of its Proceedings, and from time to time publish the same, excepting such Parts as may in their Judgment require Secrecy; and the Yeas and Nays of the Members of either House on any question shall, at the Desire of one fifth of those Present, be entered on the Journal.

Neither House, during the Session of Congress, shall, without the Consent of the other, adjourn for more than three days, nor to any other Place than that in which the two Houses shall be sitting.

Section 6. The Senators and Representatives shall receive a Compensation [illegible] of the Treasury of the United States. They shall in all Cases, except Treason, Felony and Breach of the Peace, be privileged [illegible] Attendance at the Session of their respective Houses, and in going to and returning [illegible] be questioned in any other Place.

No Senator or Representative shall, during the Time for which he was elected, be appointed to any civil Office under the Authority of the United States, which shall have been created, or the Emoluments whereof shall have been encreased during such time; and no Person holding any Office under the United States, shall be a Member of either House during his Continuance in Office.

Section 7. All Bills for raising Revenue shall originate in the House of Representatives; but the Senate may propose or concur with Amendments as on other Bills.

Every Bill which shall have passed the House of Representatives and the Senate, shall, before it become a Law, be presented to the President of the

It began with four million people on a strip of virgin coastland. The Atlantic Ocean lay to the east and to the west a great wall of mountains kept a continent's secret. It was a land of far horizons and it was a time for great beginnings.

After winning their independence from the English king, the Americans set about inventing the institutions that they hoped would guarantee freedom for themselves and their posterity. Not the wisest of them could, in the 1780s, possibly envision the evolution of the political process that they established for choosing a President. The vast, labyrinthian party structures with their complicated in-fighting and peculiar folklore were years away.

Looking back from 1964, it's clear that American history cannot be told only in terms of Presidential elections. Yet these battles do gather together the issues and wire them in a bunch, so it's possible to see, in the general way history allows, where the country has been by peeking in on every fourth year of the nation's past.

Only Externals Have Changed

What we find is that, over 175 years, only the externals of partisan warfare have really changed. And we are reminded that the old arguments over such things as the role of the Federal Government date back to the Founders.

There is a remarkable continuity, then, of issues and institutions. And this continuity in itself is part of the story of *Elections 1964*.

When George Washington was elected President in 1789, the idea of political parties was repugnant to most Americans. Parties, it was thought, cause internal unrest and foment revolution. But the nation was not 10 years old before it was becoming clear that political parties not only had their place in the Republic, but indeed were indispensible.

The first parties in the United States were the Federalists (the party of Washington, Adams and Hamilton) and the Republicans (the party of Jefferson and Madison). The Federalists succeeded for a few years in maintaining the fiction that they were not a party at all, while accusing their opponents of political organizing. This accusation doesn't make much sense today, but back in the 1790s a political organization was considered somehow un-American.

Their Presidents and Their Problems

Jefferson's party—the Republicans—are remembered by most people as the Democratic-Republicans, a name they formally assumed during the Presidency of Andrew Jackson. But during the nation's first decade, the word "Democratic" was an epithet, connoting rule by the mob, and was used to describe the Jeffersonians only by their enemies.

The Jeffersonian idea of society was neither a system of class strata nor a purely egalitarian arrangement. Equality of opportunity was the key by which an aristocracy of talent and virtue would rise to the top like cream in milk bucket.

Thomas Jefferson himself was fond of viewing the country as a land of yeomen, industrious, financially secure and unthreatened by unemployment. Commerce and industry should be developed only as necessary to insure the prosperity of agriculture.

Breakdown of Rigidity

There is little in the Jeffersonian program that strikes us as odd today, except perhaps the skepticism about commerce and industry. But in the 1790s the idea of a continually shifting aristocracy of talent was rather radical. In the Eighteenth Century, a man took his social station seriously and the rigidity of society, the order it provided, gave satisfaction to those at the top and bottom alike. Well, perhaps not quite alike. But the point is the poorer man was not generally discontented with his rank.

Toward the very end of the Eighteenth Century, however, there was a gradual movement away from the stable social structure to the kind of "atomized" society described by Jefferson. Still, rural and urban residents of older areas resisted the change; they prefered the principles of the Federalists.

The chief spokesman for the Federalists was Alexander Hamilton, a brilliant young lawyer who had married money and had attached himself to the interests of the wealthy urban class.

Hamilton believed the greatest danger to the United States was disintegration. He felt that an interdependent economic system throughout the states and a scheme for making the people and the states dependent upon the economic vitality of the Federal Government was the best way to assure a unified nation. The first Secretary of the Treasury secured Federal responsibility for the states' debts by issuing

Library of Congress

"It will not be too strong to say that there will be a constant probability of seeing (the Presidency) filled by characters preeminent for ability and virtue."—Alexander Hamilton.

116

Federal bonds to cover them. Thus, he believed, private creditors would have an interest in upholding the strength of the Federal Government.

Commerce was essential, according to the Federalist view, to hold the country together, and to expedite commerce Hamilton promoted legislation founding a national bank. Neither of these measures—the funding of state debts nor the national bank—were provided for in the Constitution.

Thus, Hamilton interpreted the Constitution loosely. According to the Constitution, Congress could pass laws "necessary and proper" to the exercise of its responsibilities. To the Federalists, "necessary" meant "effectively useful"; to the Jeffersonians, "necessary" meant "absolutely indispensable."

The Mobs of Paris

Interpretation of the Constitution, then, was one of the issues on which the Federalists and the Jeffersonians differed. Another was foreign policy.

War broke out between England and republican France in 1793 and Washington quickly proclaimed America's neutrality. But in the following years this neutrality came into question. Popular support for the French grew. The British angered Americans by stirring up the Indians on the Canadian frontier (where Western settlers were harassed) and by interfering with U.S. commerce.

But Washington resisted the intense emotional pressure and maintained American neutrality. Most Federalists had no special liking for France anyway and the bloody excesses of the French Revolution appalled them. To the Federalists, British society possessed a desirable order and stability; the mobs of Paris represented the height of disorder.

The Federalists represented a large body of opinion in America that had never—even during the American Revolution—quarreled with the British system. Their quarrel was only with the denial to the Colonies of deserved British rights.

The Jeffersonians, while detesting the excesses of the French Revolution, insisted that at least the people's cause was just; on the other hand, they saw stagnation in the rigid British social system that was so dear to the Federalists.

"In every government on earth there is some trace of human weakness, some germ of corruption and degeneracy. . . . Each government degenerates when trusted to the rulers of the people alone. The people themselves are therefore its only safe depositories. And to render them even safer, their minds must be improved to a certain degree." —Thomas Jefferson.

VOTING MACHINES

First used in Lockport, New York, in 1892, the voting machine has now replaced the paper ballot for more than 60% of America's voters. The reason: Greater speed, a running total, reduced chance of fraud or error, and a simple recount process.

Still, the machines are unpopular in many areas because the job of printing the paper ballots is a political plum.

Only eight states require voting by machine—New York, Rhode Island, Connecticut, Delaware, Maryland, Kentucky, New Mexico, and Louisiana. Elsewhere the decision is made locally.

Voting machines range in price from $16,000 to $19,000.

"There is nothing I dread so much as the division of the Republic into two great parties, each under its leader. . . . This, in my humble opinion, is to be feared as the greatest political evil under our Constitution."—John Adams.

"If I should conceive myself in a manner constrained to accept (the Presidency) I call Heaven to witness that this very act would be the greatest sacrifice of my personal feelings and wishes that I ever have been called upon to make."—George Washington.

The French issue divided the American electorate as few issues have, but until the Presidential campaign of 1796 the almost universal faith in Washington kept the antagonists from mixing it up whole-heartedly. When Washington retired to Mount Vernon, the opposing camps came out swinging.

The leading candidates were Thomas Jefferson of Virginia and John Adams of Massachusetts.

The year 1796 is important in the story of American Presidential elections because it was the year of the first national political campaign. The initiative which resulted in the forming of opposing parties came at the national level, and reflected the split among the Founders over what the role of the Federal Government should be and what kind of society was most desirable.

Parties themselves were found necessary because the desired society and the role of national government could not be shaped satisfactorily without them. It took teamwork to win an election and push through legislation. Teamwork meant a party. But how, in those simpler days of the Eighteenth Century, when so much was being tried for the first time, did people with strong political ideas go about organizing themselves?

The Federalists had the advantage of being in power in 1796, although Washington himself was nonpartisan. The Federalists, therefore, simply used the already existing leadership in the administration and in Congress to build their party. There were no party conventions in those days; the Federalists picked their Presidential candidate in party caucus. For those on the inside it was a comfortable, clubby arrangement.

The Jeffersonians found organizing a little more difficult. As the "out" party they had to recruit party workers with promises of patronage—and so that ennobling prod to civic duty, the promise of a political job, gained a permanent place on the American scene.

One factor that played a part in the politics of 1796 was regional consciousness. Party leaders realized that the regional affiliation of the candidates was important to the voter. Thus, even as today, a geographical "balance" was considered in selecting candidates.

Thomas Pinckney, a leading Federalist and the man responsible for a popular treaty with Spain, was turned down by the Federalist caucus because he was a Southerner. Since another Southerner, Washington, had been in office for eight years, party chieftains thought the next candidate should be a Northerner. Adams got the nod.

The result: Adams, 71 electoral votes; Jefferson, 68. As the runner-up, Jefferson was named Vice President according to the arrangement of the day, an arrangement that proved unworkable, and was soon replaced with today's system.

The key arguments in these early days were over individual liberties and the limitation of Federal power.

Ways of the Electorate

As early as 1800, politicians were becoming sophisticated in the ways of the American electorate, and they made careful studies of area voting patterns.

The Federalist strength was in New England, where a long established social structure and a strong commercial interest tended to produce a more conservative viewpoint, and in the longest-settled areas of the middle states—Long Island, New York City, the Hudson Valley, the Delaware Valley and the German communities around Philadelphia.

Jeffersonian strength occurred among minorities in New England: Religious groups who resented the hold the religion of the first settlers had on their area; the urban poor; and an amorphous collection of people who were becoming increasingly unhappy with the social rigidity and who would soon strike out for the West to make a better life for themselves.

Jefferson drew support, too, from the vast rural areas of New York, Georgia, South Carolina, North Carolina, and Central Virginia. And the Democratic Republicans were skillfully building strong party organizations in Philadelphia and around Tammany Hall in New York City. The professional and commercial classes were still Federalists, but poorer city folk were rallying to the Jeffersonian banner.

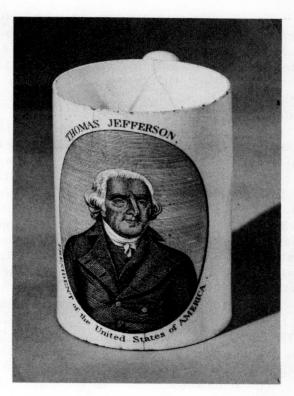

Ralph E. Becker Collection, Smithsonian Institution

An 1801 mug for parched patriots.

ELECTION OF 1800

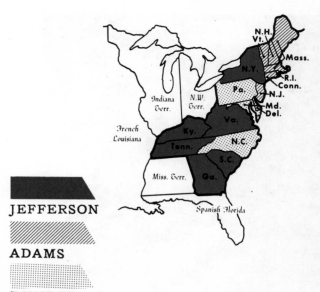

JEFFERSON

ADAMS

DIVIDED

The Western vote was very small in 1800—Kentucky and Tennessee produced only seven electoral votes. But as new states were admitted the West was to become more important to the Democratic Republicans (Ohio, 1803; Louisiana, 1812; and Indiana, Illinois, Mississippi and Alabama, from 1816 to 1819).

The 1800 campaign (the electors actually voted after the first of the year, in 1801) wound up in a tie. Seventy-three electors had voted both for Jefferson and Aaron Burr with the idea that Jefferson would be President and Burr Vice President. But the electoral system then provided no way that an elector could specify which man he wanted for which office. The election was therefore thrown into the House of Representatives where Jefferson was named President.

The experience led directly to the adoption of the Twelfth Amendment, which provides that "The Electors . . . shall name in their ballots the person voted for as President, and in distinct ballots the person voted for as Vice President."

The Jefferson success with the people was due to his party's skill in persuading voters that the Federalists presented a threat to their liberties, the widespread unpopularity of the Adams Administration, and the successful political alliance of New York and Virginia, which gave Jefferson 33 of his 73 electoral votes.

In 1804 Jefferson won in a landslide, 162 to 14. His Administration had gained popularity in its first four years by repealing various internal taxes such as the whisky tax, the purchase of the Louisiana Territory, and for liberal land settlement laws (160-acre tract for $320 payable over four years). Many Federalist voters were converted as Jefferson carried all the New England states except Connecticut.

Four years later, Jefferson's successor and former Secretary of State, James Madison, did not win so resounding a victory as the party had experienced in 1804. The 1807 Embargo, which barred American ships from leaving this country for any foreign port—in the hope of forcing Britain and France, which were dependent upon U.S. shipping, to accept the American interpretation of neutral rights—was exceedingly unpopular in shipping-minded New England. Of the New England states, only

"As there is a degree of depravity in mankind which requires a certain amount of circumspection and distrust, so there are other qualities in human nature which justify a certain portion of esteem and confidence. Republican government presupposes the existence of these qualities in a higher degree than any other form."—James Madison.

"The people being with us exclusively the sovereign, it is indispensable that full information be laid before them on all important subjects, to enable them to exercise that high power with competent effect. If kept in the dark, they must be incompetent to it. . . ."—James Monroe.

Library of Congress

Library of Congress

Vermont, rural and landlocked, remained in the Jeffersonian camp.

Not oblivious to the reasons for their decline in popularity, the Democratic Republicans determined to remove the Embargo. Less restrictive measures were substituted to keep the U.S. out of the European War. This had been Jefferson's ambition and his success. Madison did not succeed.

The Jeffersonians were especially anxious to avoid involvement in the hostilities because they foresaw in that event the ruin of their cherished agrarian society by the militant and centralized government that would be necessary to conduct a war. Nevertheless, during Madison's first Administration, a pro-war faction developed in his party. These were the War Hawks, men from the outlying areas anxious to provide security for the frontier.

Indian attacks had grown serious as settlers pushed deeper into the wilderness. European governments of the adjacent territories of Florida and Canada supplied arms to the Indians and did nothing to control their use of these weapons. The War Hawks believed the only solution was to cut off the supply of arms, and they had as their articulate spokesmen two able and ambitious young men—Henry Clay and John C. Calhoun.

Most Eastern Jeffersonians were persuaded to accept war, and Madison's war message was sustained by Congress, though against sizable opposition. The divided Congress reflected a divided country. In the election of 1812, the peace faction of the Democratic Republicans nominated DeWitt Clinton of New York and the Federalists supported him. But the South and West stood behind Madison and he was returned to the White House.

Although the war did not go well for the Americans and was at best a draw, the Democratic Republicans emerged from the conflict in a position of strength. In the dark days of December 1814, a group of delegates from New England met in Hartford, Connecticut, to consider their grievances against the Madison administration. Extremists talked of secession and this was anything but an idle proposal. Support for the war in New England had been slight; trade with Britain continued.

the United States in 1812

"If the Presidency was to be the prize of cabal and intrigue . . . bribing by appointments, or bargaining for foreign missions, I had no ticket in that lottery. Whether I had the qualifications necessary for a President was . . . very doubtful to myself. But that I had no talents for obtaining the office by such means was perfectly clear."—John Quincy Adams.

Library of Congress

But at the Hartford meeting more moderate men prevailed and no secession proposal was passed. Nevertheless their report recommended seven amendments to the Constitution and implied that these were the conditions under which New England would remain in the Union. The proposed amendments were intended to protect New England from the growing influence of the Old South and the growing frontier region. The New Englanders believed they were in a strong bargaining position because of the seriousness of the war situation.

Soon after the meeting in Hartford, however, news came of Andrew Jackson's victory at New Orleans and the treaty of peace. Although the treaty had been signed first, the people had the impression that America won the war. The Federalists were discredited as traitors, and their Hartford proposals were ignored.

The party which sought its fourth consecutive Presidential victory in 1816 was not the same party that first took office in 1801. Irrevocable facts arising from the war and the growth of the country required the Democratic Republicans to compromise some of their principles. In fact they appeared to accept many premises of their old foe, Alexander Hamilton.

The cutting-off of manufactured goods from England had spurred new industries in the country, especially in the Northeast where capital normally devoted to trade was diverted to manufacturing. Inefficient by British standards, these industries could not compete without the protection of a high tariff on imported manufactured goods. The Democratic Republicans, led by Madison, supported protectionist measures.

First Protective Tariff

Congress, in 1816, passed the nation's first tariff calculated to guard domestic producers. Meantime, Madison's party also backed the reestablishment of a national bank; the first one had been allowed to die in 1811. The bank was needed to curb the currency-issuing excesses of local banks and to provide capital for the Federal Government to meet its war debt.

Madison also favored Federally sponsored internal improvements—roads and canals—to assist the farmer in getting his crop to market and to improve domestic commerce in general. Madison refused, however, to accept legislation from Congress without prior assurance of Federal authority to underwrite such projects. This authority he required in a Constitutional amendment which was not forthcoming.

The old Jeffersonian accent on political liberty remained—no muzzling legislation had been passed during the War of 1812. The immense western migrations which continued under independent initiative, and under incredibly harsh conditions, were seen by Democratic Republicans as a continued expression of man's desire for a society in which he was free to improve his circumstances and widen his horizons.

Party on the Wane

And what of the Federalists all this time? The party of Washington, Adams and Hamilton was on the wane. Although it continued to be active within some states—especially Connecticut—it was no longer a major national influence. One reason for this is that the old issues that so divided the Federalists and the Jeffersonians in the 1790s were now largely resolved. There was a general feeling that the time had come to get on with improving the nation whose form was already assured. And new men were entering the ranks of the Democratic Republicans who were less stirred by the old arguments of the 1790s.

Acquiescence was evident among the Federalists. They had been severely beaten in the 1816 election, 183 electoral votes to 34. Only Connecticut, Delaware and Massachusetts went for the Federalist candidate, Rufus King.

With the selection of James Monroe as the Democratic Republican candidate by that party's caucus, a pattern was established. The President served two terms and was regularly succeeded by his Secretary of State, who was deemed best qualified to carry on the policies of the previous administration.

The way politicians went after votes at this time confirmed the heterogeneous makeup of the parties. Since its object was to win a majority of a population composed of various elements, the party was an alliance rather than a homogeneous body. Compromise had become an essential part of tactics. No group could have its way entirely without risking the alienation of the other groups whose support was needed.

But the Federalists had not completely given up. They hoped that the factions in the Democratic Republican party might split seriously enough to allow them to make their weight felt, and thereby regain political power or at least a share of it.

The tariff was dividing the nation sectionally. The agricultural South resented the high prices it had to pay for manufactured goods. The Eastern Democratic Republicans claimed the barrier was necessary if domestic industry was to survive. The South drew to its side the new Southern states west of the Appalachians, Louisiana and Mississippi, while the East attracted the Middle West.

The split in Congress between the sections widened when the question of the extension of slavery into the new territories came to the fore. Southern Congressmen saw in the restriction of slavery to the eleven slave states existing in 1820 an eventual curtailment of their political power. The slave was worth three-fifths of a person in the census; he thus gave added weight to the Congressional representation of the South and to Southern strength in the electoral college.

No-Fifths of a Free Man

But while being three-fifths of a person to the census-taker, the slave was no-fifths of a person when it came to political participation. He had no rights and therefore could demand no political commitment from the men who benefited from his existence. So the South enjoyed a disproportionate weight in national politics, and the Federalists hoped that they could make a comeback in a Northern party separated from the South over the slavery issue.

Party allegiance and concern for the Union were far more important in those years than any political worry or moral scruples about slavery. A plan was worked out in which slavery would be allowed in Missouri but nowhere else west of the Mississippi River north of the southern border of Missouri. The Missouri Compromise governed the slavery question in new territories until it was repealed in 1854 by the Kansas-Nebraska Act. But the debate that raged in Congress over the extension of slavery startled the nation. It came, said Thomas Jefferson, "like a fire bell in the night."

Thus in 1820, the sectional division that one day would lead to the Civil War entered politics in a major way.

In 1820, James Monroe achieved his second term with near unanimity; only one maverick electoral vote was cast against him. The Federalist caucus had selected no opponent.

In 1824 the old system of nomination broke down; there was no opposition party to appoint a candidate to oppose the administration's heir apparent. The Democratic Republican caucus refused to select the Secretary of State, John Quincy Adams, choosing instead William Crawford of Georgia, a strong states' rights man. But barely a third of the Democratic Republican Congressmen attended the caucus, and other candidates were selected by state legislatures and informal mass meetings.

Adams, Henry Clay and Andrew Jackson were selected in these ways, and the vote was split in most states. Adams' strength was concentrated in New England and New York; Jackson's in the agricultural and frontier regions of North Carolina, South Carolina, Tennessee, Alabama, Mississippi, Louisiana, Illinois, Indiana, and in the middle states of New Jersey, Pennsylvania and Maryland.

Crawford took his home state of Georgia and Virginia. Clay's strength was in the West— Missouri, Ohio and his native Kentucky. Jackson won a plurality of the electoral and popular vote, but a deal between Adams and Clay gave Adams the Presidency in the House of Representatives. Clay was made Secretary of State.

ELECTION OF 1824

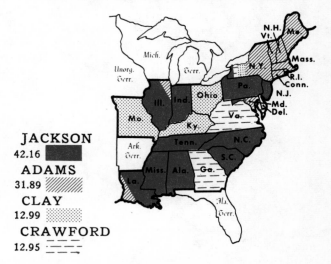

JACKSON
42.16

ADAMS
31.89

CLAY
12.99

CRAWFORD
12.95

% OF POPULAR VOTE

(No candidate received a majority of the electoral vote, so the House of Representatives chose the President from the top three contenders. John Quincy Adams was selected after winning Henry Clay's support by promising to name him Secretary of State.)

PROVIDENCE, MONDAY NOV. 17.

THE VICTORY IS WON FOR

JACKSON!!

☞ We have the pleasure of announcing to the readers of the Herald, that by the Steam-Boat Benjamin Franklin, which arrived here yesterday morning from New-York, we have received intelligence from *OHIO, KENTUCKY and INDIANA*, that the JACKSON TICKET has prevailed in these States by unexpected majorities.— This news is announced in the ADMINISTRATION PAPERS and those which have espoused the cause of the patriot farmer of Tennessee. The Administration papers from New-York, Philadelphia and Washington now confess that all is lost, and *that JACKSON is elected President by a great majority* of the electoral votes.

In addition to the above it is ascertained that *Jackson* has received FIVE VOTES in MARYLAND. In that State, the Administration claimed all but one, to the last— and the friends of Jackson did not promise themselves more than three.

If the eyes of the people of Rhode-Island are open, they will see how grossly they have been deceived by administration papers throughout the country. You were told that Pennsylvania would choose Adams electors by an overwhelming majority—that New-York would choose 24 electors for the coalition candidate—that Maryland would give her undivided vote for Adams and Clay, and that Ohio and Kentucky would give them their support. None of there assertions have been verified. The administration was unpopular; it was set up by intrigue and corruption: and it was attempted to be continued by patronage and venality. The people have weighed their rulers in the balance and they were found wanting. There was rottenness at the core, and— a profligate and corrupt administration has fallen—"never to rise again."

While this administration was crumbling to ruin, their parasites and flatterers were applauding the Cabinet to the skies, and the firm supporters of Jackson, were denominated by the venal presses of Adams and Clay, as an "*unprincipled opposition,* and the "DREGS and RABBLE of our population."

The result has been a glorious victory to the friends of General Jackson, and is an event auspicious to the future welfare of our Country.

We subjoin a list shewing the votes which are now SURE *beyond dispute, for* GENERAL JACKSON.

Maine -	1
New-York -	22
Pennsylvania	28
Maryland -	5
Virginia -	24
North-Carolina	15
South-Carolina	11
Georgia -	9
Ohio - -	16
Kentucky -	14
Tennessee -	11
Illinois -	3
Missouri -	3
Mississippi -	3
Indiana -	5
Alabama -	5
	175

The majority therefore, which Gen. Jackson will receive in the Electoral Colleges, will be at least *EIGHTY-NINE* over Adams. If to this, we add the 5 votes of Louisiana, which we are confident of obtaining and deduct them from the Adams side, we shall have a majority of *NINETY-NINE VOTES FOR THE HERO.*

Will the people of this State, throw away their weight in the scale of the Union, by adhering to a corrupt and expiring coalition? or will they distinguish themselves by early enlisting on the side of the patriot and statesman, who "has filled the measure of his country's glory?" ☞ *ON WEDNESDAY NEXT, THESE QUESTIONS MUST BE ANSWERED.*

Between 1824 and 1828, Jackson and his followers organized a national party. The issues were the rule of the people, which had allegedly been subverted by the Adams-Clay "corrupt bargain" (as it was called by the Jacksonians), simplicity in government and avoidance of corruption.

The victory of Jackson in the 1828 election was comfortable but not overwhelming. Adams amassed 44% of the popular vote. Issues tended to be subordinate. Adams had signed a tariff bill violently opposed in the South; Jackson made no clear statement in regard to the tariff.

The Adamsites had adopted the name of the National Republicans; Adams himself had approved this label in the 1824 campaign. He sought to convey a sense of unity in the country, hoping that an end to the party system had arrived with the collapse of the Federalists as a national party. "Let us uproot the baneful weed of party strife," was the way he put it, little dreaming that that "baneful weed" would grow like the fairy-tale beanstalk.

But Adams, in 1828, declined to moderate the policy of "proscription," which meant continued exclusion of Federalists from Federal patronage jobs. Proscription was the only issue that kept any unity among the old Federalists.

Simplicity in Government

Jackson's attitude toward patronage was simple. Believing in simplicity in Government, he also believed that this simplicity enabled the ordinary citizen to handle a Government job. Thus Old Hickory saw no reason not to remove officeholders of long experience and replace them with his supporters. But contrary to popular belief, his use of patronage was not excessive, and many of those replaced were incompetent or corrupt. Jackson too, incidentally, appointed more Federalists than had his four predecessors combined. The proscription issue was now dead and Federalists flowed freely into both the Democratic Republican and the National Republican parties.

Simplicity in government, avoidance of corruption and a government responsive to the will of the people were the three basic ideas of the Jacksonians. They believed that these three would insure the good society that all Americans were seeking.

The energies of Americans were now being

"No free Government can stand without virtue in the people, and a lofty spirit of patriotism; and if the sordid feelings of mere selfishness shall ursurp the place which ought to be filled by public spirit, the legislation of Congress will soon be converted into a scramble for personal and sectional advantages."—Andrew Jackson.

CAUCUS

An Algonquin Indian word, cau-cau-a-su, meaning "adviser," was adapted, or corrupted, by politicians to form the word "caucus," meaning a huddle of politicians to decide questions of policy or to select candidates. A caucus in England is a controlling group within a political party. The Algonquin Indians probably would call a caucus a pow-wow.

Ralph E. Becker Collection, Smithsonian Institution

AT THE POLLS, Harper's Weekly, Nov. 7, 1857: Where Americans have traditionally registered their differences.

directed into the growth of the country. Commerce, communications, credit, and machinery were in demand to carry forward the aspirations of the expanding society.

The upward direction of America was taken for granted. The question was how fast and in what way the growth was to occur; this is a question that has its kin today in the current controversy over the role of the Federal Government in U.S. economic expansion.

The Jacksonian approach drew much from Jefferson. The Jacksonians favored a nation of small property owners, small enterprises protected by the Government. Concentration of wealth appalled them because they believed that if some people got rich, others at the same time got poor.

Henry Clay was the leading spokesman for a Government-sponsored program of national growth. His "American System" was an integrated program of tariff protection, internal improvements (highways, canals), a national bank, and regulated land settlement. The four elements of his program were so interdependent in Clay's mind that he would not compromise any one of them. Clay was the candidate for the National Republicans in 1832, but he didn't do

as well as Adams had in 1828. His American System made too many enemies, and Jackson's method of government was popular.

In 1828 the Jacksonians had formally taken the name Democratic Republicans. By 1832 they called themselves Democrats.

Following the 1832 election, groups of anti-Jackson men began to coalesce into a national party. States' rights men around Calhoun opposed Jackson's strong Unionist tendencies. Anti-Masons (a one-shot eastern party that sought to capitalize on public anger at the Freemasons following a weird affair in which a man who announced he would expose the secrets of Freemasons, mysteriously disappeared) had carried 8% of the popular vote in 1832 and, along with the National Republicans, set about opposing Jackson.

The new grouping took the name "Whigs." The name recalled the resistance of an American Revolutionary group to the executive domination of the English king. Townsmen with commercial and banking interests had formed local party organizations which now joined the national party.

The Whigs, however, were not to remain a coalition of opponents to Jackson. States' rights,

Library of Congress

"Liberty exists in proportion to wholesome restraint."—Daniel Webster.

Library of Congress

"Sir, I would rather be right than President."—Henry Clay. (Clay later remarked that this statement had been "applauded beyond its merit.")

for one thing, could not be made a plank for a national party. There was no significant Southern support for the Calhoun doctrine of nullification—interposition of the state's authority between the people and the Federal Government —when that doctrine was brought to a Congressional test in 1832 in the dispute over the tariff of 1828.

Secondly, the Whigs began developing a positive concept of government. The importance of the executive was reduced; to the Whigs the legislative organs at the national level and in the states were more important. The legislature, they felt, more accurately reflected the popular will than an executive who could actually thwart this will by a strong exercise of his powers, namely the veto.

The Whigs had faith in the steady expansion of the economy; production would grow so that eventually there would be enough for everyone. This theory shows the Whigs to be production-minded in contrast to the Democrats who might be called distribution-minded. Concentration of wealth did not upset the Whigs. Such fortunes were considered necessary to provide the capital for growth. Since there was a shortage of hard money (gold) in the country,

an extensive credit facility was needed to supply the capital.

Belief in the need for a national bank gave the Whigs a national issue on which to engage the Democrats. Contraction of credit and the Democrats' hard money policies led, in part, to the financial panic of 1837. The Whigs sought to place the entire onus for this collapse on the Democrats.

But to succeed politically the Whigs needed more than an issue. They needed to become popular. During the 1836 campaign the Democrats repeatedly charged the Whigs with being aristocratic heirs of the Federalists. In office, so the charge went, the Whigs would revive the oppression of the people's will that was darkly linked to the Federalists.

Leading Whigs often did come from areas of greater economic development, and thus had some difficulty disposing of the Jacksonian accusation. Indeed, the Whig leadership did think of itself as a "better sort," and had difficulty accepting the support of the masses of people it associated with a rabble.

Both the Democratic accusation and the Whig uneasiness rested on a false notion of class, and arguments had been raised to support this notion. Sounding like a Marxian historian, John C. Calhoun wrote that the rising capitalist society would tend to divide into two classes: "Capitalists and operatives."

But this contention ran into some weighty denials. Alexis de Tocqueville, a French political philosopher who studied Jacksonian America, wrote that the "primary fact" about this country was "a general equality of condition among the people."

Daniel Webster, a leading Whig, also disputed the arguments for class division. As they were developing the issue of executive versus legislative primacy, the Whigs also discovered that there was no mob. The idea of class strife was fancy; it had no basis in reality.

An Underdeveloped Nation

The other chief fact about the country during this period was underdevelopment. These two facts were the things Americans were most concerned about, and how the Whigs and the Democrats related themselves to these issues determined their appeal.

Once the Whigs overcame their reluctance to be a mass-appeal party, they gave the Democrats strong opposition. During the period of 1836-1854 they were a viable and active organization and a genuine two-party system existed in the country.

The closeness of the competition between the parties may be indicated by this fact: During the five Presidential elections of the period 1836-1852, the Whigs averaged 48.26% of the popular vote, and the Democrats, 48.13% (minor parties accounted for the remaining 3.61%).

The less developed areas tended to be Democratic, and the areas of greater per capita income were generally Whig.

The changing character of the population influenced Presidential politics from 1789 to the 1840s. The ideological battles between the Federalists and the Jeffersonians were no longer relevant. Society had changed from the Eighteenth Century stable structure to one that was open, egalitarian and amorphous.

Politics now was no longer a matter of statesmen debating the issues before half the population. Candidates were selected by a method more directly reflecting the popular will—the national nominating convention, first used by Democrats and National Republicans in 1832. Government by the people was on the upswing.

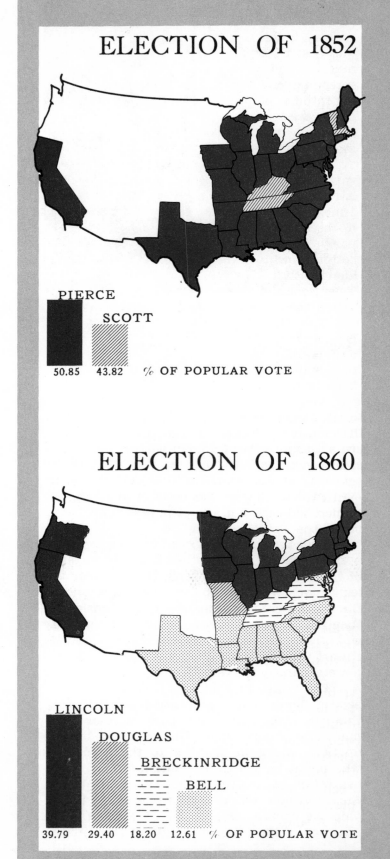

ELECTION OF 1852

PIERCE
SCOTT
50.85   43.82   % OF POPULAR VOTE

ELECTION OF 1860

LINCOLN
DOUGLAS
BRECKINRIDGE
BELL
39.79   29.40   18.20   12.61   % OF POPULAR VOTE

The part of the male population voting in 1824 was 27%; in 1828, 55%; and by 1840, 78%.

The Whigs misjudged the temper of the country in 1844. The big issue of the moment was western expansion. Since the War of 1812 America had grown dramatically. Cities were spreading out and sturdy pioneers were pushing into the new land west of the Appalachians, so far west that by 1844 Americans had been in the northern Mexican territory of Texas for more than 20 years.

In 1836 the American Texans revolted and gained independence. The Democratic administrations of Jackson and Van Buren avoided annexing Texas—although the Texans wanted it—because they feared a sectional split in their party; Eastern Democrats feared the spread of cotton-growing into Texas would drag slavery along with it. The Whig administration of John Tyler sought to annex Texas, but Congress rejected the move in a sectionally split vote.

The Democratic platform of 1844 added Oregon to the expansionist aims of the country and thereby balanced the proposed admission of a southern Texas with a northern Oregon. The tactic was successful.

Elected and in office, the Democratic President, James Polk, completed the annexation of Texas and provoked the Mexican government into causing an armed incident which led to war. Mexico was beaten. The terms of the peace treaty gave the United States an immense acquisition. With the adding of the huge Oregon Territory, which had occurred by a compromise settlement with the British in 1846, the U.S. was nearly filled out to its present shape.

Enter Free Soilers

The dispute in Congress over the extension of slavery into the territories continued. But while heated oratory filled the legislative halls, both parties were reluctant to make the issue important in the campaign of 1848.

Abolitionists and more moderate conscience-troubled people who merely opposed the extension of slavery into the territories found it difficult to accept either Democrat Lewis Cass, who was on the record for "popular sovereignty" (letting the residents of each territory decide the slavery question for themselves), or Whig Zachary Taylor who ran on a deliberately vague platform.

A third party brought together the various dissatisfied elements, endorsed the distribution of free land to actual settlers, and became known as the Free Soil Party. Its nominee was former President Van Buren who, in a generally listless campaign by all the parties, carried 10% of the popular vote—including enough Democratic votes to give the Whig candidate Taylor the Presidency.

Zach Taylor was the first career soldier to sit in the White House (Jackson and William Henry Harrison had been militia generals in the "Minute Man" tradition). When Taylor took office in March of 1849, he resolved to do something about the military government of California, a holdover from the Mexican War. His solution was straightforward. Since there was no dispute over a state's right to do as it pleased about slavery within its own borders, Taylor wanted California and New Mexico to become states right away. Two sources of possible division in the country would be thus removed from the scene.

Extremists Subdued

The Californians were eager to comply. By the time Congress, which had not been in session when Taylor was inaugurated, reassembled in December, California had organized a state government, selected representatives and adopted a constitution forbidding slavery. Confronted with this situation—one that would upset the balance created by the Missouri Compromise—Southern Congressmen balked.

California had not received the required Congressional permission to organize a state government, and the new Congress was threatened with sharp sectional division, a division reflected throughout the nation. A Southern convention met in Nashville and rumbled about secession. And an outspoken abolitionist and Free Soiler, William H. Seward, took his seat in the Senate.

Fortunately, the extremists were subdued. Henry Clay's compromise program, Webster's conservative statesmanship, and Stephen Douglas' shrewd political management brought about an accommodation.

Webster rose above smaller interests; he appealed to his colleagues to uphold the Union: "I wish to speak today, not as a Massachusetts man, nor a Northern man, but as an American. . . . .I speak today for the preservation of the Union. Hear me for my cause."

"The existence of an area of free land, its continuous recession, and the advance of American settlement westward, explain American Development."—Frederick Jackson Turner, 1893.

Congress and the country heard him. The terms of the compromise—admission of California as a free state, popular sovereignty to apply in other territory obtained from Mexico, abolition of slave trade in the District of Columbia, and a more effective fugitive slave law—were widely accepted.

A Boom Psychology

Whigs and Democrats viewed the Compromise of 1850 as a permanent settlement of the slavery question. Extremists on both sides denounced the agreement, but they had been extremists before the Compromise; they had made their conversion to abolition, or secession, earlier. But while the extremists railed and wailed, most Americans were concentrating on improving their own circumstances. They were better off than ever before and the country was gripped by a boom psychology.

The American people were, in 1850, overwhelmingly middle class—middle class in ambition, rather than middle class in fact. Extremes of wealth were few and have been overemphasized by popular notions of Nineteenth Century history.

Nor was the situation different in the South. The plantation system and the aristocratic images of Dixie are truer to *Gone With the Wind* than to the real South of 1850. Less than 6% of the white population owned slaves, and most of these owners had to work in the fields themselves. Only 1.5% of the Southern whites were of the planter-type families.

In the Northeast and in the growing Midwest, society was also largely agrarian. Only in Connecticut, Rhode Island and Massachusetts could more than half the population be considered urban.

The sectional balance achieved by the Compromise of 1850 seemed to be upheld in the Presidential elections of 1852. Both parties pledged to support the Compromise as final. Democrat Franklin Pierce gained a majority of 215,000 as more than three million voters went to the polls. The Democratic endorsement of the Compromise had been much stronger, and hence the Whigs lost many moderate votes in the South.

In 1854 new strains occurred in the sectional balance. Westward pressure made it necessary to open for settlement the as-yet-unorganized territories of the northwestern part of the Louisiana Purchase (the present area of the Great Plains states—from Kansas north to the Dakota-Canada border and west into Montana). The Kansas-Nebraska Act, organizing these lands, provided for squatter sovereignty (settlers in each area could decide the slavery question for themselves) and thus by implication repealed the Missouri Compromise. The sponsor of the bill, Stephen Douglas, maintained that this was necessary to get the legislation opening the territories passed through a Southern-dominated committee, and that the nature of the soil and climate would not support slave-based agriculture.

Settlers pushed into Kansas. There, small groups contended for control of the territorial government. Divided over the slavery issue, their disputes led to violence which was dramatically played up in the Northern press. Actually most Kansans were barely interested; the feuding was between minority factions.

Massive Retaliation

In the spring before the election of 1856, the minor incidents of violence in Kansas were augmented by an incident in the U.S. Senate. The abolitionist Senator from Massachusetts, Charles Sumner, delivered a bitter denunciation of the violence in Kansas, and blamed the Southern slavocracy for the disorder. During his speech Sumner made extreme and insulting remarks about the character of several Senators. A nephew of one of the maligned Senators, Representative Preston Brooks, was so enraged by Sumner's speech that a few days later he fell upon Sumner with a cane.

This incident caused greater hostility between the sections. The seam that held North and South together was threatening to split. The nation's greatest crisis since the Republic was born in 1789 was coming to a head.

Meanwhile, the Whigs were losing their strength. The Know-Nothings, a nativist party originally born of xenophobia and anti-Catholic sentiment stirred by the recent flood of Irish and German immigrants, had snatched some Whig strength since the election of 1852. And the abolitionist fever had split the party in many Northern states.

The strong leadership of Webster and Clay was now gone (both died in 1852). Northern citizens banded together into anti-slavery, pro-Northern economic groups. Former Whigs were attracted, including a man named Lincoln, and candidates affiliated with this combination in

The grace and balance depicted by Gilbert Stuart in his painting, *The Skater*, exemplify the nature of early American society. There was a comfortable English-like order to life in the infant nation, an order soon disturbed by new problems. . . .

. . . as more and more pioneers scaled the Appalachians to settle on the western side. This detail from Linton Park's primitive, *Flax Scutching Bee*, suggests the hard life that produced a deep skepticism of Eastern political power. In time . . .

1789

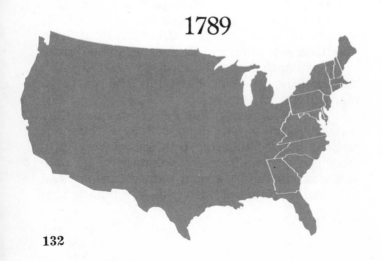

1824

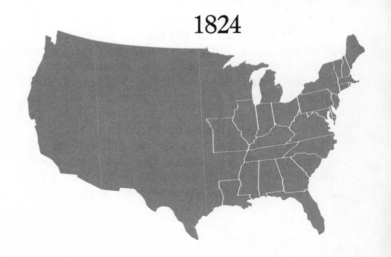

. . . the westward thrust of expansion would span the Great Plains and, by 1876, the process of filling in the wide open spaces was under way. In 1889-1890, seven states would be admitted to the Union in less than a year. Roaming Indians . . .

. . . were giving way to farmers and ranchers, and the cities were swelling with people drawn to jobs in industry. By 1912, progress was bringing prosperity to more Americans, but it was bringing new social problems as well.

Detail, Indian Encampment. Artist unknown. Courtesy of National Gallery of Art, Washington, D.C.; Collection of Edgar William and Bernice Chrysler Garbisch.

Chimneys and Water Tower, by Charles Demuth. Courtesy of National Gallery of Art, Washington, D.C.; Alfred Stieglitz Collection (Loan).

1876

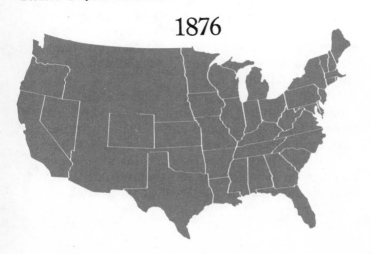

1912

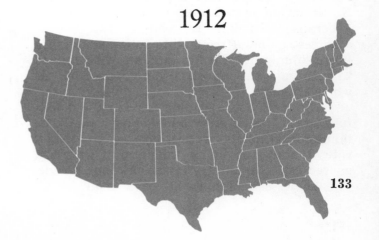

133

the mid-term elections were generally successful. The combination was called the Republican Party.

Unity in the Democratic Party dissolved over the continuing problem of Kansas. President Buchanan, a Democrat, backed a pro-slavery constitution for the state submitted without clear popular approval by the Kansas territorial legislature. Moderate leaders sought a compromise.

A bill was eventually passed in which the state constitution was returned to Kansas for popular ratification. Northern Democrats broke party ranks to join the minority Republicans in passing the bill.

Democrats Asunder

Stephen Douglas, candidate for the Senate against Lincoln in 1858, and a leader in the Democratic Party, lost Southern support during the campaign because of his statements regarding slavery in the territories. It could be excluded by a vote of the citizens in the area, Douglas said. He was returned to the Senate in a close election.

In 1860, the split in the Democratic Party was complete. Sectional feeling had been further inflamed by John Brown's raid at Harper's Ferry. The Douglas forces won convention approval of a platform upholding Congressional non-intervention in the slavery issue in the territories. Douglas was nominated for President on this platform after most Southern delegates withdrew. The radicals, who had gained control of the Southern delegation, nominated John C. Breckinridge of Kentucky on a platform of positive Congressional protection of slavery in the territories.

The Republican Party was no longer the one-idea organization composed of crusaders against slavery. It now included, or hoped to include, every major economic interest in the North. It supported internal improvements, a Federally subsidized railroad to the Pacific, a homestead law (free land to actual settlers,) a liberal immigration policy, and a tariff designed to encourage the industrial development of the whole country.

The tariff was a leading issue in the doubtful states of New Jersey and Pennsylvania. The immigration plank was calculated to attract votes among the many immigrants who had poured into the country in the previous decade. The homestead plan would be a boon for all

poor but ambitious men. The railroad was attractive to Eastern commercial and manufacturing interests.

Lincoln, the Republican candidate, was attractive to all elements in the North. He opposed slavery, but did not take an extreme view of Southerners. The Republican campaign in the North was conducted with an enthusiasm reminiscent of the exuberance of the young Whig Party in 1840. Mass meetings, torch-light parades, buttons, bunting, ballyhoo and booze enlivened the race. For the most part the economic issues were stressed in the Republican campaign; the slavery question was subordinated.

Lincoln won a majority of the electoral votes. The combined popular vote of his opponents was almost a million more than his total.

The division over the election was so serious that the losers felt they could not abide by the result, and attempted to withdraw from the nation.

In the Civil War and the decade that followed, the nation took on much of its modern form. The urban-industrial society was firmly entrenched. The rural population remained in a majority until World War I but the trend toward the cities was relentless.

Unprecedented Powers

The Federal Government assumed powers to an unprecedented extent. The Government encouraged the efforts of businessmen. The long-disputed issues of the tariff, the bank, and internal improvements were decided in favor of the business interests. Washington measures helped bring huge concentrations of capital into private hands. Investors in Government securities fared well because interest rates were high. The corporations building the transcontinental railroad received generous land grants with which to capitalize their construction. The Government also introduced a national currency; local bank notes were heavily taxed and driven out of circulation.

Industry lost its rustic aspect after 1840. The rise in immigration brought an abundant labor supply to coastal cities. The penniless Irish and German peasants who came ashore were desperately eager to work for any wages. Those who brought some resources generally took up farming in the West. This availability of cheap labor for the first time in America encouraged new industry and stimulated what already existed. By 1860 manufacturing was an urban pursuit. Carriages, tools, machinery, and furniture flowed into the market. The use of steam and heavy machinery expanded the need for iron and coal.

The transcontinental telegraph was completed in 1861, bringing all sections of the country closer together—in at least one sense—than ever before. By the end of the Civil War, Western Union emerged as the only telegraph company in the country, with 76,000 miles of wire in 1866. In 30 years the wire mileage grew twelvefold. Railroads expanded from 35,000 miles of road in the 1860s to 259,000 miles at the turn of the century. People and messages could now move from place to place at a speed unknown before and this progress would have its effect on national politics.

Compromise of 1877

The Democratic Party came out of the Civil War with diminished hopes. Until 1876 it would not be in serious contention for control of the Federal Government. The party had great problems during the Reconstruction period as Republican successes in the South kept many pre-war Democratic leaders out of office (many Southerners felt Federal help was needed to carry out various economic projects, and Federal help meant Republican help).

In the years following the Civil War the nation as a whole was prosperous as never before. However all segments of society were not sharing in the prosperity. Neither party offered a set of principles for those who were alarmed at the unequal growth of the country.

This prevailing bipartisan attitude of non-interference with free enterprise reduced the possibility of economic issues appearing in Presidential campaigns; the amorphous nature of the two major parties made clear-cut stands on economic issues politically unwise. Another reason for the absence of firm issues was the inability of either party to consistently control both the White House and Congress.

The most significant political event of the period took place in 1877; it is a generally unknown compromise, but in terms of the crisis involved, and its consequences, the Compromise of 1877 ranks with the great compromises of 1820 and 1850. More than any other event, the

Library of Congress

"I do not allow myself to suppose that either the convention or the (National Union League) have concluded to decide that I am either the greatest or best man in America, but rather they have concluded that it is not best to swap horses while crossing the river, and have further concluded that I am not so poor a horse that they might not make a botch of it in trying to swap." —Abraham Lincoln. (Picture shows Lincoln in 1860, when he had just begun to raise a beard.)

Ralph E. Becker Collection, Smithsonian Institution

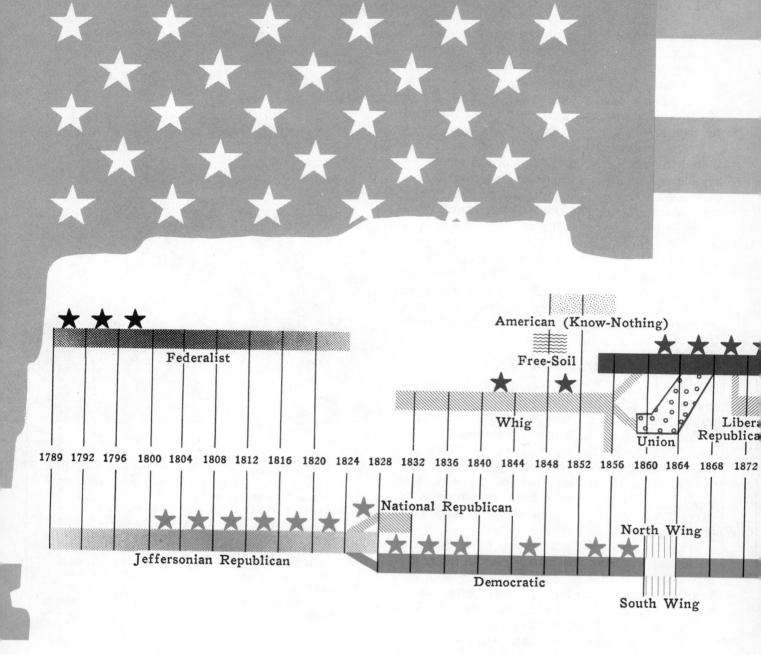

American (Know-Nothing)

Free-Soil

Federalist

Whig

Union

Liber
Republica

National Republican

North Wing

Jeffersonian Republican

Democratic

South Wing

1789 1792 1796 1800 1804 1808 1812 1816 1820 1824 1828 1832 1836 1840 1844 1848 1852 1856 1860 1864 1868 1872

The Pursuit of Power

The evolution of political parties in the United States, as illustrated here, is explained in this chapter and the preceding one. The chart also represents significant events in party history.

One such event was the disintegration of the Whigs in the slavery crisis of the 1850s. A second occurred when the old Southern Whig element of the Republican Party abandoned the GOP at the time of the Compromise of 1877 (see page 135). The Republicans suffered another, temporary, desertion when the liberal, eastern Mugwumps left the party to support Grover Cleveland in 1884.

The stars indicate the party in power.

American Political Parties

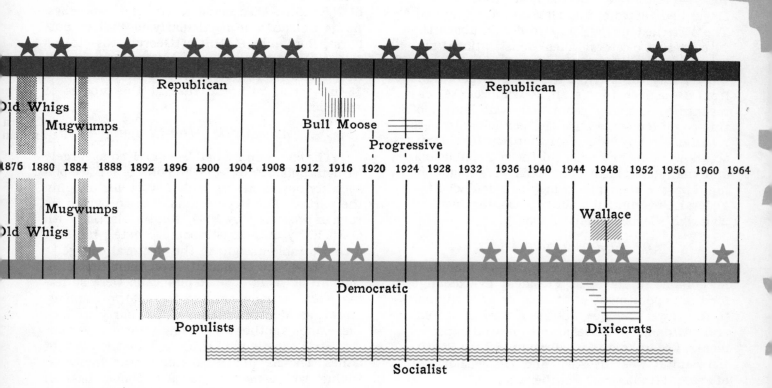

Republican

Old Whigs

Mugwumps

Bull Moose

Progressive

Republican

| 1876 | 1880 | 1884 | 1888 | 1892 | 1896 | 1900 | 1904 | 1908 | 1912 | 1916 | 1920 | 1924 | 1928 | 1932 | 1936 | 1940 | 1944 | 1948 | 1952 | 1956 | 1960 | 1964 |

Mugwumps

Old Whigs

Wallace

Democratic

Populists

Dixiecrats

Socialist

1789-1964

agreements in 1877 fixed a one-party political structure on the South.

In 1876 both parties had named men associated with reform as their standard bearers in the Presidential election—Democrat Samuel J. Tilden, governor of New York, and Republican Rutherford B. Hayes, governor of Ohio. There was almost no difference in the principles of the two men. The difference was in emphasis, as it often is in American politics.

The Democrats were stronger for ending Reconstruction, while the Republicans emphasized its economic legislation and repeated the pledge to guarantee equal rights to the Negro.

Tilden polled 4,300,000 votes to Hayes' 4,036,000, and Tilden definitely had 184 electoral votes—one short of the 185 needed for election. Hayes had 165 votes and 20 votes were disputed. There seemed no fair way to decide about the 20 contested electoral votes. Constitutional ambiguity and party division in Congress made impartiality unlikely. After long negotiations from December to March, a compromise was reached. For many years little was known of this compromise because the participants were reluctant to have it known that Southern Democrats were dealing with Northern Republicans, and that Republican politicians were abandoning a part of their platform which defended the Federal Government's active encouragement of civil rights legislation in the South.

The Troops Leave Dixie

The terms of the compromise included: Acceptance of Hayes as President in exchange for the appointment of at least one Southerner to the Hayes Cabinet, Southern control of Federal patronage in Dixie, ample internal improvements, Federal aid to a railroad in which Southern capital was invested, and the withdrawal of Federal troops from Southern states.

By removing Federal troops, the Republican negotiators deprived Republican regimes in the Southern states of their principal resource for maintaining power in the face of the Democratic opposition, which by 1877 included most Southern whites.

Stemming from this bargain were consequences of continuing significance today.

The leaders of the Southern Democrats were primarily interested in the economic development of the South. Their business outlook gave them a common interest with conserva-

tives of both parties of the North. In the course of the negotiations, the Southerners were able to win support of enough Northern Democratic conservatives to amass the political pressure necessary to gain the economic terms of the compromise. In order, however, to retain their strength in the South they had to have political crumbs to throw to the white-supremacy rank and file. The removal of troops from the South implied Republican acceptance of the Southerner's right to rule his own house, and in effect repudiated the Republican pledge to uphold Negro rights.

But the agreement did not come easily. Tilden's supporters did not like the idea of their man being dumped for a deal, and at a Democratic caucus Representative Fernando Wood of New York City made several fiery speeches. As he finished one particularly incendiary outburst, Benjamin H. Hill of Georgia rose to his feet and drawled: "Perhaps the gentleman is not aware of the conservative influence of a 15-inch shell with the fuse in the process of combustion."

Enthusiastic Mud-Slinging

The compromise had been arrived at largely without public knowledge and on the surface politics continued apace, with few issues dividing the parties. The Republicans, blessed by the return of prosperity by 1880, won the election with Garfield by only 10,000 popular votes, but had a comfortable margin in the electoral college.

In 1884, the Democrats won their first election in 28 years. The Republicans were suffering from factionalism and the reform element, known as Mugwumps, bolted the party to back Cleveland, another New York reform governor.

Enthusiastic mud-slinging took the place of issues. The Republican nominee was James G. Blaine, whose mother was a Catholic. Late in the campaign an incident was blown up by the Democrats to suggest that Blaine had permitted the Catholic Church to be slandered in his presence. The incident occurred in pivotal New York State and may have swung the state, and the election, to the Democrat, Grover Cleveland.

Cleveland was honest, determined and often stubborn. He stood against a paternalistic government that gave special favors to anyone. The worker and the corporation were equal individuals in the eyes of the government, he announced. He vetoed handouts of various sorts—

NAST'S ANIMALS

Editorial cartoonist Thomas Nast (1840-1902), best known for his devastating attacks on the New York political machine of Boss William Tweed, invented the symbols of both major political parties. His first drawings of the Republican elephant and the Democratic donkey are reproduced here. The term "Copperhead Papers" on the donkey refers to newspapers that opposed the use of martial law during the Civil War in areas outside the combat zone.

The word "Copperhead" was an epithet applied to Northern Democrats who opposed Lincoln's strict policies on the home front and who later favored lenient policies toward the defeated South. Nast's donkey, by the way, was identified in the cartoon by the somewhat less generous name of jackass. Nast didn't equivocate.

His political preferences did undergo some changes, however. He left the regular Republicans for the Mugwumps and then switched to the Democrats before finally winding up as a Republican again. After losing his savings when a brokerage house failed, Thomas Nast wound up as U.S. general consul in Guayaquil, Ecuador, where he died in 1902.

veterans pensions (many of them based on fraudulent claims), pork barrels and similar measures—and created a definite issue in 1888.

Concerned about the revenue surplus as a depressing agent on the economy and an enticement to Congressional extravagance, Cleveland was determined to reduce the tariff. Congress deadlocked over the issue, which was then projected into the campaign. Although conservative eastern Democrats were disgruntled over Cleveland's proposed cutting of the tariff, Southerners and Westerners enthusiastically endorsed it. The continuing hard times were affecting the political climate in these areas.

W. J. Bryan on an 1896 china plate.

Popular opinion was rising to challenge the high tariff as an imposition on the hard-pressed consumer. In the campaign the Republicans defended their protectionist principle. The election was close, with both sides employing ballot-box frauds. Benjamin Harrison, grandson of ninth President William Henry Harrison, won an electoral majority of 233 to 168, derived from his success in the East (notably Pennsylvania and New York) and the Middle West. Cleveland, however, had a popular majority of 5,540,000 to 5,440,000.

American society in the last years of the Nineteenth Century was no longer as open and egalitarian as it had been 30 years earlier. The immigrant clerk in the local drygoods store who had married the owner's daughter in the 1870s now owned a vast department store and forbade his daughters to be more than polite to his salesmen.

Opportunity for the individual was becoming less apparent. Americans were still ambitious to get ahead—the farmer did not want only to subsist for he was a market farmer, a businessman. The skilled worker was likewise anxious to improve himself. Unskilled labor had become decidedly urban and lived continually at the edge of subsistence. Strains were appearing in the social fabric.

In the West and South the unrest over economic conditions led to the rise of a new political party, built around local farm societies that sprouted in the 1880s. Farmers and the rural poor banded together in affirming that they could expect nothing from either of the major parties, and that they ought to form their own political organization.

The Populist platform in 1892 conceived broad changes to attack poverty and widen economic opportunity for all. Its planks included nationalization of railroads, telephone and telegraph systems, inflatable silver coinage, a graduated income tax, and Federal credit on crops. Labor planks were included to gain additional support.

An Unpopular Tariff

During the Harrison administration a new tariff, higher than ever, was made law. The measure was extraordinarily unpopular, and the tariff was the only issue between the two major parties in 1892. Otherwise their platforms were very similar.

Cleveland, again the Democratic candidate, won a convincing victory. He did not, however, carry a majority of the popular vote because agrarian politician James B. Weaver of Iowa, the Populist candidate, polled over 8% of the popular vote and won electoral votes in six mountain and plains states.

The actions of the Cleveland administration did not still the voices of protest. Instead they grew louder. The promised Democratic reduction of the tariff did not occur, and the soft money policies dear to the debtor groups were thwarted. By the election year of 1896, the Democratic Party was in an uproar. Alarmed by the rise of Populist sentiment in their sections, Southern and Western delegates determined to seize control of the party from the East, and in so doing, incorporate the platform of the Populists into their own and to nominate a man favoring the free coinage of silver. The silver problem was the leading issue among the rural elements.

At the Democratic convention, a magnificent and emotional oration on behalf of the free silver plank by Nebraskan William Jennings Bryan won the hearts of the agrarians. Almost completely he represented the hopes and anxieties of rural America, and he swept the convention. The Populists endorsed the Democratic platform.

A Little Bit of Luck

Against the broad reform program offered by the Democrats, the Republicans repeated one theme: Only the Republicans could bring prosperity to the country; election of the Democrats would bring property confiscation, disorder, and all kinds of misery.

The GOP had the good luck of the return of prosperity to the farmers in the closing weeks of the campaign and McKinley was elected.

Prosperity and a glorious little war were the principal strengths of the Republicans in the election of 1900. The Democrats opposed the extension of American colonialism which resulted from the defeat of Spain in 1898. Prosperity had continued and the Democratic protests lost much of their force. In 1898 two and half times as much gold was produced as in 1890, and the currency supply was expanded far beyond the proposals of the Democrats in 1896. McKinley's victory in 1900 was decisive—he won by 850,000 votes and carried 52% of the popular vote, which was 6% more than Bryan's total.

Swashbuckling Teddy Roosevelt, who became President after McKinley was assassinated in September, 1901, reflected the changing political outlook of his times, and he was to become a foremost leader of this change.

Between 1870 and 1910 the U.S. population more than doubled, as did the older middle class —the independent professional and businessmen. The farm population did not match this growth but the working class trebled. The striking feature of this period was the eightfold increase of the new middle class of white collar workers—clerks, small managers, sales people and technicians. This new group in combination with the older middle class formed the "respectable element" of the towns and cities. There were ties between this expanded middle class and the farmers of the more prosperous regions in the Middle West.

In the early 1900s they gave voting strength to a new reform movement, eventually called Progressivism.

Among these people at the turn of the century there was a cheerful feeling that opportunity was still present and that abundance would continue. But there was also a growing uneasiness.

The labor upheavals of the early 1890s and the Populist protest had unsettled the middle class, because the threat of severe social divisions seemed very real. Labor radicalism, the agrarian protest, and an indifferent capitalism seemed to be centrifugal forces bidding to pull society into contending factions, as was already happening in Europe. This did not occur in the United States because between 1900 and 1914 important elements made unconscious compromises. They were the farmer, labor, the businessman, and the middle class.

Both the farmer and the laboring man were willing to accept the capitalist system if its harsher aspects could be removed. They didn't want to destroy business; they wanted a bigger share in it.

Businessmen themselves began to review their responsibilities to the general walfare. With "public opinion" first becoming a factor to be weighed in the early years of this century, businessmen decided some compromises were in order. True, not all businessmen were of such a mind, but the most influential among them were.

Sharing the Abundance

Finally, the fourth element in the emerging progressivism was the middle class, which seemed to feel that all Americans could share in the abundance provided by the free-enterprise system if steps were taken to curb excessive concentrations of economic power.

Already in the late 1890s, progressive groups had won local victories. In Wisconsin, disgruntled rural voters put Bob La Follette in the statehouse after he asked them: "Shall the American people become servants instead of masters of their boasted material progress and prosperity?"

But the appearance of a national leader of the progressive movement would come more slowly. Resistance was greater in national politics than in the long discontented areas like Wisconsin. In Theodore Roosevelt, the progressives found their man.

Teddy Roosevelt exemplified the idea of change with moderation. When he assumed the Presidency he was aware of the need for change, but he moved slowly. He knew how important it was to persuade the business interests to accept moderate change and he went quietly about winning broad support.

By the election of 1904 Roosevelt had control of the party, and after the election he sought to make it progressive. After a dull campaign he was re-elected by 2.5 million votes. The large Socialist vote (400,000) gave the President a strong argument that some reform was necessary.

During his administration, T.R. brought about changes to satisfy the progressive elements without alienating the conservative business groups. The Government policed railroad trusts, actively promoted the conservation of natural resources, and raised health and sanitary standards of food and drug packaging.

Roosevelt's Choice

William Howard Taft was Roosevelt's own choice to succeed him. In politics Taft was mildly progressive, perhaps a hair to the right of T.R. But by the end of his term he had alienated the Midwestern progressives—whose spokesman was La Follette (now a Senator)—and the Eastern following of Roosevelt.

Although the split in the Republican Party was not formalized until the conventions of 1912, the breach was already obvious in 1910, when Roosevelt announced his political program called the New Nationalism. Specifically he spelled out his "square deal": Graduated income and inheritance taxes, workman's compensation for accidents, regulation of child and female labor, tariff regulation, and a firm regulation of corporations.

The leadership of the Republican Party was under the control of the conservatives, who were loyal to Taft. When the leaders rejected nearly all the Roosevelt delegates who claimed contested seats at the Republican convention, Teddy walked out crying fraud. He took half the party with him and nearly all of its popular appeal (see Chapter VI).

For the first time since 1892, when the Democrats won their last victory, there would be a strong third party in the field.

The Democrats, understandably, convened with a sense of victory pervading their ranks.

A combination of progressive and machine Democrats selected Woodrow Wilson as their candidate. The former president of Princeton University had had a liberal record as governor of New Jersey, where he had sponsored progressive reforms like those already established in Wisconsin under La Follette.

In the campaign that followed, the contest was largely between the Democratic and Republican versions of "progressivism." Wilson, repeatedly voicing his suspicion of bigness, reworked an old theme that brought a popular response. Big business, he said, ought to be reduced in size and big government should be avoided to give the small businessman a better chance to succeed. Laws were needed, Wilson declared, "which will look after the men who are on the make . . . the men who are sweating blood to get their foothold in the world of endeavor."

BULL MOOSERS, EVERY ONE

Teddy Roosevelt's 1912 Bull Moose Party attracted many bright young people who were to figure importantly in American life later on.

Among them: Harold Ickes, Secretary of the Interior, 1933-1945; William Allen White, editor and author; Nebraska Senator George Norris, a chief supporter of the Federally owned power complex, the Tennessee Valley Authority; Alfred M. Landon, GOP Presidential nominee in 1936; Frank Knox, Landon's running mate and FDR's Secretary of the Navy, 1940-1945;

Henry A. Wallace, FDR's Vice President and later the standard bearer for the arch-liberal Progressive Party in 1948; Felix Frankfurter, a Supreme Court Justice appointed by FDR in 1939; Norman Thomas, perennial Socialist candidate for President, 1928-1948; Francis Biddle, U.S. Attorney General, 1941-1945; and Dean Acheson, Truman's Secretary of State, 1949-1953.

The Bull Moose convention, by the way, was the first to which women were admitted, reflecting the party's support of the movement to gain voting rights for women.

The election results were taken to be a clear mandate for change. The combined vote of the Democrats, the Progressive Republicans and the Socialists (Eugene V. Debs was the latters' candidate) was 11,300,000 of 14,800,000 ballots cast, or 74%. The Socialists accounted for 6% or nearly a million votes, their historic high point. The Socialist vote was the bogeyman which the Progressives could point to as the only alternative to their more moderate reforms.

Wilson had appealed more directly to the "little man," both in the cities and the hinterland. During most of his first term, however, he didn't try to press all the progressive notions of the day upon the country. Nevertheless, the tariff was substantially reduced, a graduated income tax was made law, and measures were introduced to improve the flow of currency and credit.

Candidates From the Bench

By 1916 it was obvious that the Bull Moose Party, never much more than a Roosevelt instrument, was collapsing. Unless the Democrats, who were usually a minority, offered a forceful reform program to the electorate, they would probably lose to the reunited Republicans in November. Confronted with this prospect, Wilson pressed for more social legislation. Accordingly, Workman's compensation for Federal employes and a child labor law were passed by Congress in 1916 under Wilson's vigorous sponsorship. And the war in Europe was also an issue.

The Republicans in 1916 offered Charles Evans Hughes, who had an unquestionable liberal record and who resigned from the Supreme Court to accept the nomination.

The Democrats squeezed through to victory over the united Republicans. Wilson's vote jumped three million from his 1912 count to 9,130,000, a total which exceeded Hughes' vote by barely 600,000. The margin in the electoral college was 23. Wilson strength was in the South and the West and he inferred from his victory a mandate to continue his policies of "progressivism and peace." Six months later the country was at war.

Insistence on German respect for America's neutral rights, and the German refusal to honor those rights, provided the official justification for plunging into the European conflict. But there were other factors.

Businessmen, farmers, workmen and bankers were prospering on the heavy wartime purchases of the Allies. Most importantly, there was a notion firmly rooted in the conscience of the American people and the President that went something like this: Even as the United States was progressing toward middle-class democracy, so the world would become a community of peaceful middle-class democracies.

Barriers to a Rosier World

Wilson's Fourteen Points—on which peace was to be based—accurately reflected the kind of world community many Americans envisioned. Only ignorance, poverty and evil leaders, it was believed, could thwart the development of this rosier world. The German leadership became, in the American mind, a clique of powerful men who were frustrating the true direction of history. As much as the "progressive" feared that war would halt reform, it was viewed as a necessary evil to bring about permanent reform—and permanent peace. Long an exclusively American movement deriving from American problems, the reform movement suddenly took on an international character.

When peace could not be achieved on the basis so many Americans yearned for, there arose a swift and violent reaction against continued internationalism. The unfair peace could not last, many thought; America should withdraw from commitments that might infringe on its freedom of action. Thus, a country that had been internationalist in war became isolationist in peace.

Wilson attempted to defend the compromises of the Versailles Treaty by insisting that a new peace-keeping organization, the League of Nations, would take care of the repugnant stipulations. Progressives joined forces with the conservative isolationists to defeat the treaty's approval in the Senate and repudiate Wilson. Americans did not want to be involved in international affairs at all.

By the Presidential election year of 1920, progressive enthusiasms had decidedly waned. But though Progressivism as a political movement lapsed, one ambition of the reformers—success for every man—remained strong in the country. Material goods were becoming even more the indices of success. Mass production, refined by the demands of war production, now made cheap consumer goods and services generally available.

Business raced ahead. And Americans were less anxious for social changes than they were to get on with the business of living. The middle class abandoned the reform movement and concentrated on individual achievement. Warren G. Harding, the Republican candidate, represented this outlook almost exactly.

Harding captured 16,152,000 votes to his opponents 9,147,000. The Republican nominee, in winning 60.3% of the popular vote, reflected the mood of the times, especially when he said: "America's present need is not heroics, but healing; not nostrums, but normalcy; not revolution, but restoration; not agitation, but adjustment; not surgery, but serenity; not the dramatic, but the dispassionate; not experiment, but equipoise; not submergence in internationality, but sustainment in triumphant nationality. . . ."

Ineffectual Administrator

Harding's administration was vague and conservative like his campaign. In office he was too friendly to be discriminating, and he allowed his friends to take advantage of him. He died in 1923, just as the extent of the corruption—greater than any since Grant's time—was being revealed. Harding's successor, Calvin Coolidge, was unquestionably honest and was in no way connected with the unfolding scandals. Coolidge differed in another way, also: He was clearly a conservative. Limited Government interference with the economy and with society as a whole was central to his policy.

Under Coolidge there seemed to be no possibility of further corruption among Republicans and every possibility for prosperity. He was readily selected his party's candidate in 1924.

The Democrats, meanwhile, were badly divided over the Ku Klux Klan and the Prohibition issues. Prohibition had become law in 1919. A compromise candidate, John W. Davis, was eventually selected after prolonged wrangling. The Democratic platform offered no challenging issues to the Republicans, who instead directed their attack on a third party which offered a real alternative to the voters. The Progressive Party was an unsteady combination of renewed farm and labor discontent. The mild socialism and the agrarian progressivism of the party platform did not win broad appeal. Progressive strength was further reduced when crop prices, which had been dropping since the end of World War I, went up and induced many a farmer to stay within the Republican Party.

Coolidge won a decisive victory. His 15,725,000 votes nearly doubled the Democratic total of 8,378,000. Robert La Follette, the Progressive Party candidate, gained nearly 5,000,000 votes, but Coolidge still had a majority.

Prosperity continued for most Americans for four more years and in 1928 the Republicans met with full expectancy of retaining the Presidency. Herbert Hoover, the GOP candidate, typified many of those standards that were particularly admired in the 1920s. He had been an engineer who stood for efficiency, a self-made businessman who had risen from a small town to make a fortune, and a humanitarian who was convinced that private and voluntary effort would eliminate much human suffering.

Al Smith, the Democratic choice, had known a different career. Rising from the slums of New York City, he was the first Catholic to try for the White House. He spoke with an accent learned on Manhattan's lower East Side. These were disadvantages in an America where

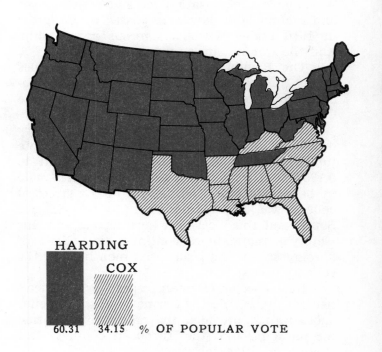

ELECTION OF 1920

HARDING

COX

60.31   34.15   % OF POPULAR VOTE

the prevailing outlook was that of the small town and the rural areas. But an even greater disadvantage to Smith was Coolidge prosperity. The Democratic Party platform was little different from the Republican, and even the traditional low tariff position had been abandoned. The Democrats seemed on their way to becoming the same "me too" party they had been before 1896.

Since the era of McKinley prosperity, the United States had had a natural Republican majority, made up of four groups: Farmers, the middle class, labor and the Negro. This meant that, except in an extraordinary situation, such as the Republican split in 1912, and the peace issue and Wilson's vigorous reforms in 1916, a Republican sat in the White House. After 1929, these groups swung over to the Democratic Party and stayed there for more than 20 years.

The farmer switched over because he finally got the Federal subsidies he had wanted since the Populist agitation.

"The world needs to be reminded that all human ills are not curable by legislation, and that quantity of statutory enactment and excess of government offer no substitute for quality of citizenship."—Warren G. Harding, who campaigned McKinley-style on his front porch in Marion, Ohio, and received delegations of voters from near and far.

The middle class turned Democratic because it became disillusioned with the Republican leadership's concept of the Federal Government—that the Government's primary function was to encourage and assist, but not over-regulate, private enterprise.

Organized labor was convinced that a sympathetic Democratic leadership now existed.

The Negro was now conscious of himself as a poor man first and a Negro second, and he voted no longer for the party of the Emancipation but for what he believed to be the party of the poor man. Since 1900, Negroes had been migrating to the North, where the suffrage was less restrictive, in great numbers. By 1932, the Negro population in the North and East was nearly three times what it was in 1900, while in the South the number of Negroes had grown by only one-sixth.

Dark, Dark Days

The Great Depression of 1929 began as a financial collapse which affected only speculators and investors. The financial collapse, however, meant a curtailment of credit which in turn led to cutbacks in production, reduced employment, and deflation.

By 1931, the economic depression had turned into a social crisis of grim proportions. Unemployment had not ceased to mount. Labor was affected first, then the middle class. Men who had never been unemployed for long periods found themselves unable to find work and unable to support their families. Hoover administration measures seemed unsuccessful, the businessman was discredited, and the people were ready to vote the businessman out of Government.

The man voted into office considered his election a clear mandate for change, but he had no clear program. His name was Franklin D. Roosevelt.

During the campaign, Roosevelt had spoken in buoyant generalities suggesting he was willing to move toward active Federal participation in the economy. Once in office he began to shape a remarkable program. His first move restored stability to the banking system and revived the confidence of businessmen and bankers—at least those businessmen and bankers who weren't ruined by Roosevelt's stringent measures.

Then, during the hundred days following

his inauguration, he unfolded a series of proposals that gave form to the New Deal. They included an agricultural recovery program, unemployment relief, Federal regulation of securities, creation of a Tennessee Valley Authority, prevention of mortgage foreclosures on homes, railroad recovery legislation, and an industrial recovery program. These proposals, or modifications of them, became law in the following years.

The scope of innovation in the New Deal program accelerated as the months and years passed. Although he made early gestures to attract the support of businessmen, Roosevelt felt they had deserted him. Thus, it became politically expedient to turn to the farmer, organized labor and minority groups for support. To do so he adopted an extraordinary policy of reform.

By the time the Presidential campaign of 1936 opened, Roosevelt's radical reform program was clear.

A vast coalition of farmers, laborers, hard-pressed middling people and the poor gave FDR an overwhelming victory over Republican Alf Landon. Roosevelt's percentage of the popular vote (60.8%) exceeded even Harding's in 1920, and still stands as a record.

It's well, in these affluent times, to reflect upon the New Deal and the Depression with some circumspection. The 1930s were exceedingly harsh years for millions of industrious and ordinarily self-reliant Americans. Not every nation, given the same desperate conditions, would have emerged from such a period with all its political institutions intact—and foes of FDR question whether the United States did, either.

But it was no less than a triumph of the American spirit that the great majority of Americans never lost faith in their political system. The two major parties polled more than 97% of the vote in the two elections in the depths of the Depression, 1932 and 1936. Not a few historians credit this faith to the persistent optimism of the man in the White House.

After 1936, international events began to intrude more frequently into the American consciousness so that by the election of 1940 they were a major issue. But isolationism was still a strong sentiment in the United States in the 1930s.

FDR was conscious of this attitude; he paid close attention to the public opinion polls, especially after war broke out in Europe. It was to be a serious problem for him in the election of 1940, when he ran for a third term against Wendell Willkie.

ELECTION OF 1932

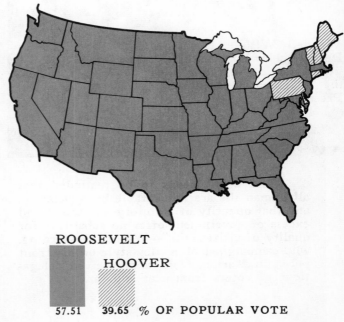

ROOSEVELT

HOOVER

57.51   39.65 % OF POPULAR VOTE

Willkie was a curious combination of a thoughtful liberal and an ambitious businessman. Although president of a utilities corporation, he did not attack the New Deal as a whole. Rather, he criticized specific programs, like the Tennessee Valley Authority. Willkie's in-between approach attracted a large following among Republicans who believed that the party could not win a national election with a strictly anti-New Deal attitude. He appealed greatly to many middle-class Americans who didn't object to many New Deal changes, but expected more encouragement of business and investment. Willkie attacked the bad management of the New Deal rather than assaulting the whole of it.

With the domestic issues of the campaign reduced largely to a matter of method, foreign affairs became the major issue of the campaign. The nominating conventions met as the military situation in Europe took a disastrous turn for England and France. France had collapsed and the Franco-German armistice had been signed a week before the Republican convention at the end of June.

Both parties supported the national defense program, upheld aid to Britain, and hemispheric defense. Willkie scored heavily when he challenged Roosevelt's promise to stay out of a foreign war. He said that if FDR's promise to keep out of such a conflict were no better than his promise to balance the budget, then the boys were "already almost on the transports."

This was effective and Roosevelt was obliged to make a definite pledge: "I have said this before, but I shall say it again and again and again: Your boys are not going to be sent into any foreign wars." It was a hard promise for the President to make. He was convinced that America had a vital interest in the maintenance of the collective security of the Western European democracies. Thus, he was a strong advocate of aid to Britain.

The Japanese raid at Pearl Harbor got Roosevelt off the hook. And it united American opinion as no amount of persuasion could have.

Throughout most of World War II, personal incomes exceeded available civilian goods and services by about 30%. Some of this surplus income was converted into savings through the series "E" war bond program. But taxes did much more to drain off the people's extra purchasing power, with taxes falling on lower income groups for the first time.

The highest income groups, however, were assessed far more heavily, with the top rate rising to 94%. People in the top 5% on the income

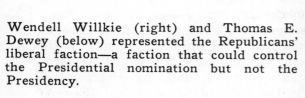

Wendell Willkie (right) and Thomas E. Dewey (below) represented the Republicans' liberal faction—a faction that could control the Presidential nomination but not the Presidency.

scale suffered a relative economic loss of large proportions, as their share of disposable income fell from 26% in 1940 to 16% in 1944. Few individuals or businesses—save the shady operators—were able to make fortunes from the war. Thus, a considerable amount of economic levelling took place.

The Republicans looked forward to the election of 1944 with enthusiasm. The midterm elections had been held as the United States and its Allies suffered a series of military disasters, and the Roosevelt administration appeared confused in the crisis. The Republicans had gained seats in both houses of Congress in 1942. The GOP, out of the White House for 12 years, selected a young candidate, Governor Thomas E. Dewey of New York, to oppose the aging FDR.

Truman Over Wallace

Roosevelt was chosen by the Democrats without opposition, but a contest developed over the Vice Presidential choice. Vice President Henry Wallace, whose radical ideas made him the darling of the more extreme New Dealers, was opposed by the Southerners and the city machines as an impractical visionary and a political liability in a country that appeared to be moving to the right. Instead of Wallace, the Democrats compromised on a border-stater, with a consistent New Deal record in Congress, the economy-minded chairman of the Senate War Expenditures Investigating Committee, Harry Truman.

Dewey struck hard at the conflict and inefficiency within the administration. But he accepted many of the policies of the New Deal.

Roosevelt retorted by attacking the Republican isolationist record and by promising a continuance of the social and economic benefits of the New Deal after the war. The war, by this time, was going successfully as Allied forces penetrated Germany and American troops landed in the Philippines. President Roosevelt was re-elected by a margin of 3,594,000 popular votes (25,612,000 to 22,018,000), the smallest majority any successful candidate had had since World War I.

Six months later Roosevelt was dead and Truman succeeded him as President. The new Chief Executive took office with a deep sense of personal inadequacy as he faced the job of ending the war and building a durable peace.

Peace did not bring the unemployment and depression that some had predicted. Instead

A candidate's life is not an easy one. Aboard his campaign train in 1948, Tom Dewey smiles after someone in the crowd hurled a tomato that exploded off the platform and splattered his suit.

Harry Truman was a man of unsuspected powers when he became the American head of state and the Democratic head of party.

||||||||||||||||||||||||||||||||||||||||||||||||||||||||||||||||||||||||||

MACHINE

This word entered politics in the 1820s when it was used to refer to the legislative process.

The application of "machine" to an efficient, boss-controlled party organization grew up in the 1850s and 1860s. At that time horse-drawn fire engines were known as machines, and the expression "to run with the machine" meant to chase the fire engine.

After 1857, William Marcy Tweed, the notorious "Boss Tweed," rose to a dominant place in New York City politics. His fire company was an important factor in his political organization, and hence "running with the machine" came to mean following the party boss and his cronies.

"Machine" came into general use after the Civil War. It was nailed down as a political term in 1876, when Thomas Nast used a fire-fighting machine in an editorial cartoon to represent the Tammany Hall political organization in New York.

||||||||||||||||||||||||||||||||||||||||||||||||||||||||||||||||||||||||||

there was a spectacular boom. Even so, serious domestic problems did arise. The savings and credit accumulated during the war brought a sudden heavy demand for consumer goods at the war's end. With consumer goods and services scarce, the Truman administration's efforts to hold prices at their wartime levels failed.

Organized labor struck the major industries —autos, coal, electrical manufacturing, steel— for higher wages to keep the worker abreast of rising living costs. Wages went up and pushed prices still higher in the process.

By the midterm election of 1946, real earnings had fallen by 12% since July, 1945, and Republicans took advantage of the popular discontent. With telling effect, they rallied a heavy protest vote to their side with the slogan, "Had Enough? Vote Republican." The GOP captured both houses of Congress. Only once (1930) in the years since 1918 had opposing parties controlled Congress and the Presidency.

The hostility between Truman and the lawmakers stalled legislation. The only significant act was the Taft-Hartley Labor-Management Relations Act which relaxed some of the previous restraints on employers and restricted somewhat the union prerogatives that had accumulated during the New Deal. The law was passed over Truman's veto.

Although the outcome of the dispute over Taft-Hartley assured Truman firm union backing, the possibility of his success in the campaign of 1948 seemed slim.

End of the Coalition

For one thing, the foreign situation was no anodyne for a public already distressed by domestic problems. Americans were finding out that the victory over the Axis powers had not cured the world of all its ills. The winning coalition, held together by the necessities of war, could not remain united to face the problems of peace. Russia was bent on trouble-making.

But domestic issues were to be the important ones in the 1948 Presidential campaign. Dewey was again the Republican candidate— the convention passed over the choice of the party's more conservative wing, Robert A. Taft. Dewey favored the new American participation in foreign affairs, and accepted much of the Democratic domestic program, with the promise to act more efficiently and at less cost. The New York Governor's running mate was another governor, Earl Warren of California. Moderate

Republicans everywhere thought they had the man who could combine the ideas of Willkie with the practicality of an experienced politician. So did most Democrats.

The Democratic Party's strength was depleted by desertions to the left and to the right in 1948. Henry Wallace, long an impassioned New Dealer, led despairing radicals out of the party because he felt it was moving too slowly in some areas. In a frenzied convention, Wallace was picked as the candidate of the newest "Progressive" party.

At the Democratic convention, a strong civil rights plank was adopted to assist Northern Democrats in gaining the Negro vote. The plank, however, turned Southerners against Truman. The Southerners bolted and nominated Senator Strom Thurmond of South Carolina for President on a States' Rights ticket.

Beset by strong opposition from the Republicans and intra-party defections, Truman seemed to be in a hopeless position. But the political seers had failed to reckon with the remarkable vote-getting skills of the man from Missouri.

The Target Was Congress

Instead of engaging in a dubious contest with Dewey, Truman went after the Republican Congress. Speaking in a blunt and informal way, he set off on an intensive personal tour that brought him directly to the voters. While successfully identifying himself as the "little man's President," he convinced important groups that their grievances were the fault of the GOP-controlled 80th Congress. The large support he won among Northern Negroes, discontented farmers and organized labor won him the election—and Democratic control of Congress.

In the years that followed World War II, the American people suffered a series of shocks. Friendly feeling toward Russia turned to hostility and fear. In September, 1949, Americans learned that Russia possessed atomic weapons. By the end of that year, a Communist regime had taken over the mainland of China.

Earlier, the Russians had failed to force the Western powers out of Berlin. But in June, 1950, Western containment of communism was challenged where the West was weakest—in Asia. The Red government set up in the northern half of the Korean peninsula at the end of World War II, invaded its American-sponsored neighbor to the south.

President Truman's decision to commit American troops to the defense of a minor outpost of the West seemed to put muscle into the U.N. pledge to defend the security of small nations, and gave proof to the Russians that clear Communist expansion through force would be met with force.

Truman refused to allow the war to be extended into China, as advocated by General Douglas MacArthur. The Chief Executive and his advisers were convinced that the principal struggle against communism was in Western Europe with its concentration of heavy industry —not in industrially weak Asia.

In the spring of 1951, Truman fired MacArthur. The popular outcry at this action was three to one in favor of the General; MacArthur represented a strong American preference for a decisive solution to their problems.

The policy of containment and its corollary, a limited war, tried the public's patience.

Several incidents of bribery and favoritism had been turned up in the Government during Truman's second administration. These examples of corruption offered the Republicans new ammunition with which to convince voters that the Democrats were inefficient and extravagant administrators.

Washington was "a mess" and the Korean War was dragging into its third year when Americans turned their attention to the Presidential campaign of 1952. To clean up "the mess" and end the war, Americans turned to Dwight D. Eisenhower.

▌▌▌▌▌▌▌▌▌▌▌▌▌▌▌▌▌▌▌▌▌▌▌▌▌▌▌▌▌▌▌▌▌▌▌▌▌▌

NEW DEAL

This famous phrase associated with the administration of Franklin D. Roosevelt was invented neither by FDR nor his speechwriters. The term was borrowed from Mark Twain's novel, *A Connecticut Yankee in King Arthur's Court.* The book's hero declared that when half a dozen men cracked the whip over a thousand people, "what the nine hundred and ninety-four other dupes needed was a new deal." Roosevelt himself acknowledged this source of the term.

▌▌▌▌▌▌▌▌▌▌▌▌▌▌▌▌▌▌▌▌▌▌▌▌▌▌▌▌▌▌▌▌▌▌▌▌▌▌

Former President Eisenhower at a fund-raising dinner for Richard Nixon's California gubernatorial campaign in 1962. Ike's party wore out his coattails.

Eisenhower—moderate in outlook and genial in personality—represented an attitude appealing to most Americans. Here was a man who had successfully handled jobs of awesome responsibility during World War II and after, a soldier and diplomat who had not only radiated optimism, but whose manner suggested he had good reason for his hopefulness. He was a man easy to have confidence in.

As soon as he was nominated for President by the Republican Party, he set about healing the wounds created in the convention floor fight between his backers and the supporters of Senator Robert Taft (see Chapter IV). Eisenhower's pick of Senator Richard M. Nixon, well known for his active pursuit of Communists in the Government, was the first step toward mending the rift. Patronage was pledged to the Taftites, and suitably broad statements about domestic policy also helped mollify the conservative wing of the party.

On foreign policy, however, he would not yield to the conservatives. He accepted the idea of containment and a limited commitment in Asia.

The Democratic candidate, Governor Adlai E. Stevenson of Illinois, sought to make the campaign a high-level debate of the problems facing America. But aside from the intellectually curious and, it was said, some curious intellectuals, few voters were interested in a detailed recitation of problems, however eloquently presented. They wanted solutions. Eisenhower did not offer specific answers, but he did have an uncomplicated, trustworthy quality that people liked. Perhaps, they thought, this decent man will find a decent way out of things.

Eisenhower won a resounding personal triumph, running far ahead of his party as the Republicans gained only an eight-seat margin in the House and had to settle for a tie in the Senate.

President Eisenhower, the first Republican chief executive in 20 years, brought no startling changes to Washington. The substance of Democratic handiwork was not repealed. *Limited* Federal supervision of the general welfare was accepted. The Republicans codified the haphazard structure of the New Deal, increased administrative efficiency, and liquidated unneeded agencies.

By 1956, the major Republican campaign issues of 1952—corruption, communism and Korea—had been disposed of. True, other problems persisted: First, there were the frustrations in foreign policy. To reduce expenses the administration decided to cut the size of the costly land forces after the Korean truce.

To contain the Communists, reliance was placed on the superiority of America's capacity for nuclear devastation and its superior airborne delivery system. The piecemeal Communist advances in areas like Indo-China did not seem worth the risk of a full-scale nuclear war, especially when it became evident that Russia's nuclear arsenal was approaching Uncle Sam's in destructiveness.

Secondly, at home, the question of the Negro's civil rights came to public attention. In 1954, the Supreme Court ruled that the practice of separating the races in public schools precluded equal educational advantages to Negroes. Mob action in some Southern communities attracted widespread attention, particularly in Little Rock, and President Eisenhower was obliged to send in Federal troops to maintain order.

But Americans didn't blame these disturbing incidents on their President. And, although he suffered two serious illnesses in the preceding year, he was renominated and re-elected—this time with a majority even greater than the one in 1952. But again he outran his party. In 1956 the Republicans failed to regain the Congressional majority they had lost in 1954.

As the months passed, the United States slid into the worst recession since World War II, and Uncle Sam's superiority in the arms race came into doubt. Missiles were replacing manned bombers as the most efficient means of delivering atomic warheads. In October and November of 1957, the Russians dramatically asserted a formidable claim to superiority in missile systems when they launched two earth-circling satellites.

Civil rights and missiles were to be the key issues in the Presidential election of 1960, when Democrat John F. Kennedy defeated Republican Richard M. Nixon in the closest vote of modern times.

But unsettled that year and still unsettled in 1964 are the two issues that in some form have recurred in U.S. Presidential campaigns since the nation's founding. These issues are the role of the Federal Government and civil rights. Hamilton and Jefferson were perplexed by them, too.

If 44 Presidential elections haven't led to the resolution of all our deep-rooted problems, they have nevertheless demonstrated a diverse people's capacity for self-government. America's political institutions still stand after 175 years of trial. This says it all.

John F. Kennedy gives the country a new phrase—the New Frontier—in his speech in Los Angeles accepting the 1960 Democratic Presidential nomination.

Vice President Richard M. Nixon and Vice President-elect Lyndon B. Johnson leave the White House for the inauguration ceremonies in January, 1961. The orderly change of power is the beginning and the end of the story.

Appendices

I. Presidents and Vice Presidents

(Note—Vice Presidents are in italics.)

NAME	PREVIOUS OCCUPATIONS	RESIDENCE	TERM OF OFFICE	AGE ON TAKING OFFICE
George Washington	Surveyor, farmer, soldier	Va.	1789-1797	57
John Adams	*Lawyer, colonial legislator, diplomat*	*Mass.*	*1789-1797*	*53*
John Adams	Lawyer, colonial legislator, diplomat	Mass.	1797-1801	61
Thomas Jefferson	*Lawyer, inventor, author*	*Va.*	*1797-1801*	*53*
Thomas Jefferson	Lawyer, inventor, author	Va.	1801-1809	57
Aaron Burr	*Lawyer, politician, Senator*	*N.Y.*	*1801-1805*	*44*
George Clinton	*Lawyer, Congressman, governor*	*N.Y.*	*1805-1809*	*65*
James Madison	Lawyer, author, Sec. of State	Va.	1809-1817	57
George Clinton	*Lawyer, Congressman, governor*	*N.Y.*	*1809-1812**	*69*
Elbridge Gerry	*Lawyer, Congressman*	*Mass.*	*1813-1814**	*68*
James Monroe	Lawyer, Senator, diplomat	Va.	1817-1825	58
Daniel D. Tompkins	*Lawyer, legislator, governor*	*N.Y.*	*1817-1825*	*42*
John Quincy Adams	Lawyer, Senator, diplomat	Mass.	1825-1829	57
John C. Calhoun	*Lawyer, Senator, Sec. of War*	*S.C.*	*1825-1829*	*42*
Andrew Jackson	Soldier, farmer, Congressman	Tenn.	1829-1837	61
John C. Calhoun	*Lawyer, Senator, Sec. of War*	*S.C.*	*1829-1832†*	*46*
Martin Van Buren	*Lawyer, Senator, Sec. of State*	*N.Y.*	*1833-1837*	*50*
Martin Van Buren	Lawyer, Senator, Sec. of State	N.Y.	1837-1841	54
Richard M. Johnson	*Lawyer, Congressman, Senator*	*Ky.*	*1837-1841*	*55*
William Henry Harrison	Soldier, Congressman, governor	Ohio	1841*	68
John Tyler	*Lawyer, governor*	*Va.*	*1841*	*50*
John Tyler	Lawyer, governor	Va.	1841-1845	51
James K. Polk	Soldier, Congressman, governor	Tenn.	1845-1849	49
George M. Dallas	*Lawyer, Senator, diplomat*	*Pa.*	*1845-1849*	*52*
Zachary Taylor	Soldier	Tenn.	1849-1850*	64
Millard Fillmore	*Lawyer, teacher, Congressman*	*N.Y.*	*1849-1850*	*49*
Millard Fillmore	Lawyer, teacher, Congressman	N.Y.	1850-1853	50
Franklin Pierce	Lawyer, Congressman, Senator	N.H.	1853-1857	48
William R. King	*Lawyer, Congressman, Senator*	*Ala.*	*1853**	*66*
James Buchanan	Lawyer, author, Sec. of State	Pa.	1857-1861	65
John C. Breckinridge	*Lawyer, Congressman, Senator*	*Ky.*	*1857-1861*	*36*
Abraham Lincoln	Merchant, lawyer, Congressman	Ill.	1861-1865*	52
Hannibal Hamlin	*Lawyer, Congressman, Senator*	*Me.*	*1861-1865*	*51*
Andrew Johnson	*Mayor, governor, Senator*	*Tenn.*	*1865*	*56*
Andrew Johnson	Mayor, governor, Senator	Tenn.	1865-1869	56
Ulysses S. Grant	Soldier, Sec. of War	Ill.	1869-1877	46
Schuyler Colfax	*Newspaper editor*	*Ind.*	*1869-1873*	*45*
Henry Wilson	*Shoemaker, teacher, Senator*	*Mass.*	*1873-1875**	*61*

NAME	PREVIOUS OCCUPATIONS	RESIDENCE	TERM OF OFFICE	AGE ON TAKING OFFICE
Rutherford B. Hayes	Lawyer, Congressman, governor	Ohio	1877-1881	54
William A. Wheeler	*Lawyer, Congressman*	*N.Y.*	*1877-1881*	*57*
James A. Garfield	Lawyer, professor, Congressman	Ohio	1881*	49
Chester A. Arthur	*Lawyer, customs official*	*N.Y.*	*1881*	*50*
Chester A. Arthur	Lawyer, customs official	N.Y.	1881-1885	50
Grover Cleveland	Lawyer, mayor, governor	N.Y.	1885-1889	47
Thomas A. Hendricks	*Lawyer, mayor, governor*	*Ind.*	*1885**	*66*
Benjamin Harrison	Lawyer, soldier, Senator	Ind.	1889-1893	55
Levi P. Morton	*Banker, Congressman*	*N.Y.*	*1889-1893*	*64*
Grover Cleveland	Lawyer, mayor, governor	N.Y.	1893-1897	55
Adlai E. Stevenson	*Lawyer, Congressman*	*Ill.*	*1893-1897*	*57*
William McKinley	Lawyer, Congressman	Ohio	1897-1901*	54
Garret A. Hobart	*Lawyer, state legislator, party official*	*N.J.*	*1897-1899**	*52*
Theodore Roosevelt	*Rancher, Asst. Sec. of Navy, governor*	*N.Y.*	*1901*	*42*
Theodore Roosevelt	Rancher, Asst. Sec. of Navy, governor	N.Y.	1901-1909	42
Charles W. Fairbanks	*Newspaper reporter, lawyer, Senator*	*Ind.*	*1905-1909*	*52*
William H. Taft	Lawyer, judge, Gov. of Phillippines	Ohio	1909-1913	51
James S. Sherman	*Lawyer, Congressman*	*N.Y.*	*1909-1912**	*53*
Woodrow Wilson	Lawyer, Congressman, governor	N.J.	1913-1921	56
Thomas R. Marshall	*Lawyer, governor*	*Ind.*	*1913-1921*	*58*
Warren G. Harding	Editor, Senator	Ohio	1921-1923*	55
Calvin Coolidge	*Lawyer, governor*	*Mass.*	*1921-1923*	*48*
Calvin Coolidge	Lawyer, governor	Mass.	1923-1929	51
Charles G. Dawes	*Lawyer, economist*	*Ohio*	*1925-1929*	*59*
Herbert C. Hoover	Engineer, administrator, Sec. of Commerce	Iowa	1929-1933	54
Charles Curtis	*Lawyer, Congressman, Senator*	*Kan.*	*1929-1933*	*69*
Franklin D. Roosevelt	Lawyer, governor	N.Y.	1933-1945*	51
John N. Garner	*Lawyer, Congressman, Senator*	*Texas*	*1933-1941*	*64*
Henry A. Wallace	*Agriculturalist, editor*	*Iowa*	*1941-1945*	*52*
Harry S Truman	*Haberdasher, judge, Senator*	*Mo.*	*1945*	*60*
Harry S Truman	Haberdasher, judge, Senator	Mo.	1945-1953	60
Alben W. Barkley	*Lawyer, Congressman, Senator*	*Ark.*	*1949-1953*	*71*
Dwight D. Eisenhower	Soldier, college president	N.Y.	1953-1961	62
Richard M. Nixon	*Lawyer, Congressman, Senator*	*Calif.*	*1953-1961*	*40*
John F. Kennedy	Congressman, Senator, author	Mass.	1961-1963*	43
Lyndon B. Johnson	*Teacher, Congressman, Senator*	*Texas*	*1961-1963*	*52*
Lyndon B. Johnson	Teacher, Congressman, Senator	Texas	1963-	55

*Died in office.
†Resigned.

II. AMERICAN PRESIDENTIAL ELECTIONS

(Note—The winner is listed first.)

ELECTION	CANDIDATES	PARTIES	POPULAR VOTE	ELECTORAL VOTE
1789	George Washington	Federalist	not recorded	69
	John Adams	Federalist	,, ,,	34
	Ten others	Locally supported	,, ,,	35
1793	George Washington	Federalist	not recorded	132
	John Adams	Federalist	,, ,,	77
	George Clinton	Anti-Federalist	,, ,,	50
	Thomas Jefferson	Anti-Federalist	,, ,,	4
	Aaron Burr	Anti-Federalist	,, ,,	1
1797	John Adams	Federalist	not recorded	71
	Thomas Jefferson	Democratic-Republican	,, ,,	68
	Thomas Pinckney	Federalist	,, ,,	59
	Aaron Burr	Democratic-Republican	,, ,,	30
	Nine others	Locally supported	,, ,,	48
1801	Thomas Jefferson	Democratic-Republican	not recorded	73
	Aaron Burr	Democratic-Republican	,, ,,	73
	John Adams	Federalist	,, ,,	65
	Charles C. Pinckney	Federalist	,, ,,	64
	John Jay	Federalist	,, ,,	1
1805	Thomas Jefferson	Democratic-Republican	not recorded	162
	Charles C. Pinckney	Federalist	,, ,,	14
1809	James Madison	Democratic-Republican	not recorded	122
	Charles C. Pinckney	Federalist	,, ,,	47
	George Clinton	Federalist	,, ,,	6
1813	James Madison	Democratic-Republican	not recorded	128
	DeWitt Clinton	Federalist	,, ,,	89
1817	James Monroe	Democratic-Republican	not recorded	183
	Rufus King	Federalist	,, ,,	34
1821	James Monroe	Democratic-Republican	not recorded	231
	John Quincy Adams	Democratic-Republican	,, ,,	1
1824	John Quincy Adams	Democratic-Republican	108,740	84
	Andrew Jackson	Democratic-Republican	153,544	99
	William H. Crawford	Democratic-Republican	46,618	41
	Henry Clay	Democratic-Republican	47,136	37
1828	Andrew Jackson	Democrat	647,231	178
	John Quincy Adams	Nat. Republican	509,097	83
1832	Andrew Jackson	Democrat	687,502	219
	Henry Clay	Whig	530,189	49
	John Floyd	Whig	} 33,108	11
	William Wirt	Anti-Mason		7
1836	Martin Van Buren	Democrat	761,549	170
	W. H. Harrison	Whig	} 736,656	73
	Hugh L. White	Whig		26
	Daniel Webster	Whig		14
	W. P. Mangum	Whig		11

Appendix II

ELECTION	CANDIDATES	PARTIES	POPULAR VOTE	ELECTORAL VOTE
1840	William Henry Harrison	Whig	1,275,016	234
	Martin Van Buren	Democrat	1,129,102	60
1844	James K. Polk	Democrat	1,337,243	170
	Henry Clay	Whig	1,299,062	105
1848	Zachary Taylor	Whig	1,360,099	163
	Lewis Cass	Democrat	1,220,544	127
	Martin Van Buren	Free Soil	291,263	
1852	Franklin Pierce	Democrat	1,601,274	254
	Winfield Scott	Whig	1,386,580	42
	John P. Hale	Free Soil	155,825	
1856	James Buchanan	Democrat	1,838,169	174
	John C. Fremont	Republican	1,341,264	114
	Millard Fillmore	American (Know Nothing)	874,534	8
1860	Abraham Lincoln	Republican	1,866,452	180
	Stephen A. Douglas	Democrat	1,375,157	12
	John C. Breckinridge	Democrat	847,953	72
	John Bell	Union	590,631	39
1864	Abraham Lincoln	Republican-Union	2,213,665	212
	George McClellan	Democrat	1,805,237	21
1868	Ulysses S. Grant	Republican	3,012,833	214
	Horatio Seymour	Democrat	2,703,249	80
1872	Ulysses S. Grant	Republican	3,597,132	286
	Horace Greely	Democrat & Liberal Rep.	2,834,125	66
	Charles O'Connor	Straight Democrat	29,489	
1876	Rutherford B. Hayes	Republican	4,036,298	185
	Samuel J. Tilden	Democrat	4,300,590	184
1880	James A. Garfield	Republican	4,454,416	214
	Winfield S. Hancock	Democrat	4,444,952	155
1884	Grover Cleveland	Democrat	4,874,986	219
	James G. Blaine	Republican	4,851,981	182
1888	Benjamin Harrison	Republican	5,439,853	233
	Grover Cleveland	Democrat	5,540,309	168
1892	Grover Cleveland	Democrat	5,556,918	277
	Benjamin Harrison	Republican	5,176,108	145
	James B. Weaver	Populist	1,041,028	22
1896	William McKinley	Republican	7,104,779	271
	William Jennings Bryan	Democrat & Populist	6,502,925	176
1900	William McKinley	Republican	7,207,923	292
	William Jennings Bryan	Democrat & Populist	6,358,133	155
	Eugene V. Debs	Socialist	87,814	

Appendix II

ELECTION	CANDIDATES	PARTIES	POPULAR VOTE	ELECTORAL VOTE
1904	Theodore Roosevelt	Republican	7,623,486	336
	Alton B. Parker	Democrat	5,077,911	140
	Eugene V. Debs	Socialist	402,283	
1908	William H. Taft	Republican	7,678,908	321
	William Jennings Bryan	Democrat	6,409,104	162
	Eugene V. Debs	Socialist	420,793	
1912	Woodrow Wilson	Democrat	6,293,454	435
	William H. Taft	Republican	3,484,980	8
	Theodore Roosevelt	Progressive	4,119,538	88
	Eugene V. Debs	Socialist	900,672	
1916	Woodrow Wilson	Democrat	9,129,606	277
	Charles E. Hughes	Republican	8,538,221	254
	A. L. Benson	Socialist	585,113	
1920	Warren G. Harding	Republican	16,152,200	404
	James M. Cox	Democrat	9,147,353	127
	Eugene V. Debs	Socialist	919,799	
1924	Calvin Coolidge	Republican	15,725,016	382
	John W. Davis	Democrat	8,386,503	136
	Robert LaFollette	Progressive & Socialist	4,822,856	13
1928	Herbert Hoover	Republican	21,391,381	444
	Alfred E. Smith	Democrat	15,016,443	87
	Norman Thomas	Socialist	267,835	
1932	Franklin D. Roosevelt	Democrat	22,821,857	472
	Herbert Hoover	Republican	15,761,841	59
	Norman Thomas	Socialist	881,951	
1936	Franklin D. Roosevelt	Democrat & American Labor	27,751,597	523
	Alfred M. Landon	Republican	16,679,583	8
	Norman Thomas	Socialist	187,720	
1940	Franklin D. Roosevelt	Democrat & American Labor	27,244,160	449
	Wendell L. Willkie	Republican	22,305,198	82
	Norman Thomas	Socialist & Progressive	99,557	
1944	Franklin D. Roosevelt	Democrat, Amer. Labor & Liberal	25,602,504	432
	Thomas E. Dewey	Republican	22,006,285	99
	Norman Thomas	Socialist	80,518	
1948	Harry S Truman	Democrat & Liberal	24,105,695	303
	Thomas E. Dewey	Republican	21,969,170	189
	J. Strom Thurmond	States' Rights Democrat	1,169,021	39
	Henry A. Wallace	Progressive & American Labor	1,156,103	
	Norman Thomas	Socialist	139,009	
1952	Dwight D. Eisenhower	Republican	33,824,351	442
	Adlai E. Stevenson	Democrat & Liberal	27,314,987	89
1956	Dwight D. Eisenhower	Republican	35,585,316	457
	Adlai E. Stevenson	Democrat & Liberal	26,029,752	73
1960	John F. Kennedy	Democrat	34,221,349	303
	Richard Milhous Nixon	Republican	34,108,647	219

III. Suggested Reading

The Concept of Jacksonian Democracy: New York as a Test Case by Lee Benson, Princeton University Press, 1961.

American Political Parties: Their Natural History by Wilfred E. Binkley, Alfred A. Knopf, 1962.

Woodrow Wilson and the Politics of Morality by John Morton Blum, Little, Brown, and Co., 1956.

Politics in America by D. W. Brogan, Anchor Books, 1960.

The Road to Reunion, 1865-1900 by Paul H. Buck, Vintage Books, 1959.

John Kennedy: A Political Profile by James MacGregor Burns, Harcourt, Brace & Company, 1959.

American Government Today by Gaylon L. Caldwell, W. W. Norton & Company, Inc., 1963.

The Enterprising Americans by John Chamberlain, Harper & Row, 1963.

The Politics of National Party Conventions by Paul T. David, Ralph M. Goldman, and Richard C. Bain, The Brookings Institution, 1960.

Rendezvous With Destiny by Eric Goldman, Alfred A. Knopf, 1952.

The Federalist Papers by Alexander Hamilton, James Madison, and John Jay (Clinton Rossiter, ed.), Mentor Books, 1961.

The Americans: A New History of the People of the United States by Oscar Handlin, Little, Brown, and Company, 1963.

1600 Pennsylvania Avenue: Presidents and the People Since 1929 by Walter Johnson, Little, Brown, and Company, 1963.

The Presidency of John Adams: The Collapse of Federalism, 1795-1800 by Stephen G. Kurtz, University of Pennsylvania Press, 1957.

Revolt of the Moderates by Samuel Lubell, Harper & Brothers, 1956.

Encyclopedia of American History edited by Richard B. Morris, Harper & Brothers, 1953.

Hats in the Ring by Malcolm C. Moos and Stephen Hess, Random House, 1960.

The Genius of America: Men Whose Ideas Shaped Our Civilization by Saul K. Padover, McGraw-Hill Book Company, Inc., 1960.

A Statistical History of the American Presidential Elections by Svend Petersen, Frederick Publishing Company, 1963.

The Presidents and the Press by James E. Pollard, The Macmillian Company, 1947.

Nominating the President: The Politics of Convention Choice by Gerald Pomper, Northwestern University Press, 1963.

A History of Presidential Elections by Eugene H. Roseboom, The Macmillian Company,

The Making of the President 1960 by Theodore H. White, Atheneum Publishers, 1961.

Reunion and Reaction: The Compromise of 1877 and the End of Reconstruction by C. Vann Woodward, Anchor Books, 1956.

III. Suggested Reading

The Concept of Jacksonian Democracy: New York as a Test Case by Lee Benson, Princeton University Press, 1961.

American Political Parties: Their Natural History by Wilfred E. Binkley, Alfred A. Knopf, 1962.

Woodrow Wilson and the Politics of Morality by John Morton Blum, Little, Brown, and Co., 1956.

Politics in America by D. W. Brogan, Anchor Books, 1960.

The Road to Reunion, 1865-1900 by Paul H. Buck, Vintage Books, 1959.

John Kennedy: A Political Profile by James MacGregor Burns, Harcourt, Brace & Company, 1959.

American Government Today by Gaylon L. Caldwell, W. W. Norton & Company, Inc., 1963.

The Enterprising Americans by John Chamberlain, Harper & Row, 1963.

The Politics of National Party Conventions by Paul T. David, Ralph M. Goldman, and Richard C. Bain, The Brookings Institution, 1960.

Rendezvous With Destiny by Eric Goldman, Alfred A. Knopf, 1952.

The Federalist Papers by Alexander Hamilton, James Madison, and John Jay (Clinton Rossiter, ed.), Mentor Books, 1961.

The Americans: A New History of the People of the United States by Oscar Handlin, Little, Brown and Company, 1963.

1600 Pennsylvania Avenue: Presidents and the People Since 1929 by Walter Johnson, Little, Brown, and Company, 1963.

The Presidency of John Adams: The Collapse of Federalism, 1795-1800 by Stephen G. Kurtz, University of Pennsylvania Press, 1957.

Revolt of the Moderates by Samuel Lubell, Harper & Brothers, 1956.

Encyclopedia of American History edited by Richard B. Morris, Harper & Brothers, 1953.

Hats in the Ring by Malcolm C. Moos and Stephen Hess, Random House, 1960.

The Genius of America: Men Whose Ideas Shaped Our Civilization by Saul K. Padover, McGraw-Hill Book Company, Inc., 1960.

A Statistical History of the American Presidential Elections by Svend Petersen, Frederick Ungar Publishing Company, 1963.

The Presidents and the Press by James E. Pollard, The Macmillian Company, 1947.

Nominating the President: The Politics of Convention Choice by Gerald Pomper, Northwestern University Press, 1963.

A History of Presidential Elections by Eugene H. Roseboom, The Macmillian Company, 1957.

The Making of the President 1960 by Theodore H. White, Atheneum Publishers, 1961.

Reunion and Reaction: The Compromise of 1877 and the End of Reconstruction by C. Vann Woodward, Anchor Books, 1956.